BREAK THROUGH YOUR BS

UNCOVER YOUR BRAIN'S BLIND SPOTS AND UNLEASH YOUR INNER GREATNESS

DEREK DOEPKER

ExcuseProof.com

BreakThroughYourBS.com

Edited by:

Marjorie Kramer
Marjorie.Kramer@gmail.com

Cover Design by:

Nathaniel Dasco

Book Layout ©2013 BookDesignTemplates.com

Break Through Your BS / Derek Doepker. —1st ed.
ISBN 978-1522879831

Contents

This is All You playing a game of perceiving reflections

reflections perceived through a game played by You in All This

You're in a house of mirrors...
Do you remember?

To not know what this means right now
Means right now you're not to know
When you're ready to receive
Then you will be given

Download Your Video Training Series And Resource Guide

Get access to your training series and resource reference guide by going to **BreakThroughYourBS.com/Bonus**

Inside the bonus video training series you'll discover...

- Why the realization you're a dry erase board will be the most empowering insight you've ever had.
- How visualizing success can backfire and keep you stuck in a fantasy world while your real world sucks.
- Why remaining open-minded is not only stupid, but destructive to yourself and the rest of the world.
- The truth about "getting" all the love you could ever want from people in your life, and why you may not be feeling as much love as you could.

DOWNLOAD YOUR BONUSES

BreakThroughYourBS.com/Bonus

Introduction

This is a book about choice – **your** choice.

The limitations of your thinking that have deluded you into feeling like you don't have a choice, when you really do, will be challenged. Whether you allow those limitations to break under these challenges, or whether you fight to keep your limitations, is your choice.

The mistaken beliefs that you have choices in areas you really don't will be questioned. Whether you allow these questions to shatter your existing beliefs so you can open up to new possibilities, or whether you fight to remain "right" in your old beliefs, is your choice.

The sense of entitlement, that you can make a choice for others, will be exposed. Whether you recognize this hidden sense of entitlement and let it go, or whether you hold onto it, is your choice.

I cannot make any of these choices for you, but I will challenge you, prod you, and poke around many areas of your thoughts and emotions to stir up the bullshit that, most of the time, you don't even realize you've been carrying around.

I do this because I'm committed to truth, empowerment, and enlightenment. At the heart of all that though, I'm committed to compassion. The more understanding you have about your own bullshit, biases, and blind spots, the more compassion and understanding you'll have for others.

As the Dalai Lama XIV says, "World peace must develop from inner peace. Peace is not just mere absence of violence. Peace is, I think, the manifestation of human compassion."

In essence, this is as much a book about overcoming your limitations, and fulfilling your greatest potential as it is a book about being compassionate towards yourself so you can develop greater compassion for others. You're going to realize that no matter how smart and evolved you are, you still have so much BS that you can never point the finger at another's BS without it triggering a reminder of your own BS.

You won't ever get rid of your BS completely, but you will be able to break through it. You will be able to work with it rather than be overcome by it. Your success in breaking through your BS will allow you to help others break through their own BS.

Some of the insights you'll find in this book include...

• The most common mental traps smart people fall for – and why your intelligence can be your greatest enemy.

• How moving away from pain often brings it closer to you, and moving away from your goals can bring them closer.

• Why every excuse you have is 100% factually true but still complete and utter total freaking bullshit.

• The tricks people use to manipulate you, and how your own brain is using these tricks to help you sabotage yourself without you even realizing it.

• The truth about love – and why your attempt to love and sacrifice for others may be what's keeping you from experiencing true love fully.

• A simple mental switch you can press that turns fear into your friend, allowing fear to propel you towards your goals rather than push you away from them.

• The myth of independence and how your desire for self-sufficiency is keeping you from true empowerment.

• One mental distinction unlike anything you've ever heard that automatically moves you into a growth and progress mindset rather than a perfectionistic fixed mindset.

• The power using "CSM" for turning dreaded tasks and adversity into something you love and how it helped me escape depression, build a highly successful business, and finally embrace failure.

• How to go from just intellectually understanding something in your head to actually feeling it fully in your heart so what you feel, think, and do are all in alignment.

• Why you will never get rid of your BS, and why you should rejoice in that fact.

• And much more...

Before going further, I want to acknowledge that you're a pretty awesome person for taking the time to learn this, explore your reality, and make the choice to move towards your highest potential.

Many people in this world are so full of bullshit, they would never pick up a book that would show them how to break through their BS because they feel they "don't need it."

The willingness to take an honest look at yourself and the ways you can improve is a great act of courage. Some can approach personal development from a place of fixing what's broken, but I think true personal development is making something great *even better*. It's the difference between demolishing a house and decorating one.

Your house, in other words, your essence, is perfectly wonderful even if there's some trash that's been piling up inside to get rid of. If you don't like the condition of your house, you don't need to destroy it. Just dispose of the junk and spice it up a bit by adding more greatness to it.

Don't worry if more trash piles up, that's bound to happen. We all have untapped potential that's obscured by BS. A great thing about always having BS is that it means you can both continue to grow and learn new things for the rest of your life, and you can always remain empathetic about the imperfections of others when you realize your own imperfections.

Before going any further, I ask you take a moment to *congratulate yourself* because you're an action-taker who is on the journey to being even more of an amazing human being. Recommendations for this act of self-congratulations include: Doing a fist pump and saying, "Way to go being so awesome (and sexy)!" Doing a happy dance. Or simply closing your eyes and taking a moment to do something you may not have done in a while – honestly tell yourself, "I love you. I accept you. Thank you."

Preparing You For What You're About To Experience

This book is meant to create your own unique experience of self-discovery. If you're reading this book because you hope someone will show you how to make your life better, I have good news – you've found this person. This person is you.

While I will share insights discovered from psychological research, from the shared wisdom of great mentors and teachers both past and present, and from my own experience, at the end of the day it's not wise to blindly accept that with which you're presented. It's wise to challenge both your own assumptions and the assumptions of others. No one is free from BS, myself included.

Because I appreciate this is about your "aha" moments, much of this book will be asking you questions rather than giving answers. If you have a desire to be told what to do so you don't have to think for yourself, don't worry, you'll figure out exactly where *that* bullshit comes from and how to get over it – if you choose.

Simply put, there are times when we want to avoid having to figure things out and want to be told exactly what to do because it: A) makes life easier and B) we don't trust that we have the answers within us. This desire to get outside answers is actually beneficial at times, in that it encourages one to seek out mentors and guidance. But taken in isolation, it prevents a person from discovering things for themselves. As I'm sure you realize, other people may not know what's best for you, given your own unique situation. They may understand big picture principles, but the exact steps to take may be unique to you.

Realize that anything can be good or bad depending on the situation. A good idea, taken in isolation from other good ideas, can be destructive. For instance, a right thing done at the wrong time is a wrong thing. Alternatively, things you may consider "bad" could be good in the right situation. This is a theme you'll see explored often throughout this book. I'll keep repeating this idea that nothing is good or bad outside of context.

Disclaimer: Just in case you're a smart ass who feels that means I'm saying "murdering people" or "molesting people" is OK in the right context, realize the very words "murder" and "molest" have already created a context around the action that makes these things generally wrong. This is not an attempt to justify any action as being potentially acceptable, but rather the recognition that a whole picture needs to be considered before demonizing or praising certain acts. *Disclaimer over.*

Who Is This Derek Dude And Why Should I Listen To Him?

I'm a multiple number one bestselling author, NLP practitioner, and breakthrough coach. I've spent over 10 years researching the world's leading experts in the fields of psychology, spirituality, and philosophy. I'm dedicated to sharing what I've found that is responsible for unleashing the greatest human potential.

I've written books in personal development like *Why You're Stuck*. I've also written books in health and fitness, and on the psychology of change, such as *The Healthy Habit Revolution: How to Create Better Habits in 5 Minutes a Day* and more.

I started out with a relatively ordinary life as a musician and aspiring rock star. After getting my degree in music composition, I moved to LA and lived the glamourous life of a dead broke valet parker, sleeping on an air mattress for over two years. Besides music, I was passionate about personal development, fitness, and entrepreneurship. This led me to begin exploring ways to build a business combining my love for personal development and fitness.

After years of struggle trying to make my big breakthrough, I was very fortunate that a mentor shared a few key principles with me that put the pieces together. Within weeks, I went from broke valet parker, to number one bestselling author. The breakthrough, while in reality taking years to germinate, seemed to happen almost overnight.

Shortly after making my breakthrough, however, I crashed. Part of what happened was that I realized that nothing I accomplished seemed to matter if I couldn't do anything when someone I loved and cared about was hurting. What I did didn't matter when I looked at the world and saw so many people suffering. Even though I was doing my part to contribute to the greater good, I could never do "enough."

I started to beat myself up for this saying, "Derek, you should be appreciative. You should look at the bright side. People would kill to have the life that you have. There are people who are depressed for *real* reasons. Everything is fine in your life, and you're just being a little wimp about it. Get over it! You read personal development – stop being a negative thinker, and take responsibility for your life."

Then an idea came to me. An insight. "Wait a second. I can't help others who are lost if I haven't been lost and found my way through it. What if I'm stuck here in this depressed state to realize what got me stuck and figure out a way out of it? If I want to help others, isn't it *perfect* that I'm stuck precisely so that I can figure out a solution to share?"

I did discover what got me stuck and how to get out of it, and that's when I wrote my book *Why You're Stuck*. I regained my sense of purpose and significance, and I have continued to study, expand my knowledge, and grow for the past several years.

The story of how and why this book came about, though, is something you'll discover on your journey of reading through it... just like I discovered the reason for its creation only while going on the journey of writing it. Or perhaps another way to see it: the journey of *the book choosing* me to write it.

If You Wish To Read This Book...

You now have a few choices to make. These are agreements I ask of my readers because anything misinterpreted, misapplied, or ignored could be destructive. This protects both of our asses so you don't take something you read in this book and screw up your life with it. Even the most innocent advice could be harmful when it's not applied properly.

The agreements are:

Seek a therapist if you need serious help

This book is for entertainment and educational purposes only. You accept the risk for the use, nonuse, or misuse of this information.

Don't believe anything I say

What's shared is only my experience. My experience may also come from studying mentors as well as psychological and philosophical research. Yes, I may be totally sexy, charming, and objectively right most of the time, so you may be tempted to put me on a pedestal. But even if what I say is "true," you may interpret it differently than what I meant, thereby making it untrue for you. More importantly, I'm just as full of shit and biases as anyone else, so while I make the best attempt to not let that get in the way of the information presented in this book, my human nature means I may have my own BS put into this writing that you would be wise to avoid.

Accept challenges and judge your judgments

I will purposely challenge you and attempt to trip you up in this book. I do it out of love so that you can discover your blind spots. You grow a muscle under the challenge of resistance, and you grow your understanding when you challenge your current limited thinking. Sometimes the challenge won't be to come up with a "right" answer to a question I ask. I may present questions with no "right" answer. Your lesson is simply to notice what came up for you when presented the question and choices. There are many layers of meaning and symbolism in this book. You can add different meanings to the symbolism, and each time it can still carry a lesson with it. I may present ideas that seem crazy, but only because you have your definition of a word and I'm using a different meaning. If you don't ask yourself, "What is meant by this?" you could miss a valuable lesson.

There's always more to the story

As you'll discover, there are almost always caveats, exceptions, and distinctions with anything that is said in this book or that you hear anywhere else. Almost any statement I make has the implication of "potentially" or "under particular conditions." You may come across things in this book and go, "Well actually, Derek, that's not really how it is or what that means. This is dangerous to even suggest and is actually the problem!" I'll leave this purposely vague here and won't elaborate, because just when you start to disagree with something you come across and get triggered emotionally, you may wish to see if you remember this simple point. Perhaps in the end it all comes together.

Embrace contradictions

You'll come to have a greater understanding of paradoxes throughout this book. I may say something that completely contradicts something else I say in another part of the book, or perhaps that you've heard elsewhere from someone who you trust. Much of the time though, I contradict myself in the same sentence by stating how two completely opposing things are both true. Am I crazy, illogical, or wishy-washy because of these contradictions? No. Realize what is said in one place is meant for a certain situation, and I may recommend something different for another situation. Learn to accept that there is typically no such thing as a "one size fits all in all circumstances" solution.

Be willing to explore a range of emotions and styles

This book will have (attempts at) humor. I will make stupid jokes. I will use a lot of unnecessary sarcastic hashtags all in an attempt to keep things light at times, and poke fun at our BS. But at times things will get serious and we will explore the darkest areas of your psyche to uncover what you've been hiding away. If you're the type of person who wants everything to be light and fun, be forewarned that you must be willing to let that go and venture into the places that your humor has been distracting you from. I will use a variety of learning styles. So one moment I may be making logical cases and in another moment using poetry to teach a lesson. If you don't like the way something is presented – there's still a lesson there for you in that. Don't miss the lesson out of a distaste for the teaching style.

Take it, toy with it, or toss it – temporarily

If you like how something works for you that you read in this book, feel free to take it and use it in your life. If you're unsure or tempted to reject it, I encourage you to toy with it for a while. Perhaps it's just there to unlock your own solution. Finally, if you don't like something and it doesn't resonate with you, feel free to toss it. However, all of these things have the caveat of temporarily. Something that works great for you right now may not be the best thing for you to keep doing in three months. Then it's time to toss it. Something may not be right for you now, but that doesn't mean it's not worth coming back to in another few months, or even few days, to see if it has relevance. And finally, don't toy with things forever. That can just lead to half-assing something needlessly instead of either taking it on fully or getting rid of it. All of this is your choice. Only doing what's in the highest and best good for all regardless of what a book says – even a totally frickin' amazeballs book like this one.

Remember that you always have a choice

You may not always get to choose the external reality, but you have a choice with your response to whatever is happening – including the interpretation of what you're reading. That means this:

Even when you don't have a choice, you still have a choice. I will reiterate you have a choice always. You will be tested on this throughout the book... perhaps when you least expect it. #FairWarning

Do you agree to these conditions?

If you're reading this, I assume you do.

Let the fun and games begin...

The Lake Of Greatness

Now you have a choice…

You stand on a cliff to make a leap of faith into The Lake of Greatness.

Go back, and your eventual death awaits, for all the water has dried up.

Or jump in, and risk being consumed by the waters and drown.

You fear going back.

Yet you may fear jumping in even more.

What if the water overwhelms you and you drown?

What choice do you make?

CHAPTER 1

Are Belief Systems BS?

When a person hears the word bullshit, they often think of something that's a total lie. A made-up story. A factually incorrect statement.

The first concept you must understand is that, more often than not, your bullshit is true. I don't just mean "because you believe it's true, then it's true for you." I mean, factually, your bullshit is often objectively correct. And yet at the same time, it's still potentially a deceptive lie.

If you're confused by this... good. Confusion forces your mind to start considering new things. Confusion precedes newfound clarity. I will attempt to confuse the hell out of you quite often in this book to rock you out of old thought patterns.

I'll explain how this contradiction works logically in a moment. For now though, let's explore your beliefs.

Do you think your beliefs are true?

On one hand, if you didn't think something was true, you probably wouldn't believe it, right? However, if you're an open-minded person, you may hold some sense that what you believe isn't true or false, but more or less a subjective opinion you hold.

Before we get into how some people can be convinced their beliefs are true, let's start with a simple non-controversial question before exploring things that are more debatable.

Do you need to breathe to live?

This is an example of an objective type of question that's not really open to a matter of opinion. This is assuming we're not talking about using something external, like a machine, to keep you alive without breathing. I know it sounds silly, because few of us would disagree about the answer, but go ahead and answer the question, "Do you need to breathe to live?"

It doesn't matter your upbringing or opinion, any reasonable person can definitely state, "Of course you don't need to breathe to live!"

It's pretty hard to argue in favor of the bullshit idea that you need to breathe to live. I think almost all of us have held our breath at one point and lived to talk about it. The science clearly shows we can live for several minutes without breathing, thereby making anyone who thinks you need to breathe to live a total dumbass who just ignores good science.

Clearly I'm messing with you...

We do need to breathe in the long term to live, but we don't need to breathe in the short term to live. Answering this question with either "yes" or "no" could be considered a correct response depending on the context.

Welcome to bullshit brain trick #1 – *giving meaning to something without considering the context.*

If you answered or were even tempted to answer, that question with anything other than, "It depends..." and then wanted further clarification, you were falling for this bullshit brain trick. I even told you in the introduction that everything has the caveat "potentially" or "under the right conditions." So if you answered with either "yes" or "no," then consider how quickly you forgot this lesson. A lesson many might even say is common sense.

Now imagine two people see this question, and one person argues vehemently that you do need to breathe to live, and another argues vehemently that you don't. One is taking the long-term perspective, the other the short-term.

Who is right? Who is wrong? In even an objective, scientific-type question about biological truths, can the lack of context make both people right *and* wrong, or looked at another way, make neither of them right or wrong?

Is it any wonder that there are so many arguments and disagreements in this world among seemingly logical people?

What's the practical significance of this?

Consider this...

If you believe breathing is a "good idea," which on the surface sounds pretty reasonable, what if you carried that belief with you while your head is underwater? The attempt to do something like breathe, because it's a "good idea" that literally keeps you alive, would be the very thing that may kill you in that situation as you choke on water in your attempt to breathe.

Let this sink in...

> *Something necessary to keep you alive in one situation can literally kill you in another situation.*

This breathing under water will be a theme I keep coming back to over and over again throughout this book. Keep this in mind as an analogy to how anything that on the surface seems good can be destructive, and something that seems destructive could be good, all depending on other factors.

What this means is that no matter what good advice you've heard, it could backfire in the wrong situation. All the good, wonderful, awesome things you do in your life could potentially destroy you if they're misapplied. And misapplying could simply be a matter of not realizing you're "underwater," so to speak, when you're doing them.

What are the things people tell themselves they need to do to live, be a good person, or have success in life? Could any of these backfire?

"I need to give food to others because that's what a good person does... *so I'll kill myself by starving to death when I give all my food away.*"

"I need to take care of my kids to be a good parent... *so I'll kill my body's health because I'll neglect spending time exercising and getting enough sleep.*"

"I need to work to pay the bills... *so I'll kill my relationships because I'm trying to get in more hours at work instead of being with the people I love.*"

There was nothing "wrong" with the first part of these statements, but they're *partial* truths. They're good ideas that can be bad ideas if that's *all* a person does, and they don't know when to let go of that idea. They don't know when to stop focusing on that truth in favor of another, greater truth.

You can look at all of these examples and go, "Yeah... no shit, Derek, that's common sense that anything can be taken to an extreme. It's all about moderation. I don't need a book to tell me that!"

Well congratulations, you have a basic level of common sense that allows you to not kill yourself by excessive generosity or working yourself into being in a state of having no friends and dying alone. But do you have enough awareness to see the subtle ways you're slowly draining your happiness with little errors in judgment?

A mentor of mine, Brandon Broadwater said, "Life is won and lost with the little things." It's the subtle ways in which you sabotage yourself slowly over time, with the most innocent actions that take you off course. Most of your self-sabotage will come from doing just a little too much or just *a little* less of something than is ideal. Or you miscalculate the timing by a bit. Or perhaps it's just a little tweak in *how* something is done that doesn't quite work out.

It's like a rocket that gets 99% out of the atmosphere before coming to a halt and doesn't quite make it. What's the result? A crash. Close wasn't good enough. The 1% makes all the difference.

Typically the "good-idea-gone-bad bullshit" is subtle, and subtle is deadly because it's easy to overlook or justify.

I don't want to ask for help because I don't want to be a burden and being a burden is bad.

I don't want this person to know how angry I am because being angry is bad and I need to always keep a sense of inner peace.

I'd love to start this business, but most businesses fail, and failure costs a lot of time and money and losing time and money is bad.

I need to tell this person only nice things they want to hear because if I tell them the truth it would hurt their feelings and be bad... and after all if you don't have anything nice to say, don't say anything at all.

I'll give my close friend a ride to the airport when I really don't want to and it interferes with other priorities because I would be kind of an a-hole and most definitely a horrible/evil/bad person if I don't do something for a friend who's done so much for me.

I shouldn't have negative thoughts because they're bad and I'm a super positive person who does a lot of self-help and has evolved beyond my ego-based wants and attachments.

I would love to take better care of my health but I just don't have the time because it's important to pay the bills, take care of the kids, and do charity work because taking care of myself is a bit selfish and bad when others need me.

I'll just crack jokes all the time because people appreciate my sense of humor and they wouldn't like me if they saw I was really upset, sad, or depressed which would be bad for my relationships and happiness.

If I say no to a request, I need to spend 5 minutes explaining myself because otherwise they'll think I'm being inconsiderate and that's bad.

I don't want to show others my talents and share my gifts and greatness with the world because it would make others insecure and uncomfortable, and making people feel uncomfortable or feel unworthy is bad.

Notice in all of these examples there's an element of "this is good, that is bad."

Isn't it easy to see how being a burden, making others uncomfortable, not doing favors for friends, ignoring family to focus on oneself, or having negative thoughts could be labeled as "bad" things to be avoided at all costs? I imagine you're savvy enough to realize you might not *actually* be a burden or make others uncomfortable with some of these things, but even if you do piss people off occasionally, is that a "bad" thing?

If you label a behavior of yours or others outside of context as *inherently* good or bad, it's bullshit. The behavior only becomes good or bad, or perhaps wise or unwise, under particular conditions. In other words, nothing has meaning until it's put into context.

Context is about who's doing or receiving the action, when is done, where is it done, why is it being done, and how is it being done.

Is buying someone a gift good or bad?

What if the reason why someone buys a gift is to kiss the ass of the person receiving it and uses it as a tool for manipulation? #Stalker #Creeper

Is telling someone you love them wise or unwise?

What if this is said when they're wearing headphones and they can't hear the words?

Is punching an innocent person in the face without being forced to, acceptable or immoral?

What if the person who does this is a boxer and they're in a boxing match?

Is kicking a kitten in its adorable little face nice or mean?

What if the reason why one is kicking the kitten is because it's the only way to save the lives of 1,000 baby bunnies? Isn't it better to just kick the kitten and hope it recovers, or do you seriously want innocent bunnies to die, you insensitive animal-hating jerk?

I'll repeat this disclaimer: Murder, rape, molestation, and similar unethical behavior already have a context applied. These are behaviors done against someone else's wishes. Touching a person isn't good or bad. It's "molestation" when you add context of it being against their will and on certain parts of their body.

This is not a book on morality, but it would be worth noting that the things that are generally agreed upon as unethical are things that violate a person's *choice*. Taking choice from someone is one of the most universally agreed-upon wrongdoings. Choice is kind of a big deal.

Consider this – what if you're taking choice away from yourself with mental deceptions and you aren't even realizing it? Could you be committing a violation against your own free will by your limited thinking? If you believe slavery is wrong, what does that mean if you're choosing to be a slave to your conditioning? Are you enslaving yourself through ignorance of self-deception? Something to consider...

CHAPTER 2

2VL vs. 4VL – Upgrade Your Brain's Thinking

Everything covered in here is to help switch your brain from 2VL thinking, which you'll often default to because of society's conditioning, to 4VL thinking, which is essential to start using before going further if you want to identify, appreciate, and break through your BS.

2VL stands for "Two-value logic," and it says things are either "true" or "false." It's "either/or" thinking. It makes a lot of logical sense for some situations. I can either be in this room or not be in this room. If I'm turning, I'm either turning left or I'm turning right. As I'm sure you're smart enough to realize, not everything in life is black or white. So what type of thinking allows for shades of grey?

4VL, which stands for "Four-value logic," allows things to be either:

1. True
2. False
3. Neither true nor false
4. Both true and false

Note that 4VL doesn't actually reject "either/or" thinking. That's a heads up for what comes up later in this book. You'd be wise to really reflect on that for a moment.

"You need to breathe to live," such a seemingly true statement, is literally true, but it's also false, neither true nor false, and both true and false depending on how you want to approach that statement.

In much the same way, your excuses, limitations, justifications, complaints, criticisms, and all the other things you're telling yourself are equally true, false, neither true nor false, and both true and false. With four-value logic, you can now see why your BS can be true, and yet still be considered bullshit when you switch your perspective.

Something becomes bullshit when the *partial* truth of a statement is believed to be the *full* truth.

It's bullshit to believe that "I need to breathe to live and that's all there is to the story." This type of thinking would lead to a false conclusion of, "I'll die if I don't breathe for even a moment."

It's *not* bullshit to believe "I need to breathe to live in the long term, but there are times I don't need to breathe." This type of thinking doesn't make "I need to breathe to live" true or false. It doesn't make breathing inherently good or bad. It recognizes there are many ways of looking at that statement.

All that changes is an understanding that there's more to the story. There's a bigger picture. Since you'll never have the full truth, everything you will ever think and come across is a partial truth. As long as you're aware that anything you believe is just part of the story, you're not bullshitting yourself. As soon as you think "this is all there is to it," you're bullshitting.

You may already know this on some level, but it's often easy for some to get caught up in thinking things like weakness, pain, pressure, selfishness, restrictions, resistance, confusion, separation, helplessness, dependency, complexity, risk, obstacles, mistakes, lack of time or money, sickness, junk food, opposing political viewpoint, disapproval, chaos, death, fear, and more are somehow "bad." If you've bought into any of these things as being barriers to your greatness and a better world, the good news is you'll have plenty of bullshit to start working through as you go through this book.

It's not just that what you consider bad could be good. In the next section, we'll explore how one of the things you value the most can be the very thing that destroys you. Without understanding what's in the next section, the knowledge you gain in this book or anywhere else could actually make your life far worse instead of significantly better. Keep reading to discover the three deadly words that often sabotage people from reaching their greatness.

CHAPTER 3

What You Know Is BS

"I know that."

These three words can be very dangerous or helpful depending on the choice you make after you think them. Another variation would be, "That's common sense."

Think of a regret you've had recently – and please don't pull the "I don't have any regrets" BS. If it's more suitable to you, think of a momentary lapse in judgment you've had.

With this poor choice...

Did you know better?

Did a part of you know not to do something, and yet you still did it? Or did a part of you know to do something, but still you didn't do it?

Think of a breakthrough you've had recently.

Got it?

Was the gist of what you needed to do something totally brand new, or an old idea you finally acted upon?

As a fitness coach, rarely am I going to tell someone how to get fit with a brand new concept they don't already know. It will typically boil down to exercise, eat generally nutritious food and avoid a ton of crap food, keep stress in check, and get enough sleep. Not exactly mind-blowing stuff. And while the details on how to do these things like exercise most effectively for a particular goal may be insightful, oftentimes I could simply ask a person, "What do

YOU think you need to do?" and they'll tell me many of the right answers.

Some may have the knowledge they need to eat more greens, stop being so hard on themselves, and spend less time keeping up with the Kardashians, but this doesn't really mean a lot of jack shit if they don't do anything with that knowledge.

It's not what you know that matters, it's what you do with what you know that counts.

Realize this: You know plenty already – probably too much for your own good.

We live in an information age in which you can Google anything, and yet all that does is create more overwhelm because now it's not about what you know, it's what to do with all that knowledge. It's made even worse when you hear one thing from one source and something contradictory from another source. More information may simply lead to more confusion.

I could write a book called 1,001 Ways to Be Happier, and it would be almost worthless. Who the hell wants 1,001 things to do? Who wants to sift and sort through all those ideas? As Kimberly "Sweet Brown" Wilkins would say, "Ain't nobody got time for that." How are you going to decide which of those things are relevant to you? When do you pick doing one over the other since you can't do them all at once? The irony is you'll probably get overwhelmed, upset, and depressed just trying to figure out how to be happier when there are so many ideas out there.

Wisdom isn't just about knowing what to do, it's also about knowing what to ignore.

This means that it's far more important for you to learn how to use the information you have than to get new information and knowledge. Much of what you read in this book is a "reminder" about what you know but may forget from time to time.

Let that sink in. Would some of your time be better spent figuring out ways to remind yourself, when it matters most, of what you already know, instead of trying to get new knowledge? How many times have you known what to do or not do to get a desired outcome, but simply didn't remember it when it mattered?

I could present hundreds of "new" ideas to you in this book about how to make your life better, but while that may make me appear to be a creative genius who presents all kinds of new cool facts, at the end of the day you may be worse off for it. It's better for you to be presented old ideas for how to better your life and explore them in brand new ways so you can actually follow through with them, than learn new concepts that don't actually do anything to fix the underlying causes of the challenges you face.

> *Breakthroughs don't usually come from looking at new ideas. They more often come from looking at old ideas in a new way.*

However, consider what you really "know." Just because you know the rules of chess doesn't mean you're a good chess player. A master chess player can look over my shoulder during a match and help me by saying, "You can move that pawn there. Then you can move this rook there. Then you can move the knight over there."

I could respond with, "Yes, I know I can move those pieces there," but it doesn't mean I have any clue why I would make those moves. The master sees something I don't – the principles and strategies behind the moves. I'm aware of what can be done on a chess board, but that doesn't mean I know how to effectively use that information.

Knowledge is understanding what's possible. Wisdom is understanding how to apply those possibilities effectively.

If you come across anything, including something in this book, and dismiss it by thinking "Yeah whatevs... I know that already," that's your bullshitting brain trying to keep you stuck. It's a subtle form of pride, and pride is quite possibly the most subtle and powerful force that keeps you from reaching your potential as it focuses your mind on what you already know and do instead of what you can discover and do to grow even more.

Pride is the ultimate impediment to reaching your potential.

Rather than looking at something you already know and dismissing it because you have awareness of the concept, you can now see that you have a choice here to start digging deeper into what you may not know around a concept by considering these things:

- Am I actually doing this thing I know?
- How could I do it better?
- Am I doing it the best way or the right way?
- Am I doing it at the right time? What about at the wrong time?
- Was this once a good idea, or is it no longer serving me?
- Why am I doing this? Is that a good reason?
- How can I remember to do this when I need to?
- How can I remember not to do this when I don't need to?
- Is there an easier way of doing this?
- Who can show me new ways of approaching this?

I'll offer some generally good advice here like, "Be grateful. Count your blessings each day. Spend a minute here and there throughout the day asking yourself what you're grateful for."

What do you think and feel when you read that?

I can only imagine this concept being a "holy shit, who would've thought of that!!" insight for a complete dolt. It's not groundbreaking information. You were probably told this many times as a kid – and yet for some reason it still gets mentioned in self-help books.

I can dismiss this idea of "be grateful" with a flippant "No duh. I know this already. OMG, I can't believe this person is talking about being grateful. Like, for realsies, who doesn't know this stuff?"

Or alternatively, I can look at this exact same concept of "be grateful" and explore it deeper. Here are my real-world feelings as I explored gratitude recently.

I started by asking, *"Am I doing this now?"*

Boom! #NailedIt

I'm practicing gratitude every single day as I spend a couple minutes after I wake up jumping on a mini trampoline and considering what I'm grateful for.

Awesome! So I pat myself on the back and say, "Way to go, Derek! You're totally rocking it. You should like, write books about this or something, 'cause you've really got this whole personal development thing down, and you practice what you preach." #RockStar #IImpressMyselfAtTimes

But not so fast…

"Am I doing this the best way?"

Well shitballs…

What used to be a practice that filled me with overwhelming feelings of gratitude has now become a near emotionless routine. I just think of a few things I'm grateful for and then go on about my business. "Practice gratitude" has become a to-do item on a checklist instead of an experience. I used to be able to generate such a strong feeling of gratitude when thinking about what I was grateful for that I'd be moved to tears. Now I just hurry up and get it done with so I can have my morning coffee.

In other words, telling myself "Yeah, I already know about gratitude" and thinking I've been practicing it was a nice pile of BS. It's BS because, while it was technically true that I was practicing gratitude, I wasn't truly experiencing the practice fully and generating strong feelings of gratitude – which is really the whole effin' point of it anyway, right?

"What" I was doing didn't matter if "how" I was doing it wasn't impactful.

Yes, I was doing gratitude, but was I really "doing" gratitude? It's like flippantly saying "I love you" out of habit to someone you care about as you walk out of the door vs. grabbing them by the shoulders, pulling them in, starting into their eyes, and with every fiber of your being radiating love as you profess, "I love you."

Both are saying, "I love you" from a technical standpoint, but they're clearly not the same act.

I didn't stop there...

"Am I doing this when it matters most?"

Ugh... most of the time I just ask, "What am I grateful for?" in the morning as part of a routine. When I'm stuck in traffic, waiting in a long line, or the shit hits the fan, and I'm facing a serious crisis, the whole "be grateful" thing often flies out the window.

If someone says, "Be grateful," I can choose to file that into the "been there, done that" part of my brain or proactively choose to explore it as though I'm experiencing the concept for the first time ever. Had I simply said, "Yes, I already know to practice gratitude, and hell, I even do it," I would have missed a deeper lesson on how I was bullshitting myself.

Consider this...

What is an area of life that you've gotten complacent in? How can you do this even better?

Another common bullshit brain trick is this – *New information is more important than old information.*

One may overvalue things that seem new and exciting over the old tried, true, and sometimes downright boring. To reach your potential sometimes means repeating old ideas and tasks over and over again until these things become engrained. It's not always fun and exciting. I get bored myself when I hear the same concepts repeated multiple times, but more often than not, I get more value out of being reminded of old ideas than learning something new.

So now you have a choice. When you hear things you like "be grateful" or any other idea you may have heard before, will you dismiss it as something you "already know" or use this as an opportunity to get deep and profound lessons as you explore the old idea in brand new ways?

No one will make the choice for you. You must decide for yourself if you wish to look at things in a new way. Only you can choose to let the words "I know that" be a trigger to explore the concept even more deeply.

My role as a guide is to present things in a way you may not have seen or heard before. I can attempt to help you prioritize and organize the information you already know to give you better perspective. I may even share a few new ideas you haven't ever considered before.

However, the words in this book still have no power to shift your perspective unless you're willing to choose to see things differently. Your role as the reader and chooser of how you live your life is to be proactive in answering these questions and coming up with your own questions to ask.

"I'm trying to free your mind, Neo. But I can only show you the door. You're the one that has to walk through it." – Morpheous – The Matrix

Your learning, your breakthroughs, and your revelations are your responsibility. Don't just wait for others to show you a new way when you can choose, at any moment, to look at things a new way to be your own greatest teacher.

CHAPTER 4

Warning: Your Knowledge Is (Potentially) Dangerous

You may already be familiar with or become very comfortable with the intellectual concepts outlined in this book. Four-value logic? Got it.

Consider the context for everything so you don't get stuck in half-truths? Second nature.

Know some ways to effectively motivate and persuade yourself and others? #NailedIt

What you know, however, should (potentially) scare the shit out of you.

Here's why your knowledge can be *potentially* dangerous...

What if the greatest opponent you face is within yourself?

Is that really so hard to believe?

Is anything more capable of masterfully deceiving you better than your *own mind*?

Ask yourself, have you ever tricked yourself with plenty of logic and good intentions into doing something ultimately harmful to yourself or another?

Have you ever looked back and said, "I knew better, but still I talked myself into it... Or out of it?"

Isn't the recognition of how self-sabotaging your own mind is a reason you're reading a book called *Break Through Your BS?*

Even if the greatest opponent you face is outside yourself, do they have any *true* power over you unless they convince your mind to buy into their story? Does a terrorist actually succeed if they don't get you to feel terror? They may have physical control over you, but even the cruelest dictators can't gain significant power unless they get some people to buy into their agenda by twisting their minds to follow them *willfully*.

If you are very persuasive and intelligent, and yet still admit you've made some poor choices, what you're really saying is that you're capable of persuading yourself with intellectual arguments into doing destructive things while making it all seem like a good idea.

No one has been able to deceive me more effectively than myself. My darkest moments came from my own mind turned against me.

After I learned about persuasion, I was able to write a bestselling book and help people get healthier and fit. I was able to coach friends through many of life's challenges. I was able to motivate myself to do things like workout consistently, build a successful business, and have even more amazing and deeply connected relationships. I used this knowledge for good as I'm not a psychopathic person who would ever use knowledge of persuasion and mental manipulation for bad.

The problem is that just because I wouldn't be tempted to use this knowledge to hurt another, it doesn't mean I was free from hurting myself. I started finding very convincing arguments to myself as to why "what I do doesn't matter. The world doesn't need me. My life has no meaning. People would be fine without me. What's the point? I might as well just give up."

I can provide very convincing reasons to justify all of those sentiments if I want to. Remember that almost everything is a partial truth from a certain perspective. It's partially true to say "The world doesn't need me." If I play that game, and I can certainly choose to play it if I want, I will be damn good at providing convincing arguments to back it up and strategically ignore any other mitigating elements of truth that go along with it.

Fortunately, I wasn't ever suicidal or outwardly self-destructive – but that can easily happen for those whose minds have taken control and turned against an individual. I was, however, strongly apathetic due to my own mental tricks turned against me. I wasn't necessarily giving up on trying to do good in the world, but I was severely slowed down until I broke out of my own self-imposed bullshit.

Applied knowledge is power. The knowledge of persuasion is power. But never forget the knowledge you possess, when turned against yourself, has the power to destroy you. Everything you learn about yourself and your brain has the potential to set you free, but it also has the potential to turn against you and drive you deeper into delusion.

Like the force in Star Wars, the more you can use your knowledge and intelligence of persuasion for good, the more you can also use it, and ultimately may be tempted to use it, for harm. And sometimes the only target of that attack is yourself.

Just because you learn of ways that you may be deceiving yourself doesn't mean you'll automatically stop doing them. Just because you know all the "mind tricks" your brain plays doesn't mean you'll be set free. Just because I know how a chess master beat me doesn't mean I can defeat them. And your mind is a damn good chess player that will use every technique you learn to break your illusions to turn around and create brand new, even more convincing illusions.

This may sound strange, but consider that who "you" are and who your mind is are not one in the same. If you are your thoughts, then who is aware of those thoughts? If you are your mind, then what is it that's aware of your mind? Learn to separate "you" from the ego-based thoughts and mind you have but are not limited to.

Your mind is your enemy – *potentially*. Potentially, it's a great friend. The difference between the two potentials comes from the choices you must continuously make to either lead you to be controlled by your mind or put you in control of your mind.

This is not a one-time decision. Your mind will constantly wrestle for control. Your knowledge and intellect *alone* won't save you, because your intelligence is being wielded perhaps even more effectively by your mind to deceive you. This isn't to say that you shouldn't use your intelligence or that it's "bad." You already know by now that nothing is inherently good or bad outside of context. However, you must discover another way to make choices that goes beyond your mind's intelligence. You must use your mind but not rely solely on your mind.

That starts with the choice you have here now... do you intend to lead your mind or are you going to be ruled by your mind?

If you do not intend to lead your mind and therefore come from a place beyond your intellect, do not read further. While knowledge is not the "problem," since it by itself has no choice, gaining more knowledge will only give your mind more ammunition to destroy yourself or others. This warning is real, and all you have to do is consider the countless ways you've been your own worst enemy to realize the element of truth it contains.

"The first and greatest victory is to conquer yourself." – Plato

CHAPTER 5

Making Sense Out Of Nonsense

Once upon a time in an ancient village, a young man dreams of adventure, but he has a great fear...

If he ventures outside his homeland, he knows there are those out there who would wish to enslave him.

Torn between his desire to explore the world freely and the fear that this will lead to his enslavement, he seeks out the village elder, a wise master, for advice.

The wise old master listens empathetically to the boy's plea.

"Wise Master, I wish to have freedom, but I know there are those in the world outside my homeland who would shackle me up and take away my choice to live as I please once they see me. Can you help me?"

The wise master questions the young man, "Do you realize if you wish to venture outside of your homeland, you cannot avoid those who would try to enslave you?"

The young man replies, "Yes, master! I know those people cannot be avoided. But yet I also feel enslaved if I'm stuck in my homeland and never get to see the world. Is there any way I can explore the world without fear of being taken as a slave?"

The master strokes his long beard and replies, "Yes... there is but one way. I can share with you the secret to living free if you wish."

The young man eagerly takes the old wise master up on the offer. "Show me the secret, please, Master!"

The master takes the young man to a cabin.

The wise master grabs the young man's hands and proceeds to shackle them to the wall with heavy handcuffs.

The young man is shocked.

The young man protests, "What the eff!! This is total bullshit, dude! I wanted you to show me how to be free from enslavement, and you just shackled me to a wall!"

The wise master looks at the young man and says, "You wanted the secret to being free from enslavement. If you want to travel free, I'm giving you exactly what you desire."

Pause the story here for a moment...

How do you feel about what's happening?

Is the young man right in saying what the master did is bullshit?

Is the master some sadistic a-hole who gets off on tormenting the young man?

Or could it perhaps be the young man's limited perspective that makes him accuse the master of bullshit, when it's really the young man who doesn't see the bigger picture?

Grab your popcorn, and let's see if the next part changes your mind about anything…

Resume scene.

The young man cries out for answers. "How is enslaving me keeping me from enslavement? This makes no sense!"

The wise master replies, "You are enslaved, but only for a time. As you learn knowledge, you will be able to pick these locks. As you gain strength fighting against the shackles, eventually, you will be able to break free from these chains."

The young man begins to come around after realizing the old man doesn't wish to keep him enslaved permanently. Still he wonders, "But why do I need to know how to pick locks and break chains?"

The old master smiles. "Because young man, while you may not be able to avoid those who would shackle you, when you have the ability to break free from any shackle, no man can ever truly enslave you. Knowing this, you will be able to live free from both the enslavement of man's shackles as well as the shackles of your own fear."

The young man got the lesson. He graciously accepted his position of temporary enslavement knowing that with time and effort, these shackles would serve him to give him the knowledge and strength to break free from any other shackles that may be placed upon him.

Years later, with the master's help and training, he learned to break free. For all the remaining years of his life, he traveled as a free man, neither remaining bound to those who shackled him nor fearing those who would try.

CHAPTER 6

Limitation = Liberation

What's your lesson from the story?

The moral expressed in this story is that truth often comes in a perceived paradox or contradiction. The paradox of this story was that the key to not being enslaved is to be enslaved. To resolve the paradox, you simply add a little more distinction. The key to not being enslaved in the long-term is to allow yourself to be temporarily enslaved so you can learn to break free from enslavement.

Once you have more power than the shackles, they cannot limit you. But to develop that greater power, you may need to put on shackles and fight against them. Breaking handcuffs is literally something strongmen develop the strength to do – and that strength is developed through fighting against resistance. You can't develop the strength to break free from restraints without putting on restraints and fighting against them.

Here's the broad version of the paradox: In order to move closer to your goal, you must often move further from it... temporarily.

The young man cannot be free from the fear of enslavement unless he knows what it's like to be enslaved and break free from it. He must be enslaved temporarily to overcome both the fear and real risk of enslavement. You've heard it said you must face your fears to overcome them. This is an example of moving towards what you don't want ultimately sets you free from it.

Consider how this plays out in so many different ways...

To make a muscle strong, one must first make it weak through training and resistance. Later, strength comes.

To grow a business and make money, one may need to give away work or samples for free and lose money in order to gain trust and ultimately make money later.

To have better relationships with others, one may spend more time with themselves alone in self-reflection and self-work.

To have greater clarity and understanding, one may need to spend time in confusion and uncertainty as they explore new ideas they haven't considered before.

This doesn't make any sense if you take a narrow perspective. To become physically stronger, I'm going to fatigue my muscles, break them down, become significantly weaker, and ultimately reach a point where it might be hard to walk down a flight of stairs after working my legs. #Genius

If you didn't see the bigger picture of eventually letting go of the resistance and allowing recovery and compensation, this would seem like the most ass-backwards thing in the world. "I want to be strong and capable of lifting heavy things, so let me work myself to exhaustion so that I can barely move my own arms and legs. That's the ticket!"

As illogical as it seems in the short-term, almost everyone universally accepts that making yourself physically stronger requires making yourself physically weaker – temporarily. The question is, do you realize this same principle is playing out in almost all areas of life?

CHAPTER 7

The Slingshot Effect

This moving away from what you want in order to get it, or moving towards what you don't want in order to be free from it, is what I call the "slingshot effect."

With a slingshot, if you wish to propel something forward with a powerful amount of force, you create tension and resistance by moving the object in the *exact opposite direction* of where you want it to fly.

It's important to recognize this is about *temporary* tension. This part is **critically important** – you must be both willing to move away from what you want and also be willing to go towards what you want. Otherwise it's like lifting weights to get stronger only to never put them down, walking around with dumbbells in your hand all day, and wondering why you can't move your arms. It's not about permanent pain or resistance, but temporary pain and resistance. You gotta know when to let go and allow yourself to enjoy the fruits of your labor or else you'll torture yourself.

This slingshot effect is playing out in virtually all areas of your life. The willingness to be uncomfortable in the short-term leads to far more comfort in the long-term. However, realize that not only does moving away from your goal *potentially* get you closer to it, but the opposite is also true. The desire to avoid pain by moving towards pleasure in the short-term often leads to far more pain and loss of pleasure in the long-term.

Someone may say, "I don't want to look at my bills and bank statements because it makes me uncomfortable." They keep saying that and keep pulling the slingshot back away from pain. Then eventually something gives, the tension is released, and they've flown forward landing smack in the middle of overwhelming debt and financial ruin all because of their attempt to avoid discomfort and move towards comfort.

A person says, "I don't want to worry about my diet and its effect on my health. I'll just keep eating these doughnuts because it feels good." That choice keeps them moving away from pain in the short-term, but then boom! The tension is released. They're shot flying forward into sickness and feeling like total shit as they finally face the consequences of that pain avoidance. Maybe the slingshot doesn't release in a day, week, or even ten years, but eventually the tension is too much and it releases.

Even if it doesn't ever release, the sheer tension of holding onto the thought, "I know I can't keep this up forever" makes the comfort provided by poor choices unfulfilling. Deep down inside, you know the slingshot effect exists without me having to tell you. That means that deep down inside, you know of behaviors you're engaged in that bring you temporary comfort that could be setting you up for long-term devastation. The inner recognition of the slingshot effect may be why things that bring short-term gratification still feel "empty" while temporary discipline, even though not always fun, provides a rewarding feeling.

Your brain will often bullshit you like this: If I want to avoid pain, I must avoid pain. If I want pleasure, I must go after pleasure.

If I didn't tell you about the slingshot effect, you might even think "Yeah, that's totally the way things work." You might even say, "Yeah, that's logical, it's common sense, and I already know that."

If I said, "To get stronger, get weaker." "To avoid pain, put yourself in pain." "To have success, fail." Would you have been like, "Dayuuum, this Derek dude is crazy pants!" Can you now appreciate how even things that don't make sense logically or are "wrong" can actually make total sense and be right from a bigger perspective?

Of course, I'd imagine it's not a revelation that you may need to give up short-term comfort for long-term comfort. Most of us realize that instant gratification isn't the key to lasting gratification. You have an inner knowing about this already and probably even think about it in the areas of life you excel at. I just gave this phenomenon a cute name and the analogy to a slingshot so you will remember it consciously when it matters most – in all areas of life.

While there appears to be a contradiction in some of these statements like "be weak to be strong," or "fail to succeed," you can likely see now that they're just incomplete statements. Partial truths. Everything is a partial truth.

Keep in mind that these statements are not absolutes. Sometimes the way to move closer to your goal is to move closer to your goal. Sometimes the way to avoid pain is to avoid pain. I can't just say, "Oh ok, I'm going to torture myself and automagically it's going to lead to feeling pleasure later." These seemingly contradictory statements are conditional on a number of factors – so it's a simplification with plenty of caveats.

However, I'm sure you can see many areas where you've "slingshotted" yourself into discomfort because you made yourself too comfortable, and "slingshotted" yourself into more comfort because you were willing to be a little uncomfortable for a moment. However, this pain/pleasure paradox is only one of many slingshot effects. As you continue through this book, you'll see just how often this slingshot plays out, perhaps in ways you never imagined.

Start to consider…

What behaviors are you doing to be comfortable now that are potentially setting you up for pain down the road?

If you knew of uncomfortable things you're avoiding that would ultimately propel you to greater joy and fulfillment, what would these be?

So now you have a choice to decide if you're willing to move away from what you've been chasing and go into what you've been resisting.

Are you willing to limit yourself so that you can be set free from your limitations?

Are you willing to face what you've been trying to escape from so that you can actually be free?

Are you willing to endure confusion, chaos, and uncertainty so that you can have true clarity?

Are you willing to endure hardship, discomfort, and pain in order to have comfort and ease?

Are you willing to embrace fear, suffering, and loss so that you can experience even greater joy, fulfillment, and love?

When making your choices, remember this:

> *You can either experience pain willingly or unwillingly, and pain that's embraced by choice is much easier to tolerate than pain that must be endured by consequence.*

CHAPTER **8**

Choose Your Own Journey In BS Land

This is a simple and potentially exciting, "choose-your-own-journey" story about "damned if you do, damned if you don't." You choose your journey, I choose the outcome. Play along and you'll be enlightened. Don't play along, and you'll *still* be enlightened... if you choose to be.

You're driving down the road in a car and come to a fork veering off to the left and the right.

You don't know where either side will take you.

However, you hear scary sounds coming from both sides.

You're struck with fear.

The left side looks scary, and you hear the sound of monsters coming from that side.

The right side looks scary, and you hear the sound of monsters coming from that side.

So now you have a choice.

You can choose to go down the right side. There may or may not be monsters down there. You won't know until you check it out.

But then consider this, what's the alternative?

What other choice do you have?

To drive down the left side with its potential monsters?

Does it matter if you pick driving down the left or driving down the right side?

Which choice do you make?

Choose now and don't overthink it. After all, this is just a made-up story, and I'll tell you the made up consequences of your choice shortly.

Got it?

Are you really playing along?

For realsies, make your choice...

Ok, good. Here's what happens.

The consequence of driving down the left or right side is destruction as the monsters are waiting for you in either path and will destroy you. Staying where you're at also leads to destruction as the monsters eventually come out from each side and destroy you.

The real question is, did you pick something else besides going to the left, right, or staying where you're at? If not, why not?

Did you *choose* to backtrack and take a different route altogether? Wouldn't that be a pretty smart choice if it appears you're headed for destruction? Or did you tell yourself the scary sounds are all just in your head, so you feel you need to choose to keep pushing forward in spite of fear even when your senses are clearly indicating there's danger? Maybe you thought there's no such thing as monsters, but isn't that just an assumption? Haven't you heard that you shouldn't make assumptions?

Did you *choose* to get out of your car and explore off-road? If not, why do you feel you need to stay in your car? Did you decide your car was or wasn't capable of going off road? Who told you that? Could you have driven your car off the beaten path if you wanted to choose that?

Did you <u>choose</u> that your car had a jetpack on it, and so you flew up above the scene to scope it out? Why not? Did I say you didn't have a jetpack, or did you make that assumption? Why would you limit yourself? Who told you that a working jet propulsion system isn't something you could choose to invent and have attached to your car in a totally freakin' made-up story where YOU get to *choose* your journey?

Did you *choose* to seek out counsel from someone who's been down either side of the road? Did you get a map or search the internet to see where each path leads? Did you choose for that not to be a possibility, and if so, why would you limit yourself in a story in which you can choose your own journey?

Did you feel you had a *choice* in how the story played out, or were you buying into what you felt "Derek's version" was? Remember I only choose the consequences; you still get to choose your journey – any journey. When I told you not to overthink it, did you just go along with my command, or did you say, "Screw that, I'm going to think about this and have some fun using my imagination?"

Did you *choose* not to *choose* anything because this is just a silly story in a book you're reading and you're wondering what the hell the point of this is? Did you tell yourself what you choose doesn't matter because there's no evidence to make one choice more reasonable than another? Did you check in with your intuition, or just think logically that because this is some stupid thing in a book it doesn't really matter what you choose?

Did you want to skip past the story to just get to the point? Are you so quick to get to the point that you don't choose to explore your own thinking by playing along, even though that's the whole point of reading this book in the first place?

What if I said any choice you make would lead to your destruction? Would any choice you make matter? Of course not, because it's a made-up bullshit story. Or at least, that's one way of looking at it. That's one partial truth. You see, from another perspective, the choice you made *does* matter, even in a made-up story, because that choice teaches you something about yourself. You can learn about yourself from each choice you make, whether it's a choice you make in a story, a game, or the real world.

In this story, I decide the outcome for you. The outcome, no matter what you choose, is this: You'll be destroyed by monsters.

The story has nothing to do with making a choice that avoids your destruction. Here's a newsflash: You, or at least your physical body, is headed for destruction in the real world – guaranteed. I already know the end outcome of your life is your physical body dies. You know it too.

In this made-up story, the ultimate outcome of your destruction was already decided for you, but you still had a choice in how you played along. In real life, the outcome of your eventual physical destruction by death is already decided, but how you play in the meantime is still your choice. If the monsters in the story are simply metaphors for sickness, injury, or old age that can kill you, is there really much difference between this story and real life in terms of your eventual destruction no matter what choices you make?

If you were manipulated into thinking you only had a couple choices, consider this...

Did you let my careful use of language which asked, "What's THE alternative?" make you think there could *only* be one other alternative? Notice how the word "the" creates a subtle implication in your mind there can only be one other option.

Side note, do you think politicians ever use subtle language tactics to manipulate your thought process? "You're either with us or against us. You either choose this, or *the* alternative is you hate freedom and want to murder puppies." By the way, if you think manipulation is always bad, remember nothing is good or bad outside of context. There are plenty of good ways to manipulate yourself and others, which could be called ethical persuasion.

What if I would have asked, "What's AN alternative?" Would that have shifted your brain into considering more than one or two other options? Do you feel how the simple switch to asking "What's an alternative?" subtly creates a context that there could be more than one option? I could have even set you up with, "What are some other alternatives?" and I guarantee you may have started to see more choices.

Now if you weren't manipulated by my clever use of language to get stuck in those few choices and did come up with a crafty out of the box choice – so what?

Did you do that because I had warned you I would try to trick you earlier in this book? If I didn't give you fair warning I would mess with you, would you have been on guard and chosen the same?

And does it really matter if you didn't pick one of the options I gave you and went off somewhere besides either of those paths? Do you know the *full* story of the outcomes? All I said was either way you'd be destroyed by monsters, which is true no matter what choice you made. But did I say that picking the right side or left side would lead to *immediate* destruction?

What if both those sides had totally awesome parties going on filled with Vegas-like shenanigans (or whatever your cup of tea is)? You could've lived a long, full life hanging out on either of those paths and the monsters only would come and destroy you after you've had your fill of awesomeness. If you went anywhere besides those two paths, monsters may have quickly gone to your location and taken you out. While you're out in nowhere land thinking you're super smart because you didn't take the beaten path, you totally missed out on a helluva party. #JustSayin #ShouldHaveBeenThere #ItWasCrayCray

In this BS story, I get to say you're destroyed no matter what, and you have no choice in that matter – just like in real life you could be destroyed at any moment even if you do everything right. This is as much about the choices you don't have as the ones you do. In this life you have many choices, but avoiding your eventual death is *not* a choice you can make. Avoiding risk is *not* a choice you can make. Avoiding mistakes is *not* a choice you can make. Avoiding pain is *not* a choice you can make. Perhaps even avoiding fear is not a choice you can make.

You can't choose to go through life without making assumptions, being wrong, and having people disapprove of you. These are all monsters that you will face that will injure or kill your ego no matter what choices you make.

This may seem to make any choice meaningless, except when you consider that the choices are not about the outcome of survival of either your physical body or your ego. It's about how you're shaped by those choices, and how you shape the rest of the world with those choices. Did you forget that you might not be alone in this story? Did you forget that it's not just about what you experience, but all the other people you meet and impact going down either of those roads or anywhere else?

In a story with arbitrary consequences made up by the story teller, the choices you make can never be truly good or bad from a final outcome perspective. I can always make the outcome undesirable if I want.

This does differ from real life where you're typically given a little more evidence based on past history, what's presented before you, and some degree of understanding of how things work. It's not so far off from reality though in that what you've led yourself to believe is possible may be far more limited than what is actually possible.

On an even more subtle level, in real life you may have some type of inner or intuitive guidance – or you may even call it spiritual guidance that exists beyond you. You can't explain why, but you sense one choice may be better for you than another. We'll get to this later.

For now realize that all of these stories and examples can teach you a lesson, but they're not the "whole" story. They both are and aren't an accurate representation of real life decision making. The fact that I'm eliminating variables you may face in real life is not meant to deceive you, but get you to focus on and consider various parts of your thought process in detail. Never forget though there is always a bigger picture.

Here's some questions to ponder at any moment...

What do I choose now and why?

What did I learn from that choice?

What choice am I not seeing that exists?

What choice do I feel matters that really doesn't?

What choice do I think exists (such as how to avoid destruction) that doesn't truly exist that I can now let go of worrying about?

Now you have a choice. To reflect upon this choose your own journey story, and ask yourself what choice did I make and why? Remember, choosing not to choose is a choice. What did you learn about yourself from this?

After you've gotten a lesson from this, consider this simple fact: Even in a completely made up story, where perhaps no choice you make will lead to a desired outcome, and with no particular evidence to support one decision over another, you still learned something.

Making a choice in this hypothetical story, from one perspective, "doesn't matter" as it's not real. It's made up. It's imagined. Yet, despite the seemingly illogical nature of making a choice in a story or game, the simple act of choosing something and exploring that choice taught you something about yourself. It exposed something that you were previously blind to. If you choose to, you can have a real shift in your understanding simply by "playing the game of choice."

CHAPTER 9

Shackling Yourself In BS

"Joe, we've decided to sell you your dream Lamborghini at a crazy price of $50,000. You'd be crazy not to take this deal!"

Joe lowers his head in disappointment. He says, "I'd love to take the deal, but I don't have the money."

The car dealer looks curiously at Joe, "Bro, are you kidding me!? You're getting an amazing deal! When else would you ever get a car like this for this little money?"

Joe acknowledges this. "Yeah, I know. I'd love to take the deal, but I just don't have the money. I mean if I could wave a magic wand and make the money appear, I'd buy the car, but it's not in my account. You just can't talk me into having money I don't have. I *can't* buy the car."

"Jessie, your dream body is only three months away," the slick fitness sales rep says. "Simply sign up for our program, and you'll be given the diet and exercise plan to get you more fit than you've ever been."

Jessie's excited, but a little hesitant. "Sounds great!! But… uhh… how much time does this take?"

The fitness rep replies, "Well, for the kind of results you want to achieve, it's as little as an hour a day, 5 days a week, plus another 2 hours a week meal prepping. And that's only for the next three months before you can cut back to maintenance."

Jessie's stomach starts to sink. "I know that's reasonable for some...but I really don't have that kind of time. I'm a single mother raising three kids, and I work a full time job. Plus I don't have the energy or the discipline for a program like that. This is something I can't do."

Are either of these people bullshitting themselves?

Excuses

Remember, nothing is inherently good or bad outside of context, and that means excuses can be good and perfectly reasonable under certain circumstances.

So are any of these excuses valid? Are any of these excuses BS?

Let's look at Joe, who's offered a crazy deal on a Lamborghini...

He doesn't have the money. Like, *literally*, for reals, not even close to that much money in his account. Open bank statement, money not there, end of story. Calling BS on this would seem a bit insensitive to the truth of his reasoning, right? I mean, surely some excuses are valid.

Yet we already realized whether you need to breathe to live can be either true or false depending on how we looked at the statement. Now let's dig into the practical way this plays out in our day to day lives.

If you were Joe, what would some alternatives be that you could take to still buy the Lamborghini?

Think about it...

Make your choices...

Pause your reading until you come up with at least two.

The first thing that comes to mind for myself, and many people when buying a car, would be to see if he could get a bank loan or make payments to the dealership. Don't have the money? Just borrow it!

Now this may seem obvious because it's so commonly done. It's at the forefront of our minds to use a loan as a way to overcome an obstacle like not having enough money.

If you thought of this, congratulations! You're capable of overcoming literal objections using common sense. You probably didn't even need to read anything in this book to come up with that idea. Welcome to not being totally hopeless at life. There is hope for you yet. ;) #NoButSeriouslyYouAreAwesome

Just for a moment, consider if this solution really is "common sense" and if so, why? Is it "common sense" because we're born into the world already understanding you can take loans for things, or rather because it's so commonly done in our society that the solution is obvious? Is it that the problem doesn't even seem like a problem because of what you've been surrounded by in your environment? That is, people commonly take car loans. This is something very important to consider... and we'll dig into it more later.

Now did you have any more, outside-the-box type of ideas?

If so, this means you didn't let a momentary truth stop you from coming up with a possibility for a new potential future truth.

Opportunity is when possibility meets reality.

If you're solely focused on what is, you can't see what "could be." To see opportunity, one must be both a realist in seeing what is here now while being an idealist with inner eyes for unseen potential.

What if he didn't qualify for a loan?

No problem. Joe can make a few phone calls.

He may negotiate a deal with a rich investor friend to have her provide the funds for the loan. However, Joe has a clever idea to rent out the Lamborghini for photo shoots and to his investor friend whenever she wants to drive it, and eventually uses that to pay back the investor. Not only has he borrowed the money, but he can actually get creative enough that he doesn't have to necessarily repay the loan out of pocket. #Winning #LikeABoss

How did I come up with this off the top of my head? Because I've studied and heard stories of entrepreneurs who often come up with crazy deals and solutions to challenges. If you've studied entrepreneurs, this may seem like a relatively rudimentary solution. However if you haven't, it may seem really unorthodox. It's my exposure to other people's perspective that opens my mind to new possibilities.

One of the easiest ways to see new possibilities is to see things from other people's perspective. If you can't see a solution, look with new eyes.

Quite simply, this means the more you hang out with, study, and expose yourself to other people's ways of thinking, the more you expand your own thinking – if you're open to it.

Be sure to consider though, is it really "new eyes" if you start looking at things the way your friends, family, and co-workers, *who are just as stuck as you*, look at things? If you ask a friend who is poor, for money advice, what kind of "new" perspective do you think you're going to get? It's like teenagers getting perspective on the world from other teenagers. #Worthless

You may be familiar with the story of Richard Branson starting Virgin airlines. His flight was canceled, so he chartered a private plane, sold the extra seats to other passengers who missed the same flight he was going to take, and made his way to Puerto Rico.

Did he have the money or the resources to make this happen when his flight was canceled? No, but he realized that was his *temporary* situation. Whether or not it remained that way was his **choice**.

Would you have thought of that solution if your flight was canceled, or does a canceled flight mean you're screwed? Does the temporary reality stop you from seeing a future possibility?

"It's not the lack of resources, it's your lack of resourcefulness that stops you." – Tony Robbins

Richard was able to separate what was true in the short-term from what may be true in the long-term. You already do this with many things. It probably wasn't a revelation that you don't need to breathe in the short term. The question is, do you consciously separate your temporary situation from your long-term possibilities when looking at each of your excuses?

Separate your future possibilities from your current reality, and you'll have countless options to choose. Always remember, what's true now doesn't have to remain true.

One bullshit brain trick is assuming that you're going to be the same, or that your circumstances will be the same in a moment, a day, a week, or a year from now. The real insight isn't just that your circumstances *may change*, they are *guaranteed* to change. Nothing in this universe remains stagnant. This is either scary or liberating, depending on how attached you are to your current circumstances.

If you really like your excuses, you can hold onto them because they're often "true." This approach, *for better or worse*, will work to keep your current reality relatively stable until it reaches an inevitable breaking point. The slingshot might be slow acting in some areas of life, but don't delude yourself into thinking things will always be as they are now. Just ask someone who's had a steady job, marriage, or healthy body swept away from them in what seems like an instant.

But if you don't like your excuses, you can easily say, "Yeah, this is true *for now*, but I'll be damned if it remains true. I'm going to choose to do something about it." This approach of considering "what could be," *for better or worse,* will work to change your current reality more quickly than focusing on "what is."

You already switch between "what is" vs. "what could be" thinking regularly. It's just that, when you really like your excuses because they keep you comfortable and "right," you'll keep yourself stuck in "what is" thinking. When "what is" gets too painful, you'll naturally jump to "what could be" thinking.

> *"If you really want to do something, you'll find a way. If you don't, you'll find an excuse." – Jim Rohn*

Being in enough pain about "what is" may even be the very reason you picked up this book. You recognized that, at least in some area of life, you don't like "what is" and this got you thinking about "what could be."

The question is, do you wait for circumstances to get so bad that you decide you need to switch your thinking, or are you proactive in choosing how you think regardless of circumstances? If it's the latter, then you may have picked up this book not out of current pain, but rather because you'd rather *prevent* future pain and/or maximize fulfillment and contribution to the world by developing yourself to your greatest potential. It's the difference between eating a nutritious diet to overcome existing disease vs. preventing disease.

Each way of thinking, whether "what is" or "what could be," has its pros and cons. After all, a person could mistakenly assume they'll make tons of money in the future and make poor financial choices out of over-optimism of what could be.

Remember, no approach is "good" or "bad" unless seen in the light of the situation. It may actually be unwise for Joe to get the Lamborghini, but "unwise" and "impossible" are two very different things. He saw it as impossible because of his circumstances without realizing his present self and future self would be living in two different realities – and these realities are created by his *choices*.

He felt he didn't have a choice at all. His response was essentially "I can't" which removed his choice. He chose to give up his power to choose. Had he realized he *potentially* could have gotten the Lamborghini with enough creativity, but simply chose not to for good reasons, his response would have been "I won't" rather than "I can't." The difference between these two statements is the difference between freedom and slavery.

Saying "I can't" isn't inherently false, but it's more complete to say "I can't *right now*." Realize "I can't" puts you in shackles to your current circumstances, which will be true if you wish to choose to focus on that truth.

However, you may also choose to shift out of that thinking and consider, "What could be?" The future holds near limitless possibilities beyond your mind's consideration. Limitless possibilities, however, can be paralyzing by having so many options to consider. This is why one may wish to remain with the thought of no possibilities rather than face overwhelming possibilities.

If you've ever felt a burden with so many choices to make, or had the quality problem of not wanting to miss out on all the amazing opportunities you could take, you know that this is a real challenge. With this understanding, *you may start to get a glimpse at how limitations can actually be liberating to control the number of choices you have.*

Without a balance of the two perspectives, like the balance between day and night, you'd either feel nothing is possible or everything is possible, both of which can be enslaving.

Now let's take a look at Jessie.

She had more subjective excuses like "not enough time and discipline."

These excuses may also take the form of, "I'm not that type of person, so it won't work for me." This is an excuse that's less about your present outer circumstances and more about your inner identity. It's far more subjective than something like how much money is in a bank account.

These types of excuses can be more readily called BS, but let's not ignore that from a certain perspective, they're absolutely true. Jessie may be working really hard as a mom, and let's give single moms some credit for how much they sacrifice. Her schedule could be filled with critically important things like work and taking care of her kids.

I'd be willing to bet that Jessie, despite her belief, has far more discipline than the average person. She simply feels she doesn't because she's so drained busting her ass with all the other things she's taking care of. But all that matters is how she feels about herself, because her telling herself that she doesn't have the energy or discipline will make it nearly impossible for her to find it.

> **You won't seek out what you don't believe is there. You must first discover the unseen possibility before it can ever be seen as reality.**

Jessie's excuse that she doesn't have enough time is actually an *objective lie.* That's because we don't "have" time. It exists outside of us. This may seem like semantics, but as long as you're trying to "get" more time, you'll find it's impossible.

What you may do instead is make *choices* about how you're spending the 24 hours a day that exists outside of us. From this understanding, what Jessie is really saying is, "I'm making other things mean more to me than this workout and diet program."

Boom! Now we're dealing with the truth.

And is there anything wrong with this?

Perhaps there is, perhaps not.

It's neither my place nor yours to judge Jessie for what she makes meaningful.

However, if we explored it deeper, we might find the reason Jessie spends so much time working and raising her kids is because raising a good family matters to her. She feels she needs to be in her kids' lives, and taking time for herself would take away from that.

But what if her declining health leads to her lacking enough energy and strength to take care of her kids and play with them, having mood swings and being a worse parent, and eventually being sick and in the hospital because she hasn't taken at least some time to look after her own health? What if the example she sets of poor health choices rubs off on her kids, and now they adopt poor health habits? What if her attempt at being a good mom actually makes her a worse mom? In other words, she slingshots herself into "bad mom" by constantly moving towards "good mom."

This isn't so hard to believe. As a fitness coach, this seems to be more the norm than the exception. Obviously she doesn't need to sacrifice her job and family entirely to start taking better care of her health. Just like one may momentarily find it important to hold their breath, it's not all or nothing.

If Jessie is honest about her situation, she may find herself in this situation. "I want to be a good mom and need to take the best care of my family, but to take the best care of my family, I need to not take care of my family... *temporarily*."

This is a "no shit" type of truth, but it bears deep consideration:

> *Giving up something temporarily doesn't mean giving it up entirely. Sometimes you must give up what matters most in this moment to have even more of it in your future.*

She is trying so hard to move towards taking care of her family that she may ultimately end up doing a worse job at taking care of her family. She's neglecting the fact that she *temporarily* needs to spend time working on herself.

That could be with a diet and exercise program, and that could also mean taking time to de-stress, get a massage, go on vacation, catch up on sleep, take up a fun hobby to recharge her batteries, or other things. Just like getting weaker is necessary to make you stronger, this time away from taking care of her family could actually make her better at taking care of her family. She spends less quantity of time with her family and job, but then when she does spend time with these things, the quality of that time goes up to more than compensate for it.

The big problem with Jessie's excuses is that she's a hard worker as a single mom and therefore seems to deserve a lot of praise and validation for her reasoning. Doesn't she deserve a lot of credit for being such a hard worker and willing to sacrifice from herself for others?

Not so fast...

Sacrifice for others and hard work are often praised as good things, but remember, nothing is good or bad outside of context. Her hard work would deserve praise if she's working hard when she needs to, and also knows when to either stop working so hard, or when to work just as hard on something else that's needed to create a more balanced life.

Remember...

Hard work is destructive if you're working hard at going in the wrong direction.

Could your hard work *at times* actually be sabotaging yourself?

Are you working so hard on doing things that matter that you've forgotten about things that matter even more?

Are you working so hard on educating yourself that you aren't doing enough to implement what you learn?

Are you working so hard on implementing the things you've learned that you aren't doing enough assessing of whether or not it's really working for you?

Are you working so hard on what was taking you in the right direction that you've overlooked the fact that now it's starting to take you *off* course?

Are you working so hard on finding inner peace and happiness that you've overlooked creating change in the physical world?

Are you working so hard at making the world a better place that you've let your own inner world turn to shit?

Are you working so hard at justifying your existing bullshit that you've forgotten it's only a temporary story, and now you can choose something new?

If it feels impossible to consider all of these things, good. If it feels like there's no way you can ever "maintain" balance and harmony in your life without something being sacrificed, good. It's OK to be feeling overwhelmed. It's OK to be feeling out of balance. It's OK to be feeling like this is impossible to always make the right choice.

Let this feeling grow as you continue to the read the book, because you're going to need to draw upon this feeling for the strength to do the one thing you need to do – the secret to overcoming all of this – and it will require relentless effort on your part. Let the tension grow inside of you, because it means you're pulling back the slingshot into the realm of uncertainty, overwhelm, confusion, imbalance, and chaos only to be potentially released, bringing you even closer to balance, harmony, and peace.

Justifications

Excuses give you a reason "out" of something, and justifications are the opposite side of the coin – a reason to go "into" something. They coexist, because whatever you're excusing yourself out of, you're justifying whatever you want to do, or feel you need to do, instead.

"I don't have enough money to get training on how to improve my life, finances, or health" can excuse someone from investing in their education. This would also then be a *justification* for remaining ignorant.

This is a key point. Every "no" has something else you're saying "yes" to. Every "yes" has a near infinite number of things you're saying "no" to.

When you excuse yourself from something, you're never making the choice to "not choose." We often think in terms of "do or don't." But for everything you say no to, you're saying yes to something else. You never just "don't." You always just "do."

The power of choice is so strong, you can actually choose to give up choice. You can choose to be enslaved and be run by your circumstances, other people's wishes, and your own conditioning.

The choice not to choose is choosing to remain a slave to your conditioning. Your circumstances. Your beliefs. Your bullshit.

Yet this is still a choice. You're always choosing something. The choice not to choose is choosing to be run by your conditioning and circumstances instead of your consciousness.

Do you choose to stop being lived by your life's story and start living your life by your choices?

Why Fight For Excuses And Justifications?

Ask yourself, "Am I defending my limitations? Am I arguing for remaining in my current conditions? Am I so focused on this partial truth that I can't step back and see a bigger truth?"

Whenever you fight for keeping your limitations, you're fighting against your liberation. Defending your story is defending your slavery to it.

Defending "I'm a hard worker" forces one into a role of working hard, many times at the expense of relaxation and recovery. Defending "I'm intelligent" forces one into a role of having all the answers at the expense of admitting "I don't know many things" and embracing uncertainty. Defending "I'm a giver" forces one into a role of giving, many times at the expense of receiving.

So why do we almost all universally do this at times? Why would we argue for a lack of possibilities and live in willful ignorance to our potential greatness?

There could be plenty of good reasons...

You may feel you don't have a choice in the matter. No one has shown you where a choice exists, and you've been conditioned by your upbringing to make assumptions about what is or isn't possible.

You may feel you *do* have a choice, but not a desirable one. You're damned if you do and damned if you don't. You're making the best possible choice you feel you can even if it's not ideal. To make a different choice, even for getting something you care about, means you have to sacrifice something you care about more.

The excuse not to take care of yourself can be justified by a need to take care of others. The excuse not to help others can be justified by a need to take care of yourself. The excuse not to take a risk can be justified by a need for safety. The excuse not to be too cautious can be justified by a need to be successful, because you'll never win by playing "not to lose," and all choices have risk.

If you're honest with yourself, you may find whatever you fight for is whatever is meeting your human needs which you'll learn about in a bit. A need doesn't have to be selfish as it could be a need to contribute to a greater mission beyond you. You'll fight for whatever you believe will meet your needs the best. This is a hint at how to escape this trap which you'll discover in a bit.

Fighting Fire With Fire

Excuses or justifications aren't necessarily right or wrong until they're put into context. This means it's a good thing that you can justify into or excuse yourself out of almost anything, because almost anything can change from good to bad or bad to good, depending on the circumstances.

Since excuses and justifications can be true, at least from one limited perspective, the problem is that most don't know how to "fight" against truth. It's not like I can look at my excuses and say, "Wow... I'm totally bullshitting myself because this isn't true." The problem is, it is true.

That's why you can know you have excuses, know they're not the whole truth, but you *still* fall for them. You don't know how to fight against the truth. You can be fully aware you're self-sabotaging yourself with the nonsense you tell yourself, and yet you still don't know what to do about it.

So how can you win this battle if your limitations are, by all your logical thinking, absolutely true?

The way to "fight" against truth isn't to fight it or reject it, but to *integrate* more truth into the picture. Don't reject your excuses or justifications. Understand why you have them, and then decide what else you can consider in addition to them.

If Joe told himself, "I *do* have the money to buy this car," that would be a lie. He can't get over his excuse by lying to himself. Joe telling himself that he doesn't have the money is *the truth*. He can't fight against that truth, but he can bring in more truth. "I don't have the money *right now*, but are there possibilities I might not have considered for how to get this money? How might I do that? If I don't know, who can I talk to who might have the answer? What am I willing to do to get this money? Does it matter enough to me to find a way?"

This is simply a taste of how you can escape your excuses. Considering something else. Pretty obvious, right? Hell, you probably already knew this. So will you let pride stop you at "I know this" or choose to dig deeper into this knowledge?

So now, you have a choice...

Knowing that it's *partly* a matter of cultivating greater awareness, understanding, and perspective to overcome your limitations, how much will you proactively explore what's beyond your excuses and justifications?

Are you willing to expand your perspective?

It sounds easy enough, but remember the slingshot...

It's often said the truth hurts. This is only the case if you're not living in alignment with it and prefer to justify your current comforts.

In order to slingshot beyond your limitations, consider...

Are you willing to face what's uncomfortable and downright terrifying for the sake of having more insight and perspective?

Are you willing to see what's ugly about yourself, others, and the world in order to make it beautiful?

Are you willing to get feedback on your weaknesses, your blind spots, your failures, your inadequacies, your flaws, your mistakes, and other things you've been trying to blind yourself to in order to gain awareness of greater truth?

If so, you may choose to escape your limitations. If not, you will choose to remain bound by them.

When making your choices, remember this:

You will eventually face a greater truth, willingly or unwillingly. Those who willingly choose to see a greater truth now are given potential freedom through enlightenment, while those who choose to blind themselves are resigned to slavery through ignorance.

CHAPTER 10

Bringing Out Your Hidden BS

A t this point, you likely have a greater awareness about how you've been bullshitting yourself.

If for any reason, you don't feel like you're falling into any of these BS traps, that could mean either...

You're so caught up in your own perspective that you can't see how it's limited. In which case, your BS is keeping you from seeing your BS. In reality, it's your pride keeping you from acknowledging it. I can't choose for you to let that pride go, only you can. You must pick either pride or your greater potential. Much like a woman is either pregnant or not pregnant, this is one of those situations where either/or thinking is legit.

Or perhaps...

You are totally rocking it in life and doing great at everything, which means you're not challenging yourself enough, which means you're actually kind of not totally rocking it and aren't doing so great because you need to keep challenging yourself to grow, and if you're not growing, you're regressing. #NotGonnaLetYouGetAwayWithThatShit

We all fall for BS from time to time because your BS hides in your BS. That is, your bullshit hides in your blind spots. You can expose it when you push your boundaries and try new things – so long as you're willing to get the lessons from the experience. Challenging yourself may expose your BS, but you can still refuse to see it if you cloud your vision with pride saying "I have nothing new to learn."

I was at a seminar recently, playing a game that was meant to challenge our creativity. Long story short, I assumed to score the most points in a round, we had to go after the big wins of 25-100 point at a time. Little did I know that there was a highly unconventional way of getting far more points in a round by going after little wins of less than 5 points at a time. After the players all discovered this way, I thought, "Wow! I was so caught up in thinking I have to "go big" to get the most points that I didn't see I could go for smaller wins faster and do 5x better!"

My "go big" bias kept my creativity limited. Boom! BS exposed. But would I ever see that BS if I didn't put myself into an environment that challenged my way of thinking and doing things? Or might I have been tempted to avoid that challenge and comfort myself with thoughts that I'm a pretty creative guy who writes books about people's blind spots and therefore wouldn't have any of my own blind spots?

I could easily go either way. There are times where I think I have things figured out without even realizing I don't know what I don't know. The inner choice to either give into pride or fulfill my potential is what leads to the outer choice I make of what to pursue in life. This outer choice, or the physical action that I take in the world, leads to my results. Even though my outer environment of playing a game shifted something inside me, the first point of choice had to come from within me to challenge myself and not give into pride. In other words, the way I decide to "be," proud or teachable, affects what I "do" and ultimately what I "have." By choosing to "be" teachable, I "do" the action of challenging myself and "have" new insights.

Remember this: No victory on the outside will come without first having a victory on the inside. There may be a time where the choice that matters the most is the one you make on the inside.

How you choose to <u>be</u> matters more than what you choose to <u>do</u>.

You may not have a choice in how you live in the outer world, but you always have a choice in how you live in your inner world. No one else can take this freedom from you. Only your own mind can take away your sense of choice, which is why it's potentially the greatest threat unless you get it to be in service to you.

What if the real question oftentimes isn't "what can I do?" but rather "how can I be?"

"Good" Intentions Aren't Enough... But They Kind Of Are

Focusing on "how to be" doesn't mean what you choose to do doesn't matter. It's not cool to do stupid things because of good intentions. Good intentions don't automatically make up for bad actions. It's not all or nothing – from one point of view.

For instance, if I want to save an injured friend's life, and I perform surgery on them even though I don't know what the hell I'm doing, my good intentions are doing a disservice. If I *really* wanted to save their life, I'd also use my intelligence to realize I'm unqualified, and I would call a doctor.

The important thing to remember is that one noble intention, such as the desire to help others, taken in isolation, can actually be harmful. There are plenty of people with good intentions doing harm not because of their good intentions, but because they lack other intentions to provide balance.

The same is true with actions. Feeding starving children while letting one's family starve isn't "good" because it's isolating one good deed at the expense of another good deed. This is why it's impossible to call something "good" or "bad" outside of seeing the bigger picture. Is daytime "good" in nature if it's not ever balanced with nighttime?

This is why the *intention* to gain knowledge, develop skills, and be resourceful must sometimes also be held in addition to the intention to serve others. You may not actually be able serve others effectively without knowledge, skills, and resourcefulness – although this isn't an absolute. There are plenty of people who show up in the world without big brains sharing nothing more than a loving smile, and they do tremendous good for others with the gift of their loving heart.

Your intentions are usually the root of both what actions you take and how those actions are done. Just listen to someone give a compliment reeking of approval-seeking instead genuine appreciation. You can often literally sense the dishonestly in the words because of the intention behind them. Whether it's the tonality, timing, word choice, body language, or something else, there's often a subtly different action when there's a different intention.

All your actions are colored by your intentions. You can try to hide your intentions, but those who can "see the unseen" will recognize the difference. Much like how the same words written in a different color could appear to be exactly the same to a color blind person while the difference would be obvious to those who can see colors. This lesson goes even deeper when you realize that just because you can't see something doesn't mean it doesn't exist or isn't being projected by you.

A word of wise to the masculine types out there – the feminine can often sense intentions much better than you can. A woman's intuition is an intention-detecting machine.

A person could say, "Intentions are everything." Or "Intentions are something, but not everything." Or "Intentions are nothing."

Which of these do you believe?

Which of these is true for you?

Is there something else that's true for you?

Why is what you believe true for you?

What would you say to someone who holds a different viewpoint?

If you believe intentions matter to some degree, what do you think and feel about people who say they don't matter at all? If you believe intentions don't matter, what do you think and feel about people who say they do?

If I ask someone making any of these statements about intentions, "Why do you say that?" and have them explain their reasoning, would this change things for you?

"Intentions are everything because they're the root of all action. Nothing is done without first there being an intention from someone, somewhere. A doctor wasn't able to save people's lives until after they set the intention to learn how and set the intention to practice those skills. Intention is the first choice made that sets other actions into motion, and even habitual acts done without thinking may have started with an intention at some point."

"Intentions are something, but not everything. If intentions aren't balanced with the knowledge of how to apply an intention properly, it could be harmful. If someone has good intentions to help a student learn math, but then shows up unprepared and teaches incorrect information, the good intention actually backfires. The good intention to help is a starting point, but it's incomplete if not followed up with right action."

"Intentions are nothing, or at least very insignificant, because intentions themselves don't change anything in this world. It's only actions that make a difference. All the good intentions in the world won't save us if a disaster strikes. In fact, good intentions have led to very destructive acts. It's better to focus on just doing the right thing."

Could you agree with all of the statements, "Intentions are everything, intentions are something but not everything, and intentions are nothing," to some degree? Is it only *what* a person believes what matters, and/or is it about *why* they believe it? If someone makes a statement, could the meaning you give it be different than what the person saying the statement *intends* it to mean? Do any of these statements even have meaning until you *choose to* give them meaning?

You see, these statements have a very different meaning depending on the intention of the person saying them, and the meaning you've given to these statements. Could there be many people making statements you disagree with, that if you only could come to understand them better, you'd find you're on the same page at heart? If someone says something you disagree with, do you choose to ask for clarification and come to understand their world, or do you automatically react by going on the offensive to prove them wrong, or on the defensive to prove yourself right?

Taken even further, could your own inner conflicts, the war with your own mind that pulls you in opposing directions of wanting to do one thing and then wanting to do the exact opposite, simply just be a *misunderstanding*? If you got to know the deeper intentions behind why you do what you do, might you find it all makes total sense? If you wanted to make peace with someone, wouldn't you first need to understand their perspective?

One perspective I have about intentions is that one can hold many intentions – and must hold either broad intentions or multiple intentions or change their intentions as needed to create a long-term balance.

If you truly have an intention to do good, you'd be wise to have the intention to know when to stop helping people that you're enabling. You'd have the intention to gain the right knowledge and skills appropriate for your life. You'd have the intention to keep yourself reasonably healthy to the degree that you can control it so that you can show up in the world as your greatest self. You'd have the intention to face what makes you uncomfortable so you can grow yourself to be capable of handling life's challenges. Most of all, you'd have the intention to *actually frickin' do the things you know to do* so you're creating real impact in the world with your actions.

CHAPTER 11

Still Searching For Your BS

Perhaps you don't fall into either of the two categories I laid out at the beginning of this section. You're humble enough to admit you have plenty of BS, but still you're unsure exactly what it is or how it's affecting you. You need some more time to explore things. Here's an insight. This exploration will be a life-long process.

If you don't see how many ways you're bullshitting yourself, ask yourself, "In what ways am I holding back from challenges that will expose my blind spots? How often am I pointing out the flaws of others instead of my own? How am I making myself wrong for being the way I am instead of making myself right by improving myself?"

In short, "*How am I letting pride keep me from my potential?*"

Warning: Pride will continuously creep up on you. You may be humble and teachable now, but once things start working for you, you'll be tempted to say, "I got this!" "I know this!"

Not necessarily bad things to say, right? I mean we want some confidence and pride in our accomplishments, true? Certainly I wouldn't advocate beating yourself up and guilt tripping yourself into changing. Isn't that the whole problem with self-help that people do it because they feel there's something wrong with themselves and they have to force themselves to change instead of accepting the wonderful beings they are in this moment? Or maybe by now it's obvious that it's not self-help that's inherently the problem, but the intention of the person doing it.

Celebrating your success is important, but what matters more is not what you've done, but who you are being. Do you care more about your success, or your *striving* for success? Is it more about the outcome or the way you're playing the game? Is this an either/or? Could it be a bit of both that's important?

What if it's a slingshot thing? Success can be one side of a slingshot where, the more you move towards it, the more you're setting yourself up to fly into failure or mediocrity. This means, with the wrong intentions and focus, "success" can sabotage growth and prevent you from unleashing your greatest potential.

In the game that I was playing at the seminar, my team was scoring more points than all the other teams early on with our "win big" strategy. We were "successful." It was only after we were told there was a way to do 5x better that I realized <u>success was keeping us stuck</u>. My team got so caught up in doing things the "working well way" that I didn't realize there was a far "better way."

It was believing the BS that success is "good" that kept our team from innovating and discovering a far easier and more effective way of playing the game. We were beating the competition, but still unknowingly falling far short of our potential. The only way to discover the better way was to stop doing what worked and fail a bunch of times until we discovered a new way of playing this game. We had to let go of our pride of being the best and doing what worked in order to reach a much greater potential.

> *Sometimes you must be willing to let go of what's working well and fail to find what works even better.*

What you're doing may be working right now, but that doesn't mean it's not BS. Would you keep doing what you're doing if you discovered a far easier, faster, and better way? What if the fact that you're getting great results in life is only leading you to get complacent and attached to your current way of doing things at the expense of something much greater?

What if someone who wants to destroy you or others is willing to fail more than you are, so ultimately they become far more powerful than you, making you helpless against them? Don't delude yourself into thinking that there aren't those who would want to harm you or people you love. History shows how many innocent lives are ruined because good women and men let their pride blind them to impending destruction.

Remember, everything changes. Just because something is working now doesn't mean it will keep working. Some people let pride blind them to the potential downfall of their relationships, business, or health even when signs are evident. It's easy to see how many giants, whether people or institutions, have fallen when they slipped into pride.

While you can't avoid pride, this isn't about total avoidance. It's about not staying stuck in pride; much the same way the key to freedom isn't to avoid limitations that can actually be useful, but not stay stuck in them. You must make it temporary.

How do you keep yourself from *getting stuck* in pride?

The answer to avoiding getting caught up in pride, or anything else for that matter, isn't to choose "not to be prideful." You can't really choose "not to choose."

The question you must consider is, "What do I choose now *besides* pride?"

The short and simple answer is "growth."

How do you choose growth?

You've already chosen it by reading this book. You've already chosen it every time you've allowed yourself to be uncomfortable. You've already chosen it when you were willing to do what you weren't willing to before – assuming that willingness came from a place of wisdom.

Essentially, everything in this book is designed to help move you out of pride and into growth. Everything in this book is designed to help you do even more than that.

However, a book won't be enough. Not even a book from Derek Doepker is enough to break you out of all your BS, as awesome as that dude's books are.

What have you been shrinking away from?

Are you waiting for everything to be perfect, or are you willing to let go of what's working for you and keep failing until you reach a whole new level of possibility?

How have you been holding back?

Are you waiting for someone to make it easy for you, or are you willing to do what's hard?

Where have you been playing small because you fear your own greatness?

Do you need to keep reading this book, hoping it will give you courage for that one thing you've been holding back from, or can you act now in spite of your fear?

Do you need a book to tell you the answer, or do you already have the answer within you?

Your answers to these questions will constantly change, and the answer that shows up is where you can grow right now.

This is your next step. *This is your challenge.*

Are you willing to put this book down and do what you've been putting off to experience the break through you've been seeking?

When making your choices, remember this:

You will be challenged to grow, willingly or unwillingly. Those who willingly choose to grow themselves will be able to break through the biggest problems while those who choose to shrink themselves will be squashed by the smallest problems.

CHAPTER 12

Why You Should Love Your BS

I know I would be better off if I stopped procrastinating and did this right now...

I know I would be better off if I told this person how I actually felt instead of bottling it up inside...

I know I would be better off not worrying about what people think and doing what I love...

I know I would be better off caring more about my friends than the Kardashians...

Yet...

I...

Just...

Can't!

Sound familiar?

You know what the problem is and how to fix it, but still, something holds you back.

Wouldn't it be nice if all you needed to do to change your life was know how you're screwing up and then know what to do instead, and then magically you'd just frickin' choose to do it?

Many people are looking for what's wrong and what the solution is, yet when they find the answer, it's dismissed as "easier said than done." Granted, the reason something is easier said than done is because you spend more time talking or thinking about it than actually doing it.

It's not enough to know what to do if you don't know *how to get yourself to do it.*

What bridges the gap between knowledge and application?

What is this "X" factor?

Before I figured this out, I got stuck in a depression shortly after my business of writing books and coaching authors became successful. Keep in mind that at this time, I was well-studied on personal development. I knew I wasn't any of the thoughts that went through my head. I would meditate each day. I would practice gratitude. I did all the things those crazy people at seminars do to get themselves hyped up. I would let go of unwanted emotions. I even had outwardly good circumstances with my health, relationships, and finances – so good that 99% of the world's population would be envious of how comfortable my life was.

Yet despite a high degree of self-awareness, doing work that I loved and that fulfilled a greater mission, and having my needs met, I got stuck in apathy, self-loathing, and feeling like no amount of good that I could do would ever matter all that much.

I was well aware of the psychology of what I was doing to myself. I sort of knew how I got myself into this state, and I even sort of knew how to get myself out of this state. Yet I stayed stuck there for months because I wasn't applying this "X" factor.

Hell, I was even aware of the "X" factor, but I didn't totally appreciate it.

That's a hint...

The "X" factor became clear to me when I had an interesting thought after someone emailed me asking for coaching.

I thought to myself, "I want to coach others on how to have a better life, and yet here I am feeling like shit for months on end. What would I coach myself to do in this situation?"

Then it hit me...

One big mission in my life is empowerment. *It's to help transform the lives of others.*

While I had my fair share of challenges in life, and this wasn't my first time feeling totally apathetic and depressed, I had never really gone through the experience of getting myself stuck, feeling totally lost and confused, and then pulling myself out of it in a conscious manner.

I thought… "What if I'm stuck so that I can understand how I got stuck and how to pull myself out of it in order to teach others my lessons?"

Instantly I felt a surge of energy that I hadn't felt for months.

My situation wasn't "bad," it was *exactly* what I needed to go through to take my next step.

What was my next step?

I didn't know it at the moment, but very quickly I got the idea to write the book *Why You're Stuck*, which outlines the ways we get ourselves stuck and how to overcome them.

How could I write a book on the topic if I didn't actually go through the experience myself?

Do you want to take advice about depression from a person who either hasn't experienced it or doesn't understand it? All they'll say is some nonsense like, "Just cheer up!" The only thing this will accomplish is perhaps getting the depressed person to punch this insensitive a-hole in the face.

Consider this…

What if your setback is really just a setup for your next breakthrough? What would happen if you turned what is holding you back into your greatest ally by giving it love and appreciation rather than rejection?

I didn't appreciate my "stuckness," negative thinking, confusion, apathy, and other "bad" emotions as being exactly what I needed to move me forward. Looking back though, if I want to empower and lead others through dark times in their life, wouldn't it pretty much necessitate that I go through something similar myself to have true empathy?

What if, on some level, your BS is a good thing? What if it's there to empower you like shackles that you can break through, and in the process, you become far stronger for it? Wouldn't that make it a gift rather than a curse?

What if not being OK is perfectly OK right now? What if the greatest challenges you go through are really just a part of your "before and after" story that will inspire others to greatness when they see what you've been able to overcome?

Feeling good and being happy are like breathing – generally good practices, but you may find yourself underwater and better holding off on them for a bit. I had to hold off on happiness, clarity, and positive thinking in order to explore the darker side of life. I had to take some time to ponder why people do evil things, why we hurt ourselves, and my own dark thoughts.

Here's a newsflash: you don't want to eliminate negative thinking. You don't want to eliminate anger, sadness, frustration, confusion, and other emotions. You want to cultivate what brings those things into balance.

Getting rid of fear altogether would be *potentially* dangerous. If I only had courage and not fear, I could become foolhardy and make stupid decisions feeling like I was indestructible. Fear without courage on the other hand keeps one either paralyzed in terror or running from what they fear, which may ultimately be far more dangerous than facing it.

If you encountered a bear, the safest thing to do is to courageously face the bear instead of run from it. You can courageously face a bear even if you're feeling fearful if you appreciate that running away means it's going to chase you down. When you're *more* scared of running than standing your ground, you'll choose to face what you fear – even though you're still probably shitting yourself.

Do you appreciate both fear and courage because you need them both at times? Do you appreciate how neither is good or bad until it's put into a bigger picture? Do you appreciate how you don't have to pick between one or the other, but you can have both working together?

Act only in fear or only in courage and you'll eventually make the wrong choice. Appreciate both, and you can choose which serves you the most in the moment. Fear and courage are simply one set of emotions we choose from. You'll come to see how there are many ranges of emotions that are each working to create harmony. Anything taken in isolation can become harmful.

You may intellectually know that negative emotions serve a useful role at times, yet intellectual knowledge of this still won't fix an emotional issue. Appreciation is about your emotions – your heart, so to speak. You can't just think it to be true, you must *feel it* to be true. Otherwise you go, "Yeah, I know this, but I'm still paralyzed by fear." You'd be trying to fight an emotional battle with pure intellect.

Have you ever felt bad... and then felt bad for feeling bad?

"I feel bad for feeling bad."

"Now I feel bad that I feel bad for feeling bad."

"Ugh! I feel even worse now that I'm feeling bad for feeling bad about my bad feelings!"

The downward spiral continues with seemingly no way out.

You tell yourself, "I shouldn't feel bad. I shouldn't feel this anger, or sadness, or depression! I shouldn't feel this confusion! I'm beyond this. I'm a good, wise, well-balanced, positive person. But yet I'm feeling bad... So something is wrong with me! I'm not OK, and that's not OK!"

Stupid Obvious Reminder: Feeling bad about your bad feelings isn't the way to stop feeling bad. #NoShitSherlock

It's ridiculous, but isn't that what so many of us end up doing?

The first thing to get out of this downward spiral is to stop labeling the feelings or thoughts or condition as "bad" or undesirable. You already know you can't label things "good" or "bad" outside of looking at how it fits into a bigger context by now. Just realize you might not see the bigger picture until more time passes, or you choose to make it mean something good.

But changing your language is a slow albeit critically important way to change your feelings. Also, let's not kid ourselves and think feeling depressed is sunshine and rainbows. It's OK to acknowledge you feel like shit. You're not a freakin' robot here. You're a human who's going to get torn up about things, and that's OK!

This last part is critical...

It's OK if you're not feeling OK.

The solution is obvious...

Be good with not feeling good.

Feel the feeling of "I'm not feeling OK and that's OK."

Look yourself in the mirror and affirm it.

Can it really be this simple?

Yes, but still you may be dealing with a bit of "easier said than done."

This is because you may have plenty of practice with attaching feelings of resentment, discontent, anger, sadness, and hatred to what you don't like, and not enough practice attaching feelings of joy, appreciation, and happiness to what you don't like.

You have to retrain yourself to start to feel appreciation for *whatever* shows up in your life. You have to feel appreciation for whatever you've chosen to do. You have to feel appreciation for all your inner demons and drives. Taking it even further, this means appreciating why other people do what they do.

What if the way to stop feeling bad is to welcome and embrace with love and appreciation the very things making you feel bad? What would happen if you loved your uncertainty, suffering, and fear?

It's not an intellectual idea, but a way of being. An intention you have. Something that takes diligent effort. It's a practice, because you have to actually *practice it.* One can't truly appreciate guitar playing by reading a book on how to play guitar and getting it only intellectually. One must actually sit down and start practicing the guitar to embody the concepts.

When creating music, each note can serve a role. An F# note isn't good or bad or better or worse than a G note. Even a happy song isn't necessarily more beautiful or appreciated than a sad song. Music is beautiful because there's no judgment of one note over the next. Tension in music is valued just as much as harmonious consonance. Nature shows us its beauty by reflecting back the full spectrum of colors. You may have a favorite color, but what kind of dull world would it be if you only saw the one color you prefer?

In much the same way, to create the life you want, you must choose to embrace all the notes and colors available to create the music and movie you dream of. And even plot twists you didn't see coming can be appreciated for keeping you from getting bored.

CHAPTER 13

We All Just Want Some Apples

While this appreciation may take time to cultivate, there is a way to speed up the process of appreciation.

You appreciate what you value, and you value things when you understand them on a deeper level. In a sense, you can use your intellect to affect your emotion.

If I told you I have an apple, and you value apples because you like their taste and know that they help keep you alive, you'd appreciate an apple if I gave it to you.

If I said, "I have a special type of new apple that is the juiciest, most delicious apple you've ever had in your life," and you took a bite and confirmed it, would you value that apple way more than other apples?

You may think, "The apples I already have are good, but I'd rather have these. I might even trade in my old apples for these new apples. Not because the old ones are bad, but because these new apples are even better." You wouldn't stop valuing the old apples, you'd just prefer the new ones. This is critical to appreciate for what's coming up.

If you already had some apples of your own, and then you were told "your apples look nice, but inside they're really rotten," would you appreciate them? Probably not anymore, once you have this understanding of their rottenness. Especially if you weren't just told they were rotten, but you proved it to yourself by cutting them open and looking inside.

At first you might have loved your apples. Maybe you even clung to them and danced around giddy as a school girl about having a nice basket of these beautiful apples. But once you realize they're rotten, you don't value them.

Unless, of course, you were starving to death and didn't feel you had another option for food. You'd still value a rotten apple if it meets your survival needs and it was all you had available. You'd still *appreciate* a rotten apple more than starving to death. Why? Because you *appreciate* life. The apple is just a means to an end. What you really appreciate, even more than apples, is being alive.

Disclaimer for smart asses: I realize you need to eat more than apples to live. It's called an analogy.

All of these apples have some type of value. If you didn't have any other options, a rotten apple is still valuable if it can keep you alive. However, if all three types of apples are available, and you looked beyond the surface of the apples and appreciated the true difference between them, wouldn't you easily choose the most delicious apple?

The reason you're still eating rotten apples is because either you have what looks like nice apples that you don't realize are rotten because you haven't looked inside them, or you know you have rotten apples but don't feel better apples are available to you. "All the good apples are taken," or "I don't deserve good apples."

For many people though, it's not a matter of eating rotten apples. It's a matter of eating mediocre apples. They've settled for what's good enough to keep them alive, and they're not going to risk giving up what keeps them alive to go search for something even greater. Maybe it's just simply, "I don't want to leave my mediocre apple tree for the slim chance of finding a better apple tree in case I starve to death on that journey."

What does all this apple stuff mean? It's OK if it's not quite clear. I'm purposely keeping it vague. Confusion precedes clarity. It will make a lot more sense in the next section and the second time you read this book. You're going to read this book a second time, right?

What you're about to discover are the six human needs. Everything you do stems from trying to meet these six human needs. Just like one may eat a rotten apple to meet their physical needs if they had no other choice, one would eat a rotten apple in the form of unhealthy actions if it met their emotional needs and they felt they had no better choice.

Whenever you do something stupid that you know better than to do, it's because it was meeting one of your needs. It's like eating a rotten apple but feeling like you had to, otherwise you would starve to death emotionally if you didn't. Rotten apples suck, but starving sucks more.

When you don't do something that you keep telling yourself you should do, it's because you feel you'd be missing out on something that meets your needs best. Like trading your good or acceptable apples for some that might end up being rotten.

Understand your needs and how you're meeting them, and you'll be able to understand all the crazy illogical behavior you have and other people have. No matter how ridiculous or short-sighted something may be, you, I, and others wouldn't do it if it didn't meet at least one of our needs on some level.

CHAPTER 14

You Really Are Crazy... But So Is Everyone Else

Do you ever crave comfort? Hope you have a "steady" job, relationships, and security? Try to avoid mistakes? Analyze the hell out of everything to make sure you get it right?

Who doesn't want these things to some degree?

We all want comfort. We desire some sense of safety and security. Even the biggest risk-taking, adrenaline junkies want some degree of certainty. Maybe the reason they take risks is because they're *certain* they'll get a rush from it.

Do you ever crave variety? Love having fun? Do something new every now and then for shits and giggles? Yearn for excitement?

Who doesn't want these things to some degree?

We all want variety. As much as you like to know what's going to happen at times, secretly or not so secretly, you wish for the occasional, unexpected occurrence to keep things interesting. Some like "safer" variety like playing a board game. Some like "riskier" variety like gettin #TurntUp and #CrayCray with a bunch of party animal friends and going streaking through the quad. #GotAnOldSchoolReferenceInASelfHelpBook #Winning

No matter how much you love comfort, a part of you, slowly or quickly, starts to feel angst when things are the same old, same old for too long. As much as you may desire predictability to some degree, there will always be a little kid in you who wishes things were new, exciting, and different.

So let's think about this...

You want things to be the same and predictable, but you want things to be different and unpredictable.

You. Are. *Crazy.*

What about your relationships to other people or things...

Do you ever crave connection? Want to have other people's approval? Or at least, the approval of some sexy person you're totally into? Do you wish people liked you... even if you don't always like them? Do you ever wish you were at least a little more like other people you admire, and less weird or different? Even if you didn't give two shits about other people, do you at least enjoy having love and connection with a pet or animals or nature?

Who doesn't want these things to some degree?

We all want connection. You can bullshit yourself and say, "I don't care what anyone thinks about me." But even if you don't particularly care about other people, do you want to feel close to something? Want to feel like at least a dog or cat or horse or something on this planet is bonded with you? Doesn't a part of you want to fit in somewhere, with some people or something? To be accepted? To be approved of?

Do you ever crave being significant? Perhaps not all the time, but do you ever secretly dream of having admirers who praise how special you are? Do you want to feel you're different, in a good way, and therefore irreplaceable? That you have a unique role in this world that only you can fulfill? To have someone look at you and say "you're one of a kind" in a totally awesome way?

Who doesn't want these things to some degree?

We all want to feel significant. Some may prefer not to be in the spotlight and would often rather hide in a corner while others might be egomaniacal, selfie-taking machines. But either way, no matter how much or how little, there's a part of all of us that wants to feel like we're not just skin and bones, but someone truly special and unique. Someone that stands apart. One of a kind.

So let's think about this...

You want to fit in, but you also want to stand apart.

You want to be like others, but also different from others.

Maybe one side of the spectrum is more appealing than the other, but no matter how much you fight it, do you find that secretly you kind of wish you had each at times?

You. Are. *Crazy.*

Totally illogical, right?

Don't worry, we're all a bit crazy.

If you get upset with others or yourself for not being logical, *that's* illogical. We're emotional creatures, and it would be illogical to expect human beings to always be logical. Not only that, it wouldn't work. Behind all this craziness is actually a very sophisticated logic. The same kind of logic that says, "Breathing and not breathing are both good ideas and both bad ideas."

But still, human beings do some downright stupid stuff that seems hard to justify.

Why does someone complain about their jacked-up relationship, but then stay in it?

Why does someone worry about a heart attack, and then go stuff themselves with doughnuts?

Why does someone join a hate group, even though we all want to love and be loved?

All of these crazy behaviors are really just examples of eating rotten apples. The apples are the behavior, and the appetite is driven by the six human needs.

Learning the six human needs that motivate you will help you determine what you really want, why you want it, and even open up new possibilities for how you can achieve happiness and fulfillment right now.

Once I understood how motivation and fulfillment really worked, not only was I able to get myself to do just about anything I set my mind to, but I also actually enjoyed the process rather than having to force myself into action through willpower.

Motivation is typically reduced to the simplistic idea that we want to gain pleasure and avoid pain, i.e., the carrot and the stick. It's helpful to know that pain is roughly three times as strong as motivator as pleasure. I would also argue for the inclusion of a third motivator – love.

> *We move away from pain and towards pleasure as humans. To choose to embrace pain or withhold pleasure for some greater good, even if it costs one their life, takes something beyond our most basic human motivations – it takes love.*

While this pain/pleasure framework can be useful, it begs the question, "What causes psychological pain or pleasure?" Thanks to the work of Tony Robbins and Cloé Madanes in the field of Human Needs Psychology, we can see human motivation narrowed down to a set of six human needs.

These six human needs are:
1. Certainty (safety, comfort)
2. Variety (excitement, uncertainty)
3. Connection
4. Significance
5. Growth
6. Contribution

To elaborate on why it's hard for a person to get themselves to give something up, such as watching TV, in exchange for something else like working out, it's because they feel the old behavior meets their needs to a greater degree than the new behavior. In other words, they'd feel a loss of pleasure and/or an increase of pain by sacrificing what they're used to. This is especially true if the person associates the new behavior with something painful, as is often the case when thinking about exercise.

You can choose to prioritize your needs differently, or you can choose to do different things than what you're currently doing to meet your needs, but you can't choose to not have any of these six needs.

You can choose not to eat, but you can't choose to avoid feeling hungry. The body's need for food will force you to feel hungry. You may choose not to meet your needs, but the hunger to fulfill these emotional needs may eventually overwhelm your willpower, and you'd do crazy things to satisfy this hunger.

Let's consider this for a moment...

If someone only feels connection by being in a relationship, they'll stay in that relationship, even if it's abusive, to keep meeting that need for connection. They'll go against their ethics and values to keep meeting that need. To tell them to "get out of the relationship," is like saying "starve yourself emotionally to death by not feeding your hunger for connection."

Would you willfully starve yourself to death?

Would you stop eating rotten apples if that's all you had to eat? Probably not...

But what if you were given something else to eat?

Would you eat nice apples instead of the rotten ones if given a choice?

Of course!

If a person was in an abusive relationship but eventually found plenty of other *better* ways to meet their need for connection, they'd run away from the relationship ASAP. They'd look back and wonder, "Why did I stay in that jacked-up relationship for so long?" Little did they know, the relationship was fulfilling a need, and they couldn't stop eating that rotten apple until they found another apple to sustain them.

So if you have set-in-stone needs, the choice you have is *how* to fulfill them. Since willpower alone won't overcome a deep emotional drive, you must appreciate your needs and satisfy them in relatively healthy ways. Keep in mind, many needs can be satisfied not by changing what you do, but by changing the way you look at *what you do*. It's not what you do that matters as much as how you *feel* about what you do that determines if your needs are met. How you feel about something often depends on how you frame it mentally.

CHAPTER 15

Healthy vs. Unhealthy Means of Meeting Needs

What makes a behavior healthy or unhealthy?

Is procrastination bad?

Could it be that one person's procrastination is another person's deliberation?

The simple answer is, procrastination is typically done out of a resistance to a behavior. "I hate cleaning. I'll do it later." Or attachment to another behavior. "I love this show on Netflix. I'll clean later."

Procrastination is typically done habitually. It's become a way of life. It's not done out of conscious, deliberate choice, but rather by fear or conditioning. It's sacrificing long-term gain in favor of short-term comfort. It's an obvious slingshot waiting to happen of going towards "feeling good now," only to be released into "feeling bad later."

Deliberation, on the other hand, is mindful. It's conscious. It's not done because one feels they "have to" wait, but rather because they're proactively waiting and possibly even gathering information. One could act at the drop of a hat if the timing is right, whether they felt like it or not.

Proactive isn't always better than reactive. Activity isn't always better than passivity. So long as these things are done with deliberate choice, they could be appropriate.

The real danger is in slavery. Being a slave to your emotional appetites. Feeling like you're making a choice, but it's not really an empowered choice. It's a choice to eat rotten apples simply because you don't realize that there are better apples available to you. It's a choice to eat rotten apples because they're close, and the better apples are all the way over "there," and it takes too much effort to get them.

I heard from a woman who said she procrastinates because she's waiting for the right timing. I asked if she knew what the right timing was. She didn't. If you're waiting for the right time, and you don't know when the right time is, could it be the right time right now, and you not even know it? Does this sound like a constructive approach?

When I asked her about it, she said that the real issue was that she feared making a mistake. This is a clear sign of being attached to comfort.

The paradoxical key to freedom from this enslavement by your emotional appetites is discipline.

"Discipline = Freedom" – Jocko Willink

What kind of discipline would free a person from their appetites?

You'll learn a few techniques in this book...

But one is simply the discipline to redirect your mind and get yourself to feel short-term pain to slingshot into long-term ease.

Do you hold off on doing something you want to do because you fear making a mistake that would be uncomfortable?

Ask yourself, "What is this fear costing you? What is this attachment to comfort costing you? What have you missed out on in life because you weren't willing to make a mistake? Haven't you still made mistakes regardless? If you keep playing small, what will your life look like a year from now? What about five years from now? What's it going to feel like to look back on your life, see all the things you could have done and didn't, and regret it? How many people are going to suffer because you aren't willing to step it up, be bold, and take some risks?"

Let it sink in...

Feel. The. Pain.

If you make your comfort zone uncomfortable by literally thinking about what it's costing you, your desire for comfort, rather than causing you to play it safe, will get you to act and step out of your comfort zone. You're fighting fire with fire, baby.

> **The easiest way to break out of your comfort zone is to make your comfort zone really uncomfortable.**

What do many people try to do instead?

They try to fight against their needs. They try to resist them.

"I shouldn't be so attached to comfort... I should be willing to take risks..."

Then they feel bad about themselves for not having the courage to act in spite of fear.

What if the way to act in spite of fear is to actually appreciate how fear my serve you?

What if the very thing that could destroy you, your fear, could be turned into your friend to set you free?

CHAPTER 16

"Hold Your Breath," And Turn Fear Into Your Friend

You've heard it said "act in spite of fear."

I say "act in the spirit of fear."

Let your fear fuel you.

Be deathly afraid of what will happen if you don't step into your greatness.

Shiver in terror at the idea of mediocrity.

Tremble at the thought of how disastrous it would be for yourself, your loved ones, and the rest of the world if you don't become the warrior you are meant to be.

But you wonder...

"What if people don't like me?"

"What if it hurts?"

"What if I fail?

That's your bullshitting mind playing the "what if" game.

Keep playing the "what if" game...

But play it on *your* terms.

"What if clinging to the illusion of safety causes me to lose what matters most?"

"What if I realize what could have been only after it's too late?"

"What if playing small is the worst mistake of all?"

You lead your mind.

You choose how to play the game.

When you do this…

Your fear will not own you, you will lead your fear.

The fear will be as strong as ever…

But rather than your fear being in front of you pushing back towards mediocrity…

You have chosen to direct this fear behind you where it pushes you faster than ever into your greatness.

Your fear will be the very force that propels you to break through the barrier of your bullshit.

This is how you can play the game.

This is how you can make fear your friend…

If you choose.

If only but for a moment…

While you hold your breath…

Until you come up for air…

Don't forget to breathe again…

CHAPTER **17**

How To Not Give A Shit

I f you said, "I don't give a shit about what people think about me," I'd call you a lying liar pants.

I can say this with almost absolute certainty.

Why?

Because biologically speaking, it's part of our survival needs to be accepted in society. If you were cast out of a tribe into the wilderness, that means danger and potential death. So a little thing in your brain says, "I should be liked and approved of by other people in order to maximize my chances of survival. If I'm an outcast, then that would be dangerous."

The common fear of public speaking isn't so stupid when you realize this. Well... it is kind of stupid, but one's brain may go, "If I embarrass myself, people won't like me. If people don't like me, I won't get support from others. If I don't get support from others in a life or death situation, that's risky. Risky equals greater chance for death."

You probably won't increase your risks of dying the slightest degree from a bad public speech, but your brain can make a lot of connections, that from a certain perspective, do make sense. Of course, it's still totally a BS story that a bad public speech would lead to people not liking someone and refusing to help them, but the idea of losing the approval of others is a very real risk to your brain.

But what happens if someone says to you, "You want people to like you!"

Do you defend against it and go, "I don't care! Whateva! I do what I want! It doesn't matter what anyone thinks about me! I just do me, and you can take it or leave it!"

Or do you sheepishly admit, "Ugh! Yeah, I do care about what people think of me. I'm such a baby! I know I *shouldn't* care what other people think about me, but I do!"

Both of these responses are bullshit for very different reasons.

The first response may come from someone who's repressed their desire for connection. The desire still lingers deep inside though. Maybe they don't even literally think or feel all that much concern about the opinions of others, but with the right trigger, it can be unleashed.

The second response is honest, but did you catch the bullshit?

"I shouldn't care what other people think about me."

Ever hear that bullshit in any type of "empowering" self-help advice?

"Stop caring about what other people think, and just approve of yourself!"

It's not bad advice from a certain perspective. There's truth to it. But it's like saying you "shouldn't" make assumptions or "shouldn't" be judgmental. You can't help but to make assumptions or be judgmental. The key is to judge your judgments and assume your assumptions are occasionally false. To get rid of them altogether though is impossible, impractical, and at times, just freakin' stupid.

Assuming, judging, labeling, looking for patterns, filtering out information – all of these things are what your brain is designed to do. There'd be something wrong with you if you didn't do these things. You couldn't function in the world without making assumptions or judgments. Don't you assume when you go to a store, buy food, and eat it that it will sustain you and not be laced with poison that results in instant death? You'd drive yourself crazy trying not to ever make any type of assumptions.

In much the same way, you're designed to want people's approval, or at least a connection with other people and things. Swap person for animals if you're the type that's lost your faith in humanity and has resorted to getting connection from your cats. It's cool. I love cats. Sometimes more than people. I don't blame you.

If someone said to me, "Derek, you write books because you just want to make money!"

If I were to respond, "I don't give a shit about making money from my books, I just want to help people and fulfill my mission of empowerment!"

Who's bullshitting, them or me?

The answer is both of us would be bullshitting.

Look at the first statement very closely.

"You write books because you just want to make money."

Do you see the "tell" of bullshit?

It's *just* a single word.

The bullshit has nothing to do with the accusation of wanting to make money. I do want to make money.

The accusation that I "just" want to make money is making it *all* about money. Clearly people can have more than one reason for doing things. In my case, it really isn't just about making money. I do care about fulfilling my mission and empowerment.

Do you realize the word "just" can subtly be an "all or nothing" word? "You just want approval." "They're *just* doing that because they're idiots." "He's *just* no good, and that's all there is to it." It makes it all about one thing and nothing else.

How many times in life is something all or nothing? Don't we typically have more than one motivation for doing something even if there's just one primary motivation?

However, I'd be bullshitting too if I said, "I don't give a shit about making money." A part of me really does care about making money from my books. In fact, it's making money from my books that in part helps me help more people and therefore fulfill my mission. Making money and fulfilling my mission don't contradict each other, they actually complement each other. Saying "I don't give a shit" implies it doesn't matter at all. It does matter, it's just that it's not all the matters – or even what matters most.

You can see the bullshit in the statement "I just want to help people and fulfill my mission of empowerment!" Now *maybe* this could be true for someone in theory... but in reality I would also say that a very small reason why I'm writing the book is because people may think it's cool that I'm an author. I certainly have a part of my ego that likes feeling significant in that way. I don't know if chicks dig it, but I still cross my fingers and hope they do. Either way, that's also why I play guitar, so I got that covered. #MultiTalented #CoveringMyBases

The reason I point this out is because "justing" things *could be* a sign of BS. Of course, it's all a matter of interpretation. And as you'll find out later, using the word "just" can be a very effective means for *breaking through* BS.

Be very careful when you accuse yourself or others of doing something just for one reason alone. As you can see by now with our human needs, we have multiple reasons for doing things that can seemingly contradict one another.

> *If you're in the habit of bullshitting yourself, you'll probably bullshit others too. If you bullshit others, you're creating a habit of bullshitting yourself.*

How could one respond to the accusation, "You just want to make money!" without using bullshit?

The response could be, "Yes, I want to make money. No, I don't just want to make money. Other things are important to. Money isn't the primary reason I do it, but it is an important reason. It's one factor, and if I didn't make money, I'd still probably do this to some degree, but not nearly as much as I do because money matters to me enough to be a factor that I weigh in deciding what I do. It's not always the most important factor, but it's still an important one. If my circumstances changed, and money became even more important, then I may stop doing this in favor of doing what makes me money so I can support myself."

That's a long drawn out way of saying, "It's not all or nothing." You'll notice though how long it takes to explain the fuller truth. The length of time to explain all that shit with various nuances and caveats is why we usually simplify things at the cost of a greater truth. There's a time for elaboration and distinction, and then there's a time for cutting to the chase and hoping people are smart enough to fill in the gaps. Be mindful though those gaps almost always get some BS thrown into them.

Let's not bullshit ourselves and say money isn't important, because in our world, it means buying food and putting a roof over your head. Money = survival for many people. However, does that mean money is all that matters?

Some people go the other way and say, "Money doesn't matter. If you really believe in something, you'd do it for free." There's so much bullshit to this, it gets its own damn chapter. So I won't dive into it here.

All of this is the same if you swap out the words money or approval with nearly anything else people desire. A desire to have fun. A desire to contribute. A desire to be safe. A desire to challenge yourself to grow. We all share these desires and can be motivated by almost all of them simultaneously in the things we choose to do.

The principle is it's important to be *honest with ourselves and others* by the words we use. It shapes our thinking.

There's a very significant difference between being told "You care about what people think," and being told "You just care about what people think," or "You only care about money." One single, simple, little word makes all the difference between bullshit and truth.

> **It's only from a place of honesty that you can make a truly empowered choice.**

Here's some BS-free, straight-up honesty: I do give a shit about what people think and feel about me. I want people who read my books to like the books and like me. I hope everyone in this world things I'm "the man." I want all hot women to think I'm irresistibly sexy, but not get too crazy about me to where it's weird, but just kind of sort of in the back of my head have it be where I can think, "Yeah, she digs me" when I see a hot girl. #KeepinItReal #RadicalHonesty

Yet I also know that by writing this book, some people are going to think I'm an idiot. I'm going to open myself up to criticism. I'm going to have people leave me a bad review, write hate emails to me, and tell me how I'm a horrible person who uses needless hashtags in my writing like a dumbass. #IDoWhatIWant #DealWithIt

So how can I give a shit about people's approval, and yet still be able to put myself out there and risk rejection and hatred? How do I essentially get myself to not give a shit about what people think when I, and everybody else if we're honest with ourselves, give a shit about what people think? How do you not give a shit when you *can't help* but to give a shit?

The secret is that I give approximately 91.3 shits about what my fans think compared to 1.9 (not quite two) shits about what my haters think.

Here's an analogy...

Let's say you have $100.

Do you give a shit about it?

If you're like most people, you do.

I know I do. I'm all about it.

It doesn't matter if you're "greedy" about money. Let's just say that's a nice chunk of change to give to charity. The point is that there's value there to deserve shits being given.

So I have this hundred dollars, and someone wants to snag it from me.

Aw. Hell. Naw.

I ain't lettin' that shit fly.

I will defend my hundred bucks because I give a shit about it. I will hold it tight.

I'm not going to let someone take it. I definitely won't throw it away. I won't even waste it on overly expensive drinks when I can buy my own beer way cheaper than at this bar, thank you very much.

Why?

Because I give a shit about it.

But then someone comes along and makes an offer...

They say, "Hey Derek, would you give up your $100 for this Lamborghini?"

"$100 for a Lamborghini? Pssh... *I don't give a shit* about this $100! Take my money!"

I couldn't throw my money at them fast enough.

Hell, I would offer them another $100 as a tip for hooking me up with the deal of a lifetime.

I just said that I gave a shit about $100, but how quickly would I *not give a shit* about $100 in light of finding something that *matters more*.

Trading something of lesser value for something of more value may seem like basic economics 101. You didn't need to read this book to realize you'll give up something of lesser value for something else of greater value. So where am I going with this?

When I traded in the $100, it felt like I didn't give a shit about it. I might have even uttered the words "I don't give a shit about this $100!" when I saw the Lamborghini. But that would be bullshit.

If *you* saw me throw $100 at someone, and let's say you didn't realize I was just offered a Lamborghini, you might think, "Wow! Derek really doesn't give a shit about $100. He would just throw that money at this guy."

Did I actually *stop* giving a shit about the $100 altogether at that point? Did the money cease to have value to me? In reality, I would still give a shit about $100 no matter what I'm offered for it. I may just give way more of a shit about something else – in this case a Lamborghini. I'm focusing on what I give more of a shit about.

The way to not give a shit about something is to give way more of a shit about something else.

This is obvious when you can see it from my perspective as I tell a story, but think about the people you admire. Do you ever look at someone and go, "I wish I was like them. They're so carefree. They don't worry about what people think about them. They do what they want. They're fearless. They're bold, brave, and intelligent. They're great."

Well, now you know better...

It's true that they might not worry too much about what people think. They might not let fear stop them. They might not care too much about the things many people worry about. Their greatness makes them seem superhuman.

But they're not. They're just like you in *some* ways. They do care about what people think. They worry about their fears. They wonder if their mistakes will cause them to lose what they love. But they've found something they care about more. They've trained themselves to tap into a power within, a power to care so much more about something *beyond themselves* that their own worries and petty fears, while still there, have become as insignificant as a $100 seems compared to a Lamborghini.

Your attempt to "not give a shit" about anything won't ever work because your brain doesn't know how to choose "not doing XYZ." If you decide not to do something, you are, in reality, choosing to do something else. It's always a proactive process.

You can choose to make your appetite for approval or connection, or any of your other needs, less significant, but you can't eliminate that appetite. It's hard-wired. You can most definitely give "less" of a shit *by comparison*, but not "no shits." Just .00001 shits perhaps at minimum.

> *Attempting to not give a shit about something fundamental to your human needs won't work. You can only choose to care about something else that meets your needs <u>more</u>.*

CHAPTER **18**

Honey, I Shrunk The Bullshit

Giving more of a shit about something to give less of a shit about something else sounds good in theory, but you may have noticed a problem...

Do you wonder...?

What if giving a shit about something else just makes me give a shit about 189 things instead of 188 things, and now I'm just feeling even more overwhelmed? Isn't my problem that I give too much of a shit about so many things already? What if I don't know what I should value more with so many desirable options, and I'm torn by giving a shit about so many different things?

If you're *really* concerned about this, you're A) likely mostly in the feminine energy and B) haven't learned the *proactive* art and science of *choosing* to make things insignificant – whether temporarily or permanently.

When I say feminine, I don't mean a physical woman, as this can apply to men, and I definitely don't mean this as an insult. The feminine nature makes even little things significant. To an extreme, it "blows things out of proportion."

Typically women embody the feminine energy more than men, and this means that when they're unbalanced, everything becomes a big deal, and they give a shit about so much stuff, it's overwhelming and at times unmanageable. They don't have as many barriers in their brain to compartmentalize stuff, so giving a shit about one thing spills over to the other things they give a shit about. It's easy to become conflicted, over-burdened, and feeling like there is a constant tug-o-war, sometimes in 18 different directions, about what matters most.

The masculine is much better at "not giving a shit," or in reality giving less of a shit, because the masculine naturally embodies making things insignificant. When unbalanced, important things become unimportant. "Oh, that pain in my arm, it's no big deal. I don't need to see a doctor. I don't need to get help. It doesn't matter if I watch TV instead of being present with my family. As long as I'm physically here, it doesn't matter if I'm not emotionally here."

Too much of making things overly insignificant has an equal potential for destruction as making things overly significant. Either imbalance is destructive. Either imbalance is enslaving.

If nature indicates anything to us, it's that harmony comes with a balance of masculine and feminine. If you only made things significant, you'd overwhelm yourself with too many important things. If you just try to make things insignificant, you'd stop caring about anything at all, including what's really important.

People will rarely reach either extreme, but they can get damned close. It shows up in the feminine who is frazzled beyond belief and has lost her head, or gone to the opposite, being depressed, because she "can't win" and has given up trying. It shows up in the masculine who is almost completely apathetic and emotionless, or the opposite, being aggressive and destructive, because he's stopped caring about others and the consequences of his actions.

You already balance these two energies every time you make a choice. Choice is when you say "yes" to one thing (what you've made more significant) and "no" to everything else (what you've made less significant) in that moment.

The trick is to realize that just because you make something more or less significant for a moment, it doesn't mean it remains that way. This is the critical BS that must be overcome, and this is what I keep harping on in this book.

Just because you make breathing insignificant, say when you're underwater, doesn't mean "breathing is insignificant." It also doesn't mean "breathing is significant."

Breathing. Is. Just. Breathing.

It's simply an act that has no "good" or "bad" until you consider the situation. This is why it's important to be able to make something significant at times, and also insignificant at other times.

I will repeat this often, because you and I will both likely forget it, and we'll pay the price for it, unless we keep reminding ourselves of it. Hell, this book is mostly an attempt to remind myself of it, and in turn, help you too.

Now apply this ability to make things insignificant to anything.

Mistakes. Are. Just. Mistakes.

Fear. Is. Just. Fear.

Talking. Is. Just. Talking.

It doesn't matter whether you're giving a speech to thousands of people or having a conversation with a friend telling them your old high school pal just passed away... "Talking. Is. Just. Talking." You've done it before so many times, why should this be any different? It's "not a big deal."

What I'm doing with this subtle use of language is taking all the context away from these things. I'm stripping the actions down to their most basic parts. I'm "shrinking significance" so to speak.

It's like saying, "A human being is just a bunch of atoms and molecules."

Is this true? Sure... from one perspective. But from another perspective, aren't I making human beings seem pretty insignificant? From this line of thinking, I could go, "It's not a big deal to blow up a bunch of atoms and molecules, and since human beings are just a bunch of atoms and molecules, it's OK to blow them up."

This is the extreme form of "shrinking significance." The imbalanced form. The natural masculine tendency to make things insignificant is why men, who often embody the masculine, are more likely to end up in jail, start wars, and commit acts of aggression. The masculine types pretty much universally like to blow shit up. The masculine embodies the energy of death and destruction, but even destruction is needed to pave the way for new creation. #AnotherStoryForAnotherBook #EverythingHasItsPlace

While the possibility for this "shrinking significance" to be taken to the extreme exists like all things, can you see how, in the right situation, this ability to make things insignificant could be a useful skill to have?

Doing squats with five hundreds pounds on my back is just a matter of bending my hips and legs and then extending them. It's only a little pain. It's *just* for a minute. *It ain't nuthin' but a g thang baby.*

All of these statements are making something that could be considered significant, insignificant.

And this, my BS-busting friend, is a nice skill to have.

To apply "significance shrinking," learn these words:

- Just
- Only
- That
- There
- Those
- Small, tiny, little, and so on.

Whatever seems like a big deal will be less significant if you use the words "just" or "only."

"It's *just* for five minutes." "It's *only* one phone call." "Let's *just* do it."

That, there, and those, (as opposed to this, here, and these) are all words the create distance between you and an object.

What seems more significant...?

"This book you're reading here..."

Or

"That book you're reading there."

Notice how the first one feels more intimate? Closer? More significant?

Using language that creates distance, nothing more than a mental trick, makes something seem less daunting. If you feel intimidated by something, try adding distance from it. Unless, of course, feeling intimidated serves a practical function in the situation you're in.

*"I'll **just** go ahead and make that little phone call to Mom."*

*"I **only** need to hop in the gym and do that workout for a bit."*

*"I **only** need go knock out that little job interview and then I can go enjoy this amazing restaurant."*

You can read how to use a variation of this technique for easily overcoming overwhelm in an article I wrote here: www.pickthebrain.com/blog/3-magic-words-overcome-overwhelm

This, like any skill, will be useful in some situations, harmful in others. How do you know when it's helpful or harmful? Learn what's called for in a particular situation through education.

In a situation that calls for dominance and authority, "Can we just do this little thing please?" isn't as authoritative. In a situation that calls for easing the burden of a request, "Let's go ahead and just schedule that meeting right now" could go a long way to minimizing friction.

Learn the skills of your environment. If you have no idea WTF an environment calls for, fear not. You will be enlightened on how to handle the unknown by the end of this book.

CHAPTER 19

Extreme vs Moderate

Is the nighttime extreme?

There's no sun out at night. Without the sun, plants don't get light. Without the plants getting light, photosynthesis doesn't happen. Without the plants getting energy, they die. Without any plants, we don't get oxygen, and we all die!

So let me ask you again, is the night "extreme?" Does the night actually kill us?

It's only "extreme" if you don't realize the day is coming to balance it out.

Let's make it more practical.

Is not eating *any* food extreme?

Can you answer that without knowing for how long?

What about fasting for a day?

Some call that extreme, others realize it can be healthy. Some fast for a week and don't eat at all. I hear some people say "That's crazy," while others are like, "Pssh, a one-week fast is child's play."

In order to be a better receiver, a Native American shaman said he was told not to give anything for a year and only receive. Is that extreme? But what is a year to a lifetime? Isn't it all relative to a bigger picture?

Balance cannot be seen in a snapshot. You can only see balance over the course of time. If something is "in balance," if it stays that way, eventually it will be out of balance. If the day stayed day and never turned to night, it would throw our whole world out of balance. Day must move to night and the night must move to day to be balanced.

Balance is an act, not an outcome.

Why does this matter?

Because you're constantly trying to balance seemingly opposing human needs, but you can never be in balance. You can only be "balancing."

Things are constantly shifting around you and within you. Nothing remains the same. The moment you find balance, if you keep doing what created that balance, you will be taken out of balance eventually.

Now it may be true that *generally speaking*, it's a good practice to ease into things and make changes and adjustments respecting a gradual gradient. Relationships are often best eased into, not asking someone to marry you on the first date. Exercise is often best eased into, not running a marathon the first day of deciding to exercise after ten years. Then making gradual adjustments so the body can handle it. A sale in business is often best made as a steady process, not asking someone to buy the moment you see them by saying, "Hey! Nice to meet you! There's this book by this guy named Derek Doepker and it's totes awesome so buy it now!" Ease into it first before pushing my book on them. #IWillTrainYouWell

However, just like nothing is "good" or "bad" outside of context, nothing is "extreme" or "moderate" outside of context. This means sometimes you need to go as fast, as hard, as extreme as possible to get to the other side of your BS.

When teaching racecar driving, students are told to speed up going into turns, because to slow down is to lose traction. You have to sometimes be willing to speed up, to go as fast as possible when approaching a wall, and do what you fear the most to break through. Sometimes you've got to jump into the deep end, and sometimes you just need to dip your toes in the pool and ease in gradually. To buy into only one approach or the other is to buy into the idea that breathing or not breathing is the best. You must be able to do both.

This means the idea of a "slow, steady, balanced" approach is *sometimes* total bullshit. The best way to break through BS at times may be to go to the extreme.

Doesn't this contradict the idea of using a gradient? Doesn't this contradict the idea that you want to stretch, rather than break your comfort zone? Doesn't this contradict the idea I laid out in *insert shameless plug* my book The Healthy Habit Revolution of creating micro-habits for small, gradual changes that don't overwhelm your willpower?

Does telling a person not to breathe contradict the recommendation to breathe?

Using gradual changes is *generally* a good approach. That's "common sense." This isn't a book telling you to avoid the extremes, it's telling you to embrace them – when appropriate. The question is, are you willing to let go of a gradual approach when it's not what's best in that moment?

It's like flying in an airplane. Most of the time, you get off course and back on course through gradual, micro-adjustments. You can end up in an entirely different city, for better or worse, with only the slightest change in direction.

Yet if you found your plane in a nosedive racing towards the ground, do you gradually adjust? No, you pull up hard and fast. If you're in a fighter plane and it's being attacked, do you take gradual maneuvers or **extreme** maneuvers? You don't need to be a pilot to figure this out.

The question is, what's your "extreme?" Are you willing to do whatever it takes, no matter whether it's moderate or extreme?

One may say, "I'm willing to work extremely hard and sleep only three hours a night to reach greatness!"

So what?

That's not "extreme." To some it may be. But to this person, their extreme may be to get more sleep, take care of their body, and recharge their batteries. Taking a break for once might be the "extreme" maneuver required for workaholics.

What is your "extreme?" What is your "edge?"

Are you willing to get help?

Are you willing to give help?

Are you willing to doubt your own ideas and seek counsel from someone else?

Are you willing to ignore "good advice" and trust your own inner knowing?

Are you willing to seek out good choices when there don't seem to be any?

Are you willing to say no to something good when there are too many good choices?

Are you willing to limit yourself with discipline and restrictions?

Are you willing to let go of how you've been limiting yourself and explore something new?

Are you willing to be uncomfortable?

Are you willing to allow yourself to be comfortable?

Are you willing to quit what you've been doing to try something new?

Are you willing to persevere in what you've been doing for as long as it takes?

Are you willing to do what seems significant and "extreme?"

Are you willing to do what seems insignificant?

The only true weakness is unwillingness to do what's required.

Whatever you're unwilling to do, that is your limit.

For some, it will be discomfort with the unknown that will keep them unwilling to go out of their comfort zone. However, it's often pride that makes people unwilling. When a person says, "I'm too good for this" or "I'm above that," they've made themselves unwilling to do the very thing that may get them to their potential. Sometimes the most extreme thing is to do what's "easy."

Whatever you place beneath you because of pride will become a stumbling block to your potential.

Still, even unwillingness has its place. Unwillingness to compromise on one's values. Unwillingness to settle for mediocrity. Unwillingness to be unwilling to do whatever it takes.

Unwillingness is neither good nor bad until you consider the context. After all, in order to have a willingness to do one thing, there are many other things you must be unwilling to do in that moment.

Now you have a choice.

Are you willing to go to the extreme, and do what some may even call crazy or "forbidden," to break through your BS and unleash your greatness?

CHAPTER 20

The Secret of the Deadly Slime

"Don't go in there!"

"Why not?"

"It's forbidden!"

"Why is it forbidden?" asked the inquisitive boy.

"What's inside can kill you!" answered his older sister.

"Oh, shitballs! Well, I guess I won't ever go in there!"

The two siblings returned to their small village town making sure to keep their adventures a secret. They knew that they'd be scolded and punished severely by their parents for even getting close to the forbidden cave, which was blocked by a gate that they were just small enough to squeeze under.

The young boy, Jeremiah, lying in bed near his sister, whispered, "What's inside the cave?"

"You're too young to know," replied his sister, Anna.

"Come on!! Just tell me! I'm dying to know!" said Jeremiah.

"OK, fine. That's where the deadly slime is. If anyone touches it, they'll die," whispered Anna, making sure to keep quiet so that their parents didn't hear them talking about what was forbidden. To even speak of it was against the rules of the village.

Jeremiah grew quiet. He closed his eyes and tried to take his mind off of the slime. It's a good thing that it's forbidden to go near it, he thought. It would be far too dangerous for anyone to risk touching it.

Years passed, and Jeremiah grew older and wiser. He became a scientist and engineer. He was a master at breaking things down and putting them back together by seeing how each piece fit together. All the village loved him for his ingenuity and clever inventions.

Then one year, drought came to the village.

The modest well dried up.

People began to grow fearful for they depended on the rain.

The water reserves emptied.

Panic struck.

It was clear that nothing could save these villagers except a miracle. An act of God or nature. Only rain could save them...

But Jeremiah didn't like to wait for miracles.

He was an engineer and a problem solver. He preferred proactive solutions rather than waiting and hoping.

He sat down and started thinking to himself, "How in the world can we get water? The rain has stopped and there's no source of water for hundreds of miles. But surely there's gotta be a way. If there were a way, even if it's totally crazy, what would it be?"

Then it struck him!

"What if...?"

"No... that can't work... but maybe?"

"I have to try!"

Jeremiah held a town meeting.

"I wish to go into the forbidden cave to save our village," he proclaimed.

He was met with jeers and scolding.

"You wish to do what!? Don't you know the slime kills people! It's forbidden!! You want to let it out and kill us! ARGHH!!"

Jeremiah, a little confused by the fear considering they were all just days away from dying regardless, pleaded, "I know it's crazy, but it may be the only way to save us all. If we don't try, we're just going to die anyway! Please, may I receive permission and the key to the gate?"

The villagers started to throw fruit at Jeremiah, and some went to their houses to grab their pitchforks.

Jeremiah, being a scientist and not a diplomat, decided it was best not to try to convince the people of the village and rather let his actions speak for him. He knew that if he were right, they'd all forgive him for saving their lives.

He decided to *break through* the gate blocking the forbidden cave without the villagers' permission. Entering into the cave with his level A hazmat suit and sciencey sort of equipment, he proceeded to analyze the slime.

"Yes! Just as I thought. This shit is super deadly and would kill anyone who touches it... and that don't mean shit. This will save us all!"

Pause story...

What did Jeremiah discover?

It's stupid-obvious once you know the answer.

How do the villagers see the slime?

How does Jeremiah see the slime?

They both see the slime as deadly poison, so why is Jeremiah the only one who feels it can save everyone's life?

Remember your lessons from earlier in the book, and you'll see why he's the only person in the village not being caught up in bullshit.

Resume story...

Jeremiah went to work using his science and engineering skills. Within hours, his creation was complete. By the next day, he returned to the village with buckets full of water.

"You did it, Jeremiah!" exclaimed the villagers. "We totally knew you could! I mean, we were just kidding about that whole pitchfork thing. You know we were just bustin' your balls, right? *nervous laughter* So uh... can you hook us up with some water?"

Jeremiah, not being one to hold a grudge, gladly shared his water with all the villagers and became the town hero.

"How did you do it, Jeremiah?" asked a young boy.

Jeremiah, reminded of his own inquisitive self as a young boy, shared with this boy his insight.

"I knew even within a poisonous substance that there may be purity. I knew the slime, as deadly as it is, may also be part water. If I could find a way to process and filter out the poison, what remained would be something that, instead of taking life, would give it. I just had to be willing to see the good within the bad; to see the possibility instead of just the reality."

The End

Jeremiah didn't let a current reality interfere with a future possibility. He didn't ignore reality though either. He still used a hazmat suit to handle the slime. He recognized that, in its current state, the slime was deadly.

However, he *didn't* say, "There's *nothing* good that can be appreciated about this slime that kills everyone it touches" like the villagers said.

Jeremiah, being an engineer, knew that the poison was made up of pieces. As important as holistic thinking is at times, it was his ability to actually create separation between the parts of the whole that was needed for this situation.

If all Jeremiah saw was the big picture of poison, then all he would see is potential death. If all he saw was reality, he wouldn't see the **possibility**. If he still believed the childish idea that the cave was "forbidden," then he would never have broken through the gate and entered, and all the villagers, himself included, would be dead.

What's your lesson?

Do you label entire people, groups, ideologies, countries, and ideas as good or bad, or can you separate the parts from the whole?

Are you making certain things forbidden, including parts of your mind or feelings, or are you willing to examine with caution what you've been told is "forbidden?"

Do you both appreciate the danger while appreciating the potential?

Do you see the purity within the poison?

CHAPTER 21

Realist vs. Idealist

Was Jeremiah a realist or an idealist?

It depends on your definition. You can argue many different interpretations of these words. I'll provide my definitions.

From my definition, he is *neither* a realist nor an idealist, but at the same time, *both*.

A realist, as I'll define it here, focuses on how things are in current reality. It takes the world as it is.

This mindset is considered grounded, practical, pragmatic, and safe. It says that if something's not broken, don't fix it. If something is broken, well then, deal with it. Don't cry about it and whine about what "should be."

There's absolutely nothing wrong with this. It's totally logical and very important to be able to take this perspective.

Had Jeremiah not been a realist on some level, he might have said, "Oh, I think that slime story is just a bunch of bullshit. Let me handle it for myself and see what happens. Oops... now my skin is melting off. Well, I guess that didn't work."

Clearly then, seeing reality is important, but what if that's all he did?

The villagers were realists, and it spelled their destruction. Jeremiah saw the slime as dangerous, but he also had an idealist mindset.

An idealist, from one definition, is one who sees things as they "could be." It's the future-oriented possibilities approach.

This mindset is considered optimistic, theoretical, progressive, visionary, and it sometimes embraces risk. At an extreme, it's pie-in-the-sky thinking. It's filled with a lot of "should be."

Now this may sound confusing. If you're more on the progressive side, you may have adopted the idea that people shouldn't use the word "should." Interesting sentence, huh?

Yet extreme idealists (rarely is a person hardcore on one extreme or the other) are often living their life in how things "should be" instead of how things actually are.

"I *shouldn't* have to defend myself because people shouldn't attack me."

"I *shouldn't* have to protect my belongings because people shouldn't steal."

"You *should* respect my viewpoint because we're all entitled to our point of view."

This is getting so caught up in how things "should be" or "shouldn't be," that one forgets that this isn't how things currently are.

This is common thinking. Just look at an article talking about defense for anything, and you'll often see it pop up.

I saw responses like this on an article about an invention to help women detect if their drink has been spiked with a date rape drug.

"OMG, they're telling women to defend themselves against rape! Hello!! How about tell men not to rape women! Let's stop blaming the victim!"

I would totally agree with this sentiment, and victim-blaming unfortunately *does* happen. To this sentiment I would add even more by saying, "Yes, let's raise a society that teaches people to respect other people's *choices*. People shouldn't rape, people shouldn't steal, and no one should harm another. However, since we're not *currently* living in a perfect world and psychopaths exist, let's work *both offensively* to create a better world while also being *defensive* against current threats."

My realist says to lock my car doors and learn self-defense. My idealist says to write books like this to help change the hearts and minds of people to create a more peaceful world. *When you integrate the two, you have balance. To reject one or the other is to reject the insight and gifts it can provide.*

To pick one or the other would be like a sports team that only plays offense or defense. Defense is just there "not to lose," but you can't win with defense alone. Offense is more important to winning the game. Jeremiah needed to go on the offense.

If Jeremiah had only focused on reality, what would have happened? If he only saw things as they could be, but didn't respect the immediate danger the slime proposed, what would have happened?

Never lose sight of what is for what could be. Never lose sight of what could be for what is.

CHAPTER 22

Act or Analyze

You're sitting in the passenger seat of a car.

The light turns green.

You're not going.

"Uh hey... the light's green," you tell the driver.

"Yeah, I know. But the lights down the road are still red. I'm going to sit here and wait until *all* the lights are green."

Perplexed, you wait a moment to see if the driver knows something about this road you don't know.

Nope...

Sure enough the lights down the road don't all turn green in sync.

The light turns red again.

You wait...

The light turns green.

You wait...

Would you start to get really frickin' frustrated with your driver when you realize you're never going to go anywhere like this? Would you be tempted to kick out the driver and take the wheel instead?

Good.

This driver is your mind, and the passenger is your greatness.

Your mind is telling you to wait until you have all green lights to go. You can take the next step, but still your mind goes, "Yeah...

but what if I'm not ready for what happens later? I better play it safe and make sure everything lines up perfectly before I start moving forward."

This is your overthinking, overanalyzing, bullshitting mind trying to wait for all green lights.

Your greatness is getting pissed and is about ready to kick out your mind and start driving.

But Derek... Surely you're not advocating just jumping into things without giving any thought and consideration? Don't we need to be prepared? Don't we need to be patient and wait for the right time?

Yes, but there's a difference between running a red light because you're impatient, which is dangerous, and waiting for all the lights to be green.

Your mind can predict problems. That's wonderful.

The point isn't to stop analyzing things or to stop asking, "What could go wrong?" Considering potential obstacles ahead of time can be wise. An overly optimistic approach gets many people in trouble.

The key is to act, then analyze.

Act, then analyze, then repeat.

The first act is choosing your intention. Then keep the ball rolling.

- Green light (Act): Choose to take a road trip.
- Red light (Analyze): What if I get a flat tire?
- Green light (Act): Put a spare tire in trunk.
- Red light (Analyze): What if I get stranded?
- Green light (Act): Put food and water in car.
- Red light (Analyze): What about running out of gas or something else I can't predict?
- Green light (Act): Get an AAA membership and start driving, knowing that this is enough to take care of most

reasonable foreseeable issues. Anything else can be handled when it comes up.

What do over-thinkers do instead?

They analyze. And analyze. *And analyze...*

What if...? What about...? Have I considered...?

All while going nowhere. All while *doing nothing* about those "what ifs?" All while sitting still, worrying about issues that can be handled just fine *if* they come up, *when* they come up, but aren't an issue now – *and may never even be an issue.*

They think that they're preparing, but preparation has action. They think they're waiting for the right time, but then the light turns green, and they still don't go because they think the right time is when it's the "perfect" time, or all lights are green, which never happens. They forget they can still get to their destination with "imperfect" street lights. They forget it's OK to have the occasional stopping point and detour.

I didn't come up with the concept of "act, then analyze" because I'm a gung-ho guy who's frustrated with other people's overthinking. I came up with it because I'm a natural, "What could go wrong? What mistake could be made? What if...?" type of thinker.

This is wonderful, at times, because it means I'm willing to look at problems, a pretty important thing to do if you want to solve them – like solving the problem of over-analyzing. Or solve the problem of our brain's bullshit. I had to analyze my over-analyzing to figure out a solution. The key thing is, I couldn't just think about it, I had to do things as well.

The final green light of getting on the road requires an element of risk. Will a spare tire, food and water, and a Triple A membership prepare me for every type of problem that might arise on a road trip? No. Life could throw any number of real obstacles my way. My mind could throw any number of imagined obstacles my way.

Yet, some challenges I wouldn't even see a solution for until I get there. It's like thinking, "What if I get on the road and one of the roads is closed? I better make sure all the roads are open ahead of time."

Is that what you'd think? Or would you think, "If a road's closed, I trust either my GPS or the signs there will reroute me when I get there. I'll figure it out as I go."

> **The only full-proof plan is the plan to need to change your plans.**

One must be willing to trust that they'll be able to handle what comes up in the moment.

Did you catch it?

Did you notice the "willingness" there?

Willing. To. Trust.

In this case, the issue with the over-analyzer is they've just placed most of their trust in their *future-potential-problem* solving mind.

This is wonderful when preparing to launch a lunar shuttle.

It's not so wonderful if you need to get in the car to grab groceries and it takes you three weeks to plan the trip to the store.

One must cultivate a trust in their ability to think and act spontaneously; to trust that insight will be given to them in the present moment. To trust that answers will be shown only *after* they start their journey, not before. To trust in one's present-problem solving self.

> **The over-analyzer has a lot of trust that unpredictable problems will occur, but not enough trust that unpredictable solutions will show up with them.**

Many of us fall somewhere in between. Trusting only enough in our ability to act in the moment to keep things bearable but not enough to live boldly. Acting without over-analyzing when forced unwillingly by circumstance, but preferring to retreat back to the recesses of the mind when given a choice to willingly.

The trust to be developed is in "spontaneous doing" rather than "pre-planned thinking." Both are strengths in their appropriate place, and both are detriments when taken in isolation.

How does one develop this trust?

Stupid Obvious Insight: You develop trust in "doing" rather than just "thinking" by doing rather than just thinking.

Yes, it really is this simple.

What does this look like?

One way is putting yourself into situations where you must improvise, or simply *choosing* to improvise and be spontaneous in your life.

I love dancing. I can improvise funky ass dance moves all day long. Yet when I'm asked to go up on stage at a seminar and lead an entire group in a "follow the leader" type of dance routine, instantly I'm in my mind thinking, "What kind of moves should I do? Can I plan out a couple moves in case I run out of ideas? How am I going to start? Dammit, Derek, remember the cool moves you've seen... Ugh, I can't even think of anything right now. Think, dammit, think!!"

Then I stop, catch myself, and remember, "Yo Derek, it's just dancing. Get up there and you'll figure it out as you go."

You know what happens when I *don't think?* I *do.* I do just fine. The more I allow myself to trust I'll figure something out when I get up there, the more the answers come to me.

Then the more I put myself in those situations, the better I get at acting without analyzing. Or more accurately, acting without over-analyzing.

I may be a natural thinker, observer, planner, problem solver, but I don't have to be bound by those things. I can train my muscle of spontaneity. When this muscle is strong, then I'm prepared to handle the challenges I will inevitably face.

Many people freeze up in a crisis situation. It's too outside their context, and they simply can't process it. They haven't trained themselves to be comfortable with uncertainty, novelty, or danger. They haven't prepared themselves for when the shit hits the fan – which interestingly enough does entail a bit of pre-analyzing what you might do so that it doesn't catch you by surprise.

What if you're ever in this type of situation?

What if your life and the lives of the ones you love depend on you acting on the fly?

Spontaneity will be a good skill to have, but it's a result stemming from a more fundamental quality. Spontaneity arises out of a way of being that you must relentlessly strive for. Yet the striving to develop spontaneity will necessitate the development of this quality.

Only when you're willing to trust something *beyond your mind* will you no longer be bound by your mind. What's found beyond your mind is found now, in this moment. You find it if you choose to let go of what's been distracting you from it.

*"Use the Force, Luke. **Let go**, Luke. Luke, **trust** me." – Obi Wan Kenobi*

CHAPTER 23

How to Get Off Your Ass And Get To Greatness

H and on hot stove = Pain
    Pain = Hand *off* hot stove
    Pain moves you.
Pain *warns* you.

We fear pain even though it usually isn't dangerous, but rather is helping you *prevent* danger. Those who can't feel pain have a serious increase in risk of death because they don't realize when they're hurt. Those who can't feel pain may get bedsores – open wounds from sitting in the same position for too long as the skin erodes away.

Pain is safe, *comfort* is dangerous... potentially.

You know by now that moving towards comfort will potentially slingshot you into pain. Remember that comfort isn't inherently good or bad or to be avoided altogether. The key is, don't get too comfortable with comfort.

Comfort leads to complacency. Complacency is the cause of stagnation. Stagnation in your life leads to bed sores on your soul.

At first, you won't often feel pain from complacency. It's masked by comfort. This is why it's *so dangerous*. You don't get the warning unless you learn to pay attention to the subtle discomfort that grows inside of you from complacency.

Those who don't feel the pain of complacency may have years go by, and then they look back on their life and go, "What the hell did I do for all these years? I could have been something great. I could have done something great. Instead... I just *settled*." After years of comfort, eventually they're slingshotted into the pain of regret.

> *"We must all suffer one of two things: the pain of discipline or the pain of regret and disappointment." – Jim Rohn*

Nature comes equipped with mechanisms to elicit pain when you're not stepping into your greater potential to prevent this. Your body is *supposed* to feel like shit and break down when you don't exercise or feed it nutritious foods. Your heart is supposed to ache when you're not bonding and interacting with others. Your mind is *supposed* to get restless when you don't challenge it with new learning.

So why then are so many people capable of living in mediocrity without it causing them enough pain to get the warning of the regret they're going to endure?

Where You're At Isn't Where You're Going

The mind has several games that keep you settling for mediocrity without feeling like it's a big deal.

The first game is comparing a destination to a current location. In other words, when one looks at what they want to accomplish, they'll often make a comparison between what they want vs. what they currently have.

I'll use the topic of fitness as an example, but realize it's a principle that applies to many things.

"I want a fit body, but right now I have an unfit body."

This gap between what a person wants and what they currently have gets them thinking about changing.

But what happens when they start thinking about actually going on the journey to getting what they want? Now the fear of *pain* comes in. They start looking at a future possibility instead of a present reality, and the risk of discomfort becomes real.

"If I want this fit body, doesn't that mean I have to give up comfort and feel pain? I'd have to start to exercise... and I hate exercise. I'm not sure what to do... and that means I have to figure things out and possibly fail. I'm probably going to have to give up some of my favorite comfort foods. I'm definitely going to feel pain when I do that, but maybe I can search endlessly for a special diet program that lets me eat anything I want. I better hold off on doing anything until I find a *comfortable* way to reach my goal."

Then they compare this outcome of having a fit body and the journey that goes with it to where they're currently at...

"Things aren't so bad now. I can enjoy good foods. I can spend my money on other things besides a workout program. I mean, I don't love my body... but it's not bad enough to give up all my comforts and endure all that pain just to be a little more healthy and fit. I'm not great, but I'm *good enough*."

Who the hell would change if it meant giving up so many things one enjoys... especially when things aren't even *all that bad*?

Yet this is a trap in thinking...

Did you catch it?

Do you see comparing the present reality with a future possibility?

The present reality looks more appealing and the future possibility looks unappealing, so naturally one begins clinging to their present reality at the expense of the future possibility.

I like to say it's comparing a destination with a departure point. Comparing the destination of a fit body, which is reached, say, a year in the future, with the "departure point" of where one is at right now.

Remember, from one perspective it's not a choice between "do" or "not do," you can only "do or do." You can't "go" or "not go" on the journey of life. You're always moving towards something.

You've heard it said, "Keep doing what you've always done, keep getting what you've always got." I say, *"Keep doing what you've always done, keep going to where you've been going."*

> *"If you do not change direction, you may end up where you are heading." – Lao Tzu*

Not learning is to unlearn. Not growing is to decay. Not creating is to destroy.

This may sound extreme. It may sound like I'm not recognizing the idea of maintenance or moderation. Maintenance, though, is a game of the mind, and a useful one at times. However it's just a game.

In nature, the one constant is change. Day to night, summer to winter. You may look at your face today and think that it appears the same as yesterday, but it has changed. And you only see this change, which is *always occurring,* after a span of time. This is why the notion, "I don't want to change, I love myself how I am" is, from one perspective, bullshit. You will change whether you want to or not.

In nature, straight lines are also bullshit – they don't occur. What appears straight, upon closer inspection, is more like a wave of gradual course adjustments going from point A to point B with continuous movement and realignment.

Remember this…

The natural tendency, *without proactively choosing the alternative,* is to stagnate, regress, and ultimately move towards death – whether physical death, death of a relationship, death of a good habit, or any other type of breakdown. All things are either growing or dying. Improving or decaying. Being nourished or being starved.

If you don't move towards strength by challenging your muscles, they atrophy. If you don't move towards education, you become ignorant to the changes happening around you in the world. If you don't move towards strengthening your relationships, the bonds grow weaker and eventually break apart.

Health is a perfect example of this pull towards regression because you're always aging. If you don't choose longevity by being proactive in healthy habits, you *choose* accelerated aging.

A friend of mine and workout partner, celebrity fitness trainer Tony Horton, is often saying "aging is for idiots" because, from a certain perspective, it's a choice. The choice not to move towards good health is the choice to move towards decay and death quicker than is necessary. Aging may be inevitable, but aging poorly is often a choice.

Every single day a person is making decisions about what to eat, how to handle stressors, how much sleep to get, what kind of activity to do, and more that are affecting their health. Your health, body, relationships, finances, and other things will never remain exactly as they are now.

The person who says, "I'll go on a diet after the New Year" forgets they're already on a diet. They've been on a diet since the day they were born. Their dietary decisions, every single day, are moving them closer to good health or closer to disease and death.

Are you choosing life or death?

Yes, this is either/or thinking. Yes, it's only true from one perspective. Yes, you may play the game of "maintenance" from time to time with certain things in life and be successful.

However, **greatness is extreme**, mediocrity is moderate. If you wish for an extreme outcome, would it not require an extreme approach *at times?* Consider the validity demonstrated from natural principles and practicality to what's being said here for unleashing your greatness.

Like a plane with a propeller that drives it, one must keep momentum going because if you stall and don't regain momentum, it's just a matter of time before a crash. There's no, "I'm just going to chill in this one *exact* spot for a while I think about what I'm going to do" in a plane. You're always in motion towards something, and therefore you must always be choosing where you wish to go.

It's true, some things in life are best considered "do" or "not do." Some things are all or nothing. Some things, like launching a rocket into space, require deciding, "Do I have enough energy to go all the way?" If not, don't even bother.

"All or nothing" is the perfect game to play – at times. Sitting and waiting for the right moment has its place. There does exist helicopters and vertical takeoff planes that can sit in one spot safely.

The question is, do you know what vehicle you're flying? Do you know if you're above water and should breathe, or underwater and should hold your breath? "All or nothing" thinking could save you or kill you depending on the situation.

Are you applying "all or nothing" in the wrong situation like your health, relationships, or finances? These things are a plane that's already in the air. You've *already* left the departure point. There's no *choosing* "not to take off." There's no choosing to wait a little longer or skip the journey altogether. You're on this journey whether you want to be or not. You don't want to fall asleep in the cockpit. You need to stay alert, constantly course correct, refuel, and get to one destination or another.

Is your plane headed to where you want it to go? Somewhere else? A crash?

In a plane, you only need to be off course by one degree to end up in an entirely different city over the course of time. You only need one degree of downward pitch to eventually crash. Mediocrity is sometimes only being off course by one degree, and its subtlety is its danger because you don't feel it. One may get lost in the clouds and not realize they've been off course or in a downward dive until it's too late. This is a real common cause of plane crashes.

The way to prevent this is by paying attention to the instruments in a plane. In your life, pain can be one of those instruments of warning. Are you paying attention to it, or overlooking it?

The good news is, if most of the time one gets off course by a small degree, this means that most course corrections are only a matter of small changes. Fixing your life and unleashing your greatness can be deceptively simple, requiring only a few minor tweaks to get to the destination of greatness.

> *You will have a natural tendency to drift off course, and that's OK. Getting great things in life requires redirecting yourself towards greatness by continuously correcting your course, and many times course corrections are so subtle that they're almost effortless.*

There is no eliminating a pull towards mediocrity, or lack of motivation, or your fears. These things are part of your experience. These are natural forces, like strong winds, that may push or pull you off course. Would it be wise to "reject" or resist "wind," or rather to accept that it will be there and choose to redirect yourself to where you wish to go when taken off course? Yes, you will be taken off course at least momentarily. Although "off course" may only be an illusion.

While course corrections may be subtle, at times, if you're headed for a crash, you must be willing to make extreme adjustments. If you're *only* willing to be moderate, you might not make it to your destination. If you're only willing to do the extreme, you'll burn out like a plane running out of fuel from crazy maneuvers. This is why a willingness to do both what's extreme and what's subtle is critical as covered before.

The good news is, you can often prevent having to make extreme maneuvers if you continuously make good decisions, and if you respect having a gradual gradient of change so you don't overwhelm yourself. This is the key idea behind my book *The Healthy Habit Revolution*, and another book from former lawyer turned highly success entrepreneur Adam Markel called *Pivot*.

To prevent having to go to the extreme often, or to build up the motivation to be willing to do what's extreme, it would be wise to start playing the game of "comparing destinations."

Comparing Destinations

When you realize you're already in the air flying to some destination and have left the "departure point," then you'll make a far more accurate comparison: Which destination would I like to end up at?

Where am I going to be a year from now if I *keep* doing what I've been doing and don't make a change?

What is this going to cost me? What will this destination feel like? Look like? Be like? Is that a place I want to go to in my life?

Continuing to use health and fitness as an example...

The person who's been gaining 10 pounds each year for the past two years might not be in that much pain about being 20 pounds overweight. They think, "I'd like to lose this weight and get fit, but I don't want to give up what I enjoy. I can tolerate 20 extra pounds comfortably."

The delusion is they think they're going to stay twenty pounds overweight continuing what they've been doing. They think, "I can keep doing what I've been doing and keep getting what *I've got.*"

Instead, they need to consider, "If I keep going where I've been going, where will I end up?" Everything is in motion towards something. They need to project into the future and ask, "What's this going to be like five years from now if I *continue my current trend*, and am now *70 pounds* overweight?"

Oh. Hell. No.

That shit ain't cool.

This ability to compare two potential futures is critical for eliciting enough pain right now in order to change. This is crucial as moving toward your greatness requires painful sacrifice and discomfort. When you realize the alternative is *even more* painful in the long run, choosing greatness becomes a much more *comfortable* choice.

> *To choose mediocrity is to choose to give up nothing that matters right now at the expense of giving up everything that matters later.*

I love the idea of being more educated in a year by going to seminars, getting coaching, and purchasing training programs, but then I consider, what will this cost me? An *uncomfortably* large amount of time, money, and energy. Some sacrifice. Some discomfort. Some pain. It's a bit scary to think about. If I compared it to my current situation, I might be tempted to say, "Nah. It's OK. I'm cool with where I'm at."

But what if I compare getting this education to where I would end up being if I moved *towards ignorance* over the next year? What would *that* cost me? Probably even more time, money, and energy trying to figure things out myself, making mistakes, and paying the price for it. This means even more sacrifice, even more discomfort, and even more pain relative to getting an education.

When I see I'm heading to one destination or another, "comfortable ignorance" now becomes a far less desirable destination to choose. This is why I've invested thousands of dollars to educate myself through books, seminars, coaching, and more.

If I compared the *desired destination* of more education with my current *departure point*, my current pain might not be enough to move me. Yet if I compare potential destinations based on either where mediocrity takes me vs. where stepping into my greatest potential takes me, I'm scared shitless of settling for mediocrity.

Don't compare where you want to be with where you're at. Compare where you want to be with where you're actually going. Then you will see the cost of moving towards mediocrity compared to moving towards greatness.

CHAPTER 24

Morphine For The Mind

Regardless of whether or not you look at your current location or a future destination, you won't effectively move towards greatness if you're ignoring the painful signals that are warning you to change course. This whole approach requires the ability to actually *feel* pain fully.

If you've trained yourself out of this ability to feel pain, then you've trained yourself out of accessing one of the most powerful motivating forces you have. If you're wondering why you lack motivation, ask, "In what ways am I not allowing myself to feel pain?" Keep in mind that this isn't about unbearable pain or torturing yourself. It could simply be the painful discomfort of a deadline you set for yourself or the painful exertion of a workout.

One is *supposed* to feel pain when they don't have an open conversation with someone about something that needs to be addressed. But instead of finding comfort by resolving the issue, they find comfort, *temporarily*, by eating a tub of ice cream. One is supposed to feel pain when their life isn't fulfilling a mission. But instead of finding excitement by working towards a meaningful cause, they find excitement, *temporarily*, by playing and completing a mission on a video game. #NotHating #ILoveVideoGames

In other words, we have become a culture that has gotten really good at numbing pain with endless distractions.

Distraction is morphine for the mind.

Even pain itself can be used to distract oneself from a deeper pain.

Just look at the things people get upset over. At the time of writing this, there was recently a controversy about Starbucks having red cups for Christmas. In some people's minds, this is more worthy of placing their energy and attention into fighting than say... fighting against the injustice of children being sold into sex slavery.

Are they crazy?

No. It doesn't matter where you stand on the great red cup shenanigans of 2015. Anyone who is outraged over red cups is just like you in some way.

Before you point a finger at them, ask, how many ways you could make your own life or the world better?

Ask yourself if instead of doing something, do you prefer to complain, silently or out loud?

Ask yourself, "Even if I am doing something about the causes I believe in, am I playing full out, or do I hold back?

Do I focus on the big things that matter or distract myself with the little things?

Do I care more about what matters *some* or what matters most?

Why do we hold back on striving to resolve great problems and do great things? Because to strive to take on greater challenges entails taking on greater risk.

This phenomena can clearly be seen on the TV show *The Walking Dead* with a situation Denise found herself in. She had aspirations of becoming a surgeon, but opted instead to become a psychiatrist. A man was going to die, and she was asked to perform a surgery as she was the only one with some degree of medical training. In this situation, she was overcome by fear and anxiety because she didn't know exactly what to do. What if she tries and fails? What if this man dies at her hands?

Now on the surface, it's a silly fear as an outsider. So what if she tries and fails? The guy would die *anyway*. At least there's a chance he'll live if she makes an attempt.

Yet she feels a pressure we can all relate to. As soon as we give ourselves responsibility for saving someone or something, we take responsibility for losing it as well. It's easy to say, "I'm not *really* responsible" intellectually, but practically and emotionally, it doesn't work that way. Taking responsibility gives one an opportunity to gain and therefore an opportunity to lose.

This pressure is partly why we admire surgeons so much. They're willing to put themselves in a high pressure situation where, although they can save a life, they also have a great responsibility to not cause the loss of life. There's a looming feeling of, "If I don't do this right, if I get distracted, or if I simply am not prepared enough, this person may die at my hands." #NoPressure

This pressure can push one to be focused and unleash greatness. However, too much pressure can become paralyzing. The attempt to avoid this pressure and the discomfort that comes with it is why we hold back to some degree or another. We play small, or in most cases, modestly. Not necessarily modest by other people's standards, but by our own potential, which is far beyond what we ever give ourselves credit for.

Since we can't avoid pain, we try to minimize it by playing small to only risk losing a little. Yet it's the moment one decides to hold back and play small that they've already lost what's most valuable – the gift of their greatness.

Taking Pride In Pain

To numb pain is a common approach, but there's another interesting thing people do with pain besides avoid it. They take pride in it.

"You don't know how bad I have it! You think your life bad? Look at mine! I have way more pain than you!"

Have you ever fought to make sure people know how shitty your life is? Do you ever feel a need to defend how much pain you're in? Or does it show up as resentment for how comfortable others have it, and you remind yourself that your suffering makes you somehow better than them? At the very least, have you seen others do this?

Why do almost all of us take pride in our pain from time to time? One reason is it makes us feel significant – a need we all have. If we can't avoid pain, we might as well fight to make the pain matter. I might as well say the pain makes me matter.

Remember, pride is the ultimate impediment to your potential. Taking pride in your pain is about making you more significant, more special, more "worthy" because of your pain.

If you haven't found anything else that makes you significant besides your pain, you'll cling to it – even when it destroys you. It would be as silly and destructive as a person who says, "I'm so proud of what big breaths I can take. I refuse to stop taking them when I go under water."

Then they choke and drown.

They couldn't let go of taking big breaths because their pride makes them cling to what made them feel significant. And yet they could have easily deluded themselves into thinking, "But breathing is 'good,' so I should be proud of this and keep doing it always."

At some point, you have to be willing to give up pain to avoid destroying yourself. At some point, you have to be willing to give up pleasure to avoid mediocrity. You can't attach to either side.

You can't attach to just feeling pleasure or to just feeling pain. Remember, at some point, you have to be willing to give up breathing to live. Then at some point, you have to be willing to give up holding your breath and come up for air to live. Are you willing to both experience pain and willing to let it go?

It's like the two ways of handling emotions, suppressing them and expressing them.

Those who suppress their emotions are like those who numb themselves to pain. It's still there lurking beneath the surface until it bubbles up. It's not resolved, just hidden away temporarily.

Those who express their emotions are like those who take pride in their pain. It's not necessarily bad in a moment to express your emotions, and you may even think "expressing yourself" is a good thing. But remember, nothing is "good" or "bad."

One who always feels a need to express emotions can be run by their emotions. They've chosen to let their emotions make their choices instead of their consciousness. Just like those who've given up their sense of choice and let their mind run the show, one can "give up choice" and let their emotions take control.

Those who take pride in their pain need their pain to make choices for them. They have all kinds of stories about what they can and can't do because of their painful upbringing, painful circumstances, painful body, painful finances, or anything else they feel. Their pain is making their choices, not them, but yet they still have a choice to take back control from their emotions at any time.

While we are emotional creatures who make emotional decisions, when you realize you can choose your thoughts, actions, and environment to change your emotions, then you still have a choice, *to some degree*, in how you feel.

We want to be willing to move into pain. This is part of the slingshot. This is the person who goes, "I'm *willing* to endure this workout and this pain. I'm *willing* to make this painful sacrifice for those I love. I'm willing to be uncomfortable by going without sleep to stand guard."

But the slingshot doesn't work *just* by a willingness to go into pain. You have to have a willingness to *release it* too. You have to *let go* after you pull back the bands on a slingshot.

"Letting go" is the third way of handling emotions. To feel them fully, even more fully perhaps than when you're expressing emotions, and yet recognize you can also release the emotions. You have choice, not your emotions.

So now you have a choice.

Are you willing to let go of the pride you take in your pain and the significance it gives you and realize it's your inner greatness that's already here within you now that makes you significant?

CHAPTER 25

The Root Of Fear

Fear of failure and fear of success, and perhaps all the different types of fears, are essentially the same thing – fear of loss. Fear of losing out on meeting our needs. The fear that keeps you from unleashing your greatness is that you'll risk losing too much.

How can fear of success be a fear of loss?

The delusion is this... "If I have everything I want, then I'll be happy."

In reality, if one gets everything they want and their life finally ends up how they feel it "should" be, they'll experience far more fear than they ever have before.

That fear will be *losing* the perfect life they've always wanted and now have, which will haunt them every moment they think about how perfect things are.

What if you're subconsciously stopping yourself from getting what you desire because, deep down you know that getting what you desire means a real risk of then potentially losing what you desire?

Buddha says attachment to desire is the cause of suffering.

Those with nothing left to lose can have the most freedom as they have become free from the fear of loss, which may be the only type of fear there really is.

To have what you desire without attachment starts with letting go of wanting things to always be a particular way in a universe whose rule is that all things must change. It's the recognition that you will lose whatever you get because nothing is permanent, so there's no point in fearing its loss.

Another game to overcome the fear of loss is realizing you've only ever had one thing to begin with, and this could never be taken from you...

CHAPTER 26

Losing Is A Delusion

You won't experience the fear of loss if you realize you have nothing to lose. It means seeing what you think you "have" is really just "borrowed" for this *moment*. And realize a "moment" is relative. What is a day to a decade if not a moment in your memory? What is a lifetime to an eternity if not a moment?

You can only return to nature what was borrowed for your momentary lifetime here on this Earth. Nothing is taken for granted, because you know all must be returned to its source.

In the future, your relationships have all ended. Your body is dirt. Your possessions are buried, burned, or recycled after eons have passed. In the big picture of time, you've *already* lost everything. Fear of loss is clinging to what is *already gone*.

This is the source of gratitude. To look at your life and say:

*This vision that reads these words isn't owed to me. It could be taken at any moment, but for this moment, I get to enjoy it. Only for **now** do I get to see beauty. Any beauty I see in the future is a gift.*

*This food I eat isn't owed to me. Mother Earth could have kept it for herself, and maybe one day she will choose to, but for this moment, she shares it with me. Only for **now** do I get to eat. Any food I have in the future is a gift.*

*This next breath isn't owed to me. The trees that give their oxygen may not always be here, but for this moment, the trees and I share our breath with each other so that we each may live. Only for **now** am I being granted this exchange of life. Any breath I have to give and receive in the future is a gift.*

Thank you. Thank you. Thank you.

The greatest lie you can tell yourself is that you have something to lose when everything you have is being shared with you momentarily as a borrowed gift. How can you lose what isn't yours? In every moment, you have nothing but an overabundance of gifts constantly being showered upon you.

You're alive because at one point, you were a helpless baby headed for destruction, and someone shared their nourishment, lessons on life, and love to give you the gift of living just a little longer. Despite being a "self-sufficient" adult, you're still as helpless and dependent on an outpouring of gifts as you've ever been. You've just bought into BS that you've somehow accumulated possessions that are yours to keep instead of yours to borrow until they're called back to their source.

> *What if you choose to see this moment as a gift? What if any moment you're frustrated or feeling any pain, you use this pain simply as a reminder to say, "I forgot to be grateful, and I'm grateful for this pain showing up to remind me to be grateful."*

So now you have a choice. This is all you have. A choice. The only thing you've ever had and truly own is choice. Your "agency," which means your ability to choose, can *never* be taken from you. It can never be lost because, even if you've chosen to give it away, you can reclaim it at any moment. You can choose to reclaim your sense of choice now.

No one else but you can make you choose to volunteer on your own accord to go along with another's will, but guilt-tripping family members, friends, co-workers, or beggars may sure try with *their* choices.

No one else but you can make you choose fear and hatred over love, but there will be those who try to strike you with terror by *their* choices.

Nothing and no one but you can make you choose mediocrity over greatness, but your bullshitting mind will try to convince you it's safer with its *programming*.

Of course, you can choose to see you have more things than choice alone.

Maybe you do "have" a body, and you feel this recognition is important so you don't neglect it. Maybe you do "have" knowledge, and you feel this recognition is important so you appreciate the lessons you've learned. Maybe you do "have" something that exists beyond your body, beyond your mind, beyond even your agency, beyond what you can understand with these words.

In this case, maybe you do, in fact, have things to lose, a cost, if you go after your greatness. What if you lose your fears? What if you lose your ego? What if you lose your pride? What if you have *no choice* but to lose these things if you wish to be great?

You can look at it any which way. ***How do you choose to play the game?***

CHAPTER 27

Nothing To Lose, Nothing To Gain, Everything To...

I f nothing will ever be yours to "have," what do you have to gain? You have nothing now, and you never will have anything. To remain in a state of not having anything to lose means you must remain in a state of not gaining anything.

Remember, this requires switching your definition of "have." You may in fact "have" many possessions from one perspective that you have every right to own and keep, and yet "have" nothing but choice from another perspective. This is all a game of perception. This last sentence may be the most important one you read in this book.

So what remains when you have nothing to lose and nothing to gain?

> *If you have nothing to lose and nothing to gain, you're left with the only choice remaining – the choice of what to give.*

The game many people play is this...

I must cling to things so I don't lose them. Then I must *get more* from others, myself, and the world. I must desperately hope my mind, other people, and the world choose to fulfill my wishes because I cannot choose to fulfill all my own wishes.

Ever play this game? Ever see others play this game? How did it work out for you and them?

Deep down inside, we know we don't have a choice to keep what we have. We can choose to fight for it, but something could happen beyond our choosing. A fire could burn down a house and take nearly all of someone's possessions.

We typically want people to choose the best thing for us, or choose what's best for them if we love them. How helpless do you feel when you see someone you love choosing to harm themselves? It's infuriating to see people you care about making choices that hurt them or others, and yet there's nothing, or perhaps nothing you can perceive at this moment, that can be done about it.

There may be nothing more frustrating than wishing you would have the motivation to do something or stop doing something, and yet another part of you seems to have a plan of its own. You choose one thing, and yet it feels like your mind or emotional drives choose another. Did your mind decide, or did you simply choose to let your mind decide?

Addictions can quite literally make it impossible for someone to make a conscious choice about their behavior. And yet, even with the addict, there's a choice. Perhaps it's the choice to get help or the choice to forgive themselves for their uncontrolled behavior.

Here's another game you may choose to play.

I won't fear losing anything since I have nothing to lose, so all that remains is to feel appreciation for what's been shared with me in this moment. If I'm left with only my choice of what to give from what I'm borrowing, what would I like to give?

Do I wish to give fear, resentment, and hatred? If others can choose not to receive those things from me, than who is left to receive them except for myself?

Or...

Do I wish to give love, gratitude, and my greatness? Would others receive *these* gifts? Would I give these gifts to *myself*?

Do I wish to give happiness, and in turn feel happier myself?

Do I wish to give lessons, and in turn learn more myself?

Do I wish to give gratitude, and in turn feel greater gratitude myself?

Ask yourself, "Have I ever played this game of giving, where by giving I receive? Does it actually work, or is it just some feel good theory? Can I prove it for myself to be true?"

So now you may choose to consider...

Have you ever given someone a hand, and then felt it was you who was being helped the most?

Have you given such sincere gratitude that it brought tears to someone's eyes, and in this moment you felt more grateful than ever?

Have you ever given an act of love without expecting anything in return, and suddenly felt yourself radiating an abundance of love throughout your entire being?

> *"Love is the only thing you get more of by giving it away"* – Tom Wilson

What you might find when you play this game is that you will never "get" anything, but you will "receive" everything. You'll receive everything you give out – good or bad.

It requires a logic that exceeds the mind.

The mind says to get more is to have more, to give more is to lose more. By now you should know your mind if full of shit. If you come to doubt anything in your mind, doubt this deception.

Of course, it's a game you can play and *make true* for yourself if you wish. Your ability to choose is so strong that you can choose to make your own belief systems, your own BS, become completely true from your perspective. You are the magician, and you can create whatever illusions you want.

This "giving and *therefore* receiving" is a logic beyond the mind. A logic that says you can *have* "nothing" and yet still give "everything." A logic that says you can give more and in turn "get" or receive more by this very act of giving.

You already know how to play this giving game quite well. Your mind doesn't make sense of it, but something inside you may confirm it's true. It's the game that's played by something beyond your mind.

You already know this. This is not a revelation. It's a reminder. And still you forget about it. Why do you keep forgetting? What reminder do you need?

Some have even gone their whole lives forgetting they know how to play this giving game. This is because no one, or very few people, *gave them* the example of how to play it as a reminder. They grew up without teachers or role models to remind them of the rules of "giving and receiving."

The choice then is this, do you wish to give others this reminder of how to play the giving game?

Do you think the more you remind others of the giving game, the more you'll remind yourself?

> *The mind asks, "What can I get?" And in its getting, it never quite gets enough in return.*
>
> *The heart asks, "What can I give?" And in its giving, it always receives more than its fill in return.*

CHAPTER 28

To Receive Or To Rob? That Is The Question

Would you give to those who cannot receive? When one is ready to receive, only then it will be given.

Perhaps you feel the giving thing has merit, but you may also be a bit curious about the whole "receiving" thing.

But Derek... don't we need to choose to receive as well as choose to give? Isn't a problem that some people are such great givers but terrible receivers?

If you pondered this yourself, then I have a question for you...

What makes you think giving and receiving aren't the same?

There is no act of giving without an act of receiving co-existing at exactly the same moment. The moment something is given, it is also received. To say giving has taken place without receiving would be faulty logic from this perspective.

But Derek... I get that giving and receiving go hand in hand, but why say you can only give? Surely you can say at some point you're giving, and then at other points you're receiving if someone is giving to you. Oh wait, it's probably a four-value logic paradox thing, right? I'm sure you probably have some totally smart answer to this so now I'm going to shut up this mind chatter and prepare to have some enlightenment dropped on me.

"Giving and receiving" is one way of looking at things. A breath is giving carbon dioxide and then in the next moment receiving oxygen. Another way to consider, if only for a moment, is that *everything is giving*. Couldn't you say it's giving carbon dioxide to the air during an exhalation and then giving oxygen to the lungs during an inhalation? You could say receiving something is *giving* reception.

As much as this might sound like an attempt to be overly philosophical, it really comes back to practical application. This "always giving" game is useful for turning receiving into something that's active. Remember that we're using words to describe a reality that cannot be limited to words. Language is limited in its ability to express deeper truths.

Let's look at this practically...

Imagine you're giving a gift to someone. You really thought long and hard about this gift and feel it's perfect for them, and you leave it on their table wrapped up in a nice shiny box.

But they don't ever acknowledge it. Nothing. Not a word.

You start to wonder... did they receive it?

I mean sure, it was sitting on their table, but maybe they didn't see it. Maybe it got thrown away by accident. Then you notice next time you're at their house... there's your gift box opened up, and the gift is sitting on the table.

You see them.

They say nothing.

What. The. Eff?

Does it feel like your gift is *received*? Sure you intellectually know they have it, but they didn't acknowledge it. Doesn't something feel off about this?

Have you ever given anything and felt like, "Ugh! Not even an acknowledgment? Not even a thank you? Not even a hand wave in the window when I slow down to let you cut in front of me driving on the road, you insensitive jerk!?"

So then is it possible for someone to be a "bad receiver" by not giving acknowledgement or appreciation? Might you even say they're a "non-receiver" if they don't acknowledge the gift by even looking at it or paying it any attention?

When anything is attempted to be given to you, whether given by yourself or others, you have two choices: ***You can either give reception or give rejection.***

Notice the use of the phrasing "give reception." You're *actively giving* reception. It's strange and perhaps a bit illogical, but still it makes sense on an emotional level. You give reception by *giving* out your hands to hold the gift. Or g*iving* words of thanks. Or *giving* silence even with a nod of acknowledgement.

However, you could also choose when someone says, "Oh, you're so great!" to give in return, "Oh no, I'm nothing special!"

Boom! Rejection given.

Was a compliment actually "given?" Yes and no.

Yes, technically a compliment was given, but was it received? If it wasn't received, was it given? Or just *attempted* to be given?

Have you ever given rejection when someone tried to give you recognition?

Someone gives you a compliment, and instead of just graciously giving it a warm, welcome reception, you give it rejection by denying it, playing it off, or any other form of basically telling the other person they're full of shit and their opinion is invalid to you.

Wow! Aren't you the sweet, modest one?

Don't worry… I'm guilty too. #LiveAndLearn

Even if you don't reject the recognition from others, consider this: Have you ever had the opportunity to recognize *yourself* for your own accomplishments, but then rejected this? Are you both giving yourself recognition and giving yourself reception of it?

To receive is vulnerable. The giver has control. The receiver is passive. Well at least, if you want to play it the way most people do, that's how it would feel.

One goal with this book is to give you another choice on how to play. Yes, vulnerability, learning to receive, and letting others "have control" is important. But these words are just mind games. They have no meaning except the meaning you give them.

Rather than making the mind, which loves to feel in control, have to sit there and passively accept something, let's give the mind something *proactive* it can work towards. Let's give the mind something it can do. Let's give the mind its sense of control back when receiving not through giving rejection, but through being the bestest, most amazingest **giver** of reception and appreciation ever.

Imagine this...

Someone gives you a gift. You stop everything you're doing. Get the biggest smile on your face. Look them dead in the eyes, and as you embrace them say, "Thank you for this. You and your gift mean the world to me!"

You'll probably make the other person cry with tears of gratitude, and they're the ones who gave you the gift! Then you'll probably start to cry because you'll feel that gratitude too! Interesting how this works, right? I'm pretty sure some unicorns and butterflies will manifest around you as you embrace each other and all will be right in the world in this moment.

Imagine the love that's shared when you focus on how to give appreciation and acknowledgement for what another has given you. When you give appreciation to another, both of you receive the feeling of appreciation. In other words, **you giving joy to another is giving joy to yourself**.

Why would anyone *not want* to experience this?

Because they're playing the mind's version of the giving game. It's not true giving, it's giving with the idea of getting something back. It's not "give and receive," but rather "give and take."

"I'll do this favor for you, but I'll resent it if you don't do a favor for me later."

"I'll give to you, but if I don't get at least a 'thank you,' I'm going to be pissed off."

"I'll buy this for you so that you like me and *give me your approval.*"

Have you ever seen a needy person who tries to get people to like them? It typically doesn't work. If it does "work," it's because they've found other insecure people where they feed into each other's "give and take." And do they ever seem happy in this cycle?

Have you ever been truly fulfilled caught up in this cycle yourself?

The difference isn't in the giving, it's in the taking. Taking comes from expectation. The world or others owe me something. After all, I gave to them... so the least they can do is give me acknowledgement.

This is actually the game that those who have an easy time giving but a hard time receiving play.

"Oh no, I don't need anything. I'm just going to give to others because I'm such a kind, wonderful, giving person. I don't want to burden others by having them give to me."

Those who *pride* themselves of how much they give to others but have a hard time receiving, are actually "takers" or "robbers."

Consider this...

Is it generous, kind, and selfless to rob someone of $10 so one can give that money to someone else?

If one is willing to give to others (time, money, compliments) but not willing to receive the same in return, this is attempting to give joy to others while simultaneously robbing from others *the joy of giving.*

The givers who cannot receive are actually taking from others the opportunity to give.

If you've ever attempted to give someone a gift, and another person rejects it, haven't they taken from you the joy you would have had from this attempted giving? Did you feel your heart sink when you wanted to give to someone but they refused your gift?

Now you may think, doesn't one have a right to reject what's been given to them? How can this be "taking" or "robbing?"

Sure. That's their choice to reject your gift. It's your choice to reject theirs. There's no moral judgment here because it actually does *no harm to a true giver*. While the choice not to receive *potentially* "takes" or "robs" the joy of giving away from someone, when the giver is playing the true "giving game" from the heart, this giver *still* receives joy.

Think about it…

The true giver can never be robbed. The true giver "owns" nothing to be robbed of to begin with. Remember, to be a true giver, one must be in a state of total appreciation for everything they have with no expectations. They are playing the game of "I have nothing to lose, I have nothing to gain. I only have my choice to appreciate what is shared with me this moment."

How can anyone rob a true giver of anything if a true giver is playing the game of "having nothing?"

"Oh, this person didn't want what I had to offer? That's OK! I still feel good. I don't need them to accept my gift to feel the joy of giving. It's my willingness to give that fills me with gratitude, not their reception of what I give."

"Givers and receivers" can only give, and in turn, be receiving. There is never a disappointment or resentment among "givers and receivers."

If you ever give and feel resentful about not getting anything in return…

If you ever give and feel pissed off someone didn't acknowledge you…

If you ever give and feel anything but joy and gratitude when the other person throws the gift back in your face…

You weren't really *totally* playing the "true" giving game which is "give and receive" without expectation, rather you were playing the mind's bullshit version of "give and take." #DontWorryItsNormal #JustMeansYouAreHuman

While I said those who don't receive "rob" from those trying to give, this is both true and false. You can only *rob from yourself* the feeling of appreciation when you expect another to give you appreciation and it's not given. Only "givers and takers" can *take* from other "givers and takers." A "giver and taker" cannot rob joy from those who *choose* to feel joy and appreciation for everything that shows up in life.

If you hold no expectations that anyone owes you anything, you'll feel joy and appreciation every time you attempt to give *regardless* of whether or not the gift is received.

No one else actually "robs you" of joy. Joy is *your choice*, remember? Gratitude is *your choice*, remember? To receive by giving is *your choice*, remember? It's always *your choice*.

No one else robs you of any of these feelings, except when you've chosen to go play the game of "give and take" with them. Then you make the agreement, the mutual decision, the collective choice, to rob from them and have them rob from you. Then you could say, "They robbed me of the joy of giving!" And you'd be right, because *you've* chosen to play that game. You had chosen to play the game of "give and take" and opened yourself up to *being taken*.

But you don't have to keep playing that game. You can remember it's *just* a game, and you can choose to quit it at any time. Your mind will attempt to pull you back in that game, and you might fall for it on occasion, but do you remember the way to remind yourself of the heart's "giving game?" How do you give anything to yourself if not but to give to another? It may be "easier said than done" at first, but doesn't this just mean you need to do and practice it more?

It's easy to talk about "receiving" as if it's a simple and universally agreed upon idea and start spouting off cute quotes about "be open to receiving," but you must truly appreciate the many games, or else your mind might trick you into deluding you into thinking "taking" is "receiving."

Now that you can see how "receiving" is an act of "giving" something, let's talk about receiving even more of what you want.

CHAPTER 29

How To Actually, Like For Seriously, Get What You Want In Life

Are you reading this book because there's something you wish to have in your life?

Do you want to learn how to turn your dreams into reality?

Do you want to experience freedom from your limitations?

Do you crave to know the secrets to receiving anything you desire, like more happiness, great relationships, shit tons of money, a successful business, and excitement?

Why?

Why do you care about any of those things if you have nothing and will gain nothing?

Why do you care about that stuff if you can choose to be happy right here now with what you "have?"

Or are you still playing the mind's game of getting more and never having enough?

Still, I wouldn't be writing this book if I didn't have something to gain from it, and you wouldn't be reading it if you didn't have something to gain, right?

I won't sell you on the idea that neither of us have something to gain from our journey together, but what we have to gain might not be what we think...

Do you want to know how to get what you want?

It's simple...

Don't ask, "How can I get?" Instead ask, *"How can I give?"* #YouProbablyHadThisFiguredOut #IPrettyMuchSpelledItOutLastChapter #ItBearsRepeating

If you ask, "How can I give," then you will start to find your answer to receiving what you desire. Just remember, one must let go of all expectations of getting anything in return or else you get caught up in "give and take."

Gee Derek... thanks for nothing. I already know to give without expecting anything in return. That's common sense. The problem, like all this self-help stuff, is that it's easy to say "give without expectation" and "let go of attachment," but it's not so easy to do. Why don't you offer some practical advice that I can actually use instead of all this vague, overly emotional bullshit. #RealTalk

Well, there the mind goes playing that game again. Oh, by the way, these little sections aren't what I imagine you're saying, it's what I say to myself. It's my mind's bullshit put on page. You weren't assuming it was anything else, were you?

To respond to my own mind, I'd say this...

*Great point, mind! I appreciate you for bringing this up. I really love how you remind me of these things and keep me on my toes. You're such a great friend and ally. It IS easier said than done sometimes, isn't it? This means I need to do it more than I say it. What if it's not about how much I succeed, but how much I **strive** to succeed? What if it's not about what I do, but how I "be?" After all, my doing comes from my being. How do I need to be? What character trait can I cultivate to mitigate my selfish tendencies and go beyond my mind?*

Well, I don't have all the answers, but a wise mentor of mine, Brandon Broadwater, told me that gratitude cures selfishness. Looking back, every

time I was feeling grateful, I wasn't caught up in wanting to "get" anything but rather wanting to give out of gratitude. I felt like I had so much already that I was happy to give some of my surplus. I seem to have proven to myself that this works.

So how do I cultivate even more gratitude? I suppose I can ask my heart and soul, "What am I grateful for?" Then really keep exploring all kinds of variations of this question like, "What should I be grateful for? What can I be grateful for that I'm not seeing?" Looks like this is a great question that I can sit with and explore... always and forever. Thanks for the reminder mind!! You rock! #ILoveYourChallenges #BestiesForever

Now you're a smart person, and I know this because you're reading this book. You're a cut above the rest if you read a Derek Doepker book. You may be starting to put some pieces together. So what if I asked you, "How do you receive more?" What would your response be?

Using a little basic logic, if the way to receive is to give, then you probably guessed the way to receive more is to give more.

Now wouldn't a good question be *how* to give more?

In order to know how to give more, you might consider, "What is the source of my giving?"

You'll note that I told my mind that gratitude is the cure for selfishness. Gratitude switches the **source** one gives from. If you don't give from the right source, you can never totally get out of the "give and take" game. Even I, quite regularly, draw from the wrong source.

When I catch myself giving from the wrong source, that's when I must think... *Just remember the parable of the greedy giver. What was their source?*

CHAPTER 30

The Parable Of The Greedy Giver

Each day, villagers from nearby cities would make the trek out to the river of Limitless Supply to fill their containers with water. The river was given this name because in the thousands of years that people had occupied the area, never once had the river run dry.

One day, a modest villager was making her way to the river when she came across a man lying on the ground, exhausted from thirst and dehydration.

"Please, do you have any water you can give me?" he cried out.

The villager, looking with pity on the man, said, "I would give you water, but I have none."

The villager then proceeded to the river of Limitless Supply.

She did as she always did. She made sure to fill up only what she needed for herself and her family – sure not to take any more than her fill. She was told never to be greedy, and she was obedient. She also realized the virtue in not weighing herself down with excess water to carry.

Upon her return trip home, she passed the thirsty man who once again pleaded, "Please, do you have any water you can give me?"

The villager once again looked with pity on the man. "I do not have water I can spare, for I only have my fair share. If I were to give my water away, then either I or those I love would go thirsty."

She returned to her village.

Several hours later, another villager on her way to the river of Limitless Supply came across the same man.

"Please, do you have any water you can give me?" he cried out even more desperately.

The villager, looking with pity on the man, said, "I would give you water, but I have none."

The villager, proceeded to the river of Limitless Supply.

She did as she always did. She made sure to fill up multiple containers of water so she would have extra. She always took more than her share, and some called her greedy. Yet, she felt she might as well take as much as she could from a river that has limitless supply.

Upon her return trip home, she deliberately passed the thirsty man who once again pleaded, "Please, do you have any water you can give me?"

The villager, looked with pity on the man and said, "I do have water to spare. I have enough for you, and even enough for you to take and give to others. Let's return to the village together, and should we see anyone else in need of water, we may both have water to give them."

End story.

Was the villager who only took her "fair share" selfless? Generous? Considerate?

Was the villager who took more than her fair share selfish? Greedy? Inconsiderate?

Who was able to *give more*? Who was able to be more generous?

How often are you refusing to receive more, only to find you have less to give?

When are you refusing to ask for what you're worth and can't give as much to others as you'd like?

When are you refusing to receive rest and end up too tired and drained to give yourself, others, and the world anything of value?

When are you refusing to receive help in an attempt to do it all yourself and can't give the world a gift that can only be created through team work and collaborative effort?

In our society, those who have riches are often resented. "Rich people are greedy." "Those who want more are selfish." "Those who ask for a lot of money must not be content with what they have because they aren't spiritual enough and are unenlightened."

This. Is. Bullshit.

This doesn't have to strictly be about financial riches. Those rich in their relationships may be looked at with envy by those who have poor relationships. Those rich with knowledge may be looked at as snobs by the ignorant. Those rich will skills may be scorned by those who've preferred distractions over their development.

Yet all this resentment and jealousy will do is keep a person from receiving what they reject in another.

> *Whatever you're resenting, you're robbing yourself from receiving. What you resent in another, you resist having for yourself.*

Imagine someone looks at a nice house and feels, "What a rich jerk! They must have screwed over a lot of people to get that kind of money."

What are the odds this person will ever be financially well off? Wouldn't they keep themselves from ever becoming a "rich jerk" by remaining poor or middle class? If they did "receive" a lot of money, how long would they keep it for before they find a way to sabotage their wealth so they don't start to look at *themselves* with resentment?

But Derek... I don't resent others. I'm happy when I see another person do well. I resent myself for not being able to get the same things. These people must have something I don't... good for them, bad for me. I don't have the intelligence, charm, charisma, opportunities, self-discipline, motivation, and ridiculous good looks they have.

Thank you for sharing, mind. I appreciate that we might not have all those inherent qualities as much as others. But even you know the part about us not being ridiculously good looking isn't true. We're a #SexyBeast. However, remember it's not just about what you resent in another. Who's to say that you and another aren't one and the same, from one point of view? What you resent in yourself, you keep from receiving yourself. Let's play the game of finding all the things I appreciate about myself, as I am here now. And then I will start to receive even more. After all, those people with riches probably felt the same insecurities themselves because they too have a doubting mind, and yet, look at what they've done when they worked with their minds. Let's do this together!

Side note...

Do I try to argue with my mind and make it wrong, or do I appreciate what it has to share? I may simply tell my mind, "Thank you for sharing," and then move on. I don't make it "bad" or "wrong."

If you hate drama and conflict, what do you do in your daily life? Try to keep the peace at all times? Avoid any confrontation? Don't speak your point of view?

What if you love conflict? Do you embrace the chance to argue and prove another person wrong every opportunity you get?

Whatever you do in your outer world, you do in your inner world. To treat your mind and the arguments it brings up as "bad" means you'll either avoid what it has to say, like avoiding that one friend who you "just don't even want to get started with," or you'll engage it in all kinds of "you're wrong, I'm right" arguments. Neither works to create lasting resolution in real life, neither works to create lasting resolution in your inner life.

> *What if learning to make peace with yourself is the key to making peace with others? What if learning to make peace with others is the key to making peace with yourself? What if there is no difference between yourself and others?*

You must give your mind and its thoughts acknowledgement if you wish to receive its wisdom. However, don't confuse acknowledgement with entertaining a thought. You may still wish to let thoughts go and play a different game than what the mind prefers by simply telling it, "Thanks for sharing, I choose something else."

Back to our main topic...

I say that it's bullshit to say "rich people are greedy." But what about rich people who really are greedy? It definitely seems to happen. Just look at wealthy individuals who don't give two shits about the wellbeing of others or the planet in their climb to the top. Isn't it true that there are some very greedy, selfish people out there who step on the people they consider "below them?"

If one is a "giver and taker," then being rich opens them up for more taking. More selfishness. More fear of loss and therefore more taking and hoarding anything they can get. Pride takes over, and they'll also attempt to take away approval from others by giving rejection and insults. There are definitely some rich jerks out there.

Being rich simply makes one more capable of giving. More capable of giving what one is and has – for better or worse. So if one is a "giver and receiver" who is driven by love rather than fear, then wouldn't being rich mean they have more to give for good?

Being rich simply means you have more to give. If you're loving, you'll give "awesome shit" like gifts. If you're an ass, you'll give more "shit" to people who don't deserve it.

The idea that "we all have the same amount to give" is both true and false.

On one hand, we all have a great capacity. We all have large containers we can fill at the river of Limitless Supply to have more than our fair share, so that we have plenty to give to others. Yet whether or not we *fulfill* the capacity of these containers is our *choice.*

The notion that "we're all equal" is both true and false.

Isn't it true that some have more knowledge, more skills, more resources to give to others?

Many wish to share a message on how to live better with others, but what if they lack the skills to teach effectively? Does their empty container have anything to offer, or must they fill their container by gaining the skills of teaching and influence?

Many wish to give money to charity, but what if they lack the money to give to charity? Does their empty container have anything to offer, or must they fill their container by acquiring more money?

Many wish to care for those they love, but what if they haven't cared for themselves and are too tired and empty to give care? Does their empty container have anything to offer, or must they fill their container by caring for themselves and restoring their energy?

We all have great capacity, albeit in different qualities, yet the contents of our containers is determined by our choices.

Most people aren't walking around with completely empty containers, unless things have gotten really bad. Instead, most are walking around with "just full enough" containers for themselves, and maybe those they love the most. Not enough to make a great impact, just enough to get by and do mediocre things in the world. Just enough to not have to consider themselves, or be considered by others, "selfish." Yet in this mediocrity, one would selfishly rob the world of the gift of their greatness.

The first villager wasn't *totally* selfish. She considered her needs, and then considered her family back in the village. Where she stopped was considering this thirsty man. She didn't fill up her container enough to help this man because this wasn't her responsibility. She didn't have to help this man after all, and this is certainty her choice.

She may have even chosen to help the man at the expense of herself or her family. Yet, as she rightly pointed out, this would have just led to another person going thirsty. Why would anyone need to go thirsty if there's a river of Limitless Supply? What would even stop her from just going back and refilling her container?

Had she gone beyond herself though, and considered a bigger mission, to make sure no man or woman goes thirsty, *and considered the source of her giving was of limitless supply*, wouldn't she have decided to fill up her containers with far more?

Are you just considering what you and those closest to you need from you? These are definitely the bigger priorities. Yet with Limitless Supply, why would you limit yourself? Why would you limit what you receive when that means limiting what you can give?

> *It's when you have a willingness to give more, by your consideration of what's beyond you and your immediate concerns, that you'll receive more. You must be asking, "How can I give even more?" in order to open yourself up to opportunities that exist right now to receive even more.*

This isn't just a feel good idea of "magically" receiving more because you give more – it's downright practical for overcoming your fears that keep you from receiving what you want.

When you have a big enough reason why you're doing something, you won't let anything stop you. When you find a cause that goes beyond your own needs, you'll transcend the fear of losing out on your needs.

Would you be willing to face death to save a life of a loved one?

Your desire to do something for another gets you *outside of yourself*, and once you're outside of yourself, you're beyond the limits of the fears that exist *within you*. The way to overcome what holds you back *inside yourself* is to get *outside yourself.*

> **The bigger your cause, the greater your courage. When you're driven by a mission that's outside you and beyond your needs, the fears within you no longer bind you.**

I'm able to act most boldly when it's not about getting what I want, but fulfilling a mission. *My fear becomes irrelevant if I'm barely even thinking about myself.* This must be taken with the caveat that I still meet my long-term needs. I still must feed myself before I can effectively feed others. In a plane, one would be wise to put the oxygen mask on themselves before assisting a child.

I experienced this first hand when writing this book where concerns about reaching out to others for help seemed irrelevant when I was thinking about how much I want everyone to get the messages in this book. My concern for others negated false concern for my own ego because I was no longer primarily in my ego.

Now consider this...

If transcending your fears means getting outside yourself and placing your concern on contributing to others, does this mean you become *dependent* on other people in order to transcend your fears? It would seem then we *need* others, or a cause outside of ourselves, to fulfill the need of contribution, which is what this entire section is about. Yet, what about the idea of self-empowerment where one can find inner peace just within themselves? What about the idea of not depending on others for happiness, but finding it from within?

This still idea of fulfilling oneself is true from a certain perspective. Only we as individuals can take responsibility for our own happiness. In this way, we're independent. Our feelings are self-made choices.

However, just because it's your choice to breathe, you still "depend" on trees for oxygen, and they depend on you for carbon dioxide. This isn't a co-dependent relationship, which is unhealthy. It's an *inter-dependent* relationship. It's the way of nature. Self-fulfillment is both true *and* false.

But Derek... I don't need anyone else to be happy. I can be independent from other people even though I may depend on nature. I can live in the woods alone as a hermit and probably find a way to be content.

*Yes mind, we may not need others to generate a feeling of happiness. Yet fulfillment is something different than happiness. Some joys are off limits, "unchoosable," if you will, without other people. Without other people, how can one experience the love of holding their child in their arms? How can one know the joy of giving a helping hand to someone in need? How can one feel the immense satisfaction of laying on their death bed, knowing their impact will live on after they're gone through the lives that they've touched? Can anyone choose to experience these joys without "depending" on others to share these experiences with? You may live without another, but to live **fully** depends on sharing your life with others.*

The second villager took more than her share, and it was through this act that she became extraordinarily generous. It was through her receiving more that she was able to give more.

Was there any wrongdoing in what she did? With a limitless supply, how could she be greedy? What could she rob from anyone else if the river has a limitless supply?

Remember the question, what is the source of the giving? It's the river of Limitless Supply. It's the endless resources that you can draw upon in this world. It's the abundant supply of food, water, energy, assistance, knowledge, and more available to all of us so that no person ever needs to be without. It's perhaps something beyond even all of this.

When you're drawing from this limitless source, it's easy to practice "giving and receiving." Yet if you're drawing from a source of scarce supply, then the natural tendency is to "give and take." The thinking is that there's only so much to go around, so it's best to not to give too much for risk of losing too much. This feeling of being in a state of scarcity leads to one "doing" the game of "give and take."

The simplest way to enter into a state of true giving is to draw from a source of abundance. To be in abundance is to effortlessly "do" the game of "give and receive."

But Derek... this only makes sense in the hypothetical fantasy world you've created. Anyone can make up a story that talks about a river of limitless supply. Anyone can make up a story about abundance and say there's enough to go around for everyone. Anyone can delude themselves with fantasies... just ask me! That's what I do best. Yet you can't say this is reality when clearly there isn't enough to go around. If you give away all your food, you'd starve. We've said it ourselves that this would be unwise! Just look at how many people don't have enough. We live in a zero sum world. All you have to do is look at the "haves" and "have nots" to see it's true.

Thank you for sharing, mind. I appreciate you playing the "what is" game. It's true that there are some that have and others that don't. This is reality, but what's a possibility? Let's play "what could be." Even in a drought, we live in a world that's two-thirds water. Creative minds have discovered ways to make undrinkable water drinkable. Creative minds have developed sources of energy that take from a limitless supply of the sun rather than the limited supply of the Earth. What else could be possible?

But Derek... even if we can have enough food, water, and shelter for everyone, the Earth can't support too many people. We may end up with overpopulation. Disease may break out, and then we may have even more people suffer and die. This is what could be.

Thank you for sharing, mind. I appreciate you giving me "what could be." I'm grateful you remind me that we must be considerate to balancing many factors and appreciate what the Earth can handle. Consider this: those who've played the game of abundance, the game of "almost anything is possible," have found solutions to our world's seemingly impossible problems that those who played the game of scarcity could never imagine. Those who've played the game of scarcity felt safer in the short-term, but ended up with more suffering in the long-term. So shall we play the game of scarcity or the game of abundance?

But Derek... you know this isn't my choice to make of whether we play the game of scarcity or abundance. I do as you command. What game would you like me to play?

Thank you for reminding me, mind, that now I have a choice. Do I play the game of scarcity or the game of abundance?

So now *you* have a choice – Will you play the game of scarcity or abundance?

CHAPTER 31

How To Stop BSing Yourself

Now you know the game of "giving and receiving."

Is this a game you wish to play, or do you want to play the game of "give and take?"

If you wish to play the game of *true* giving, the game of "giving and receiving," then...

You should always be *open to receiving* more so you can *give more*, true?

You must always be willing to receive what others wish you to have, correct?

You would always choose to give reception instead of rejection to what's given to you, right?

Bullshit.

If you've bought into the idea that "I must always be a good receiver," then you've bought into the same bullshit that says "I must always breathe to live." If you didn't catch the word "always" and went along with it, you've bought into the BS that something is good or bad outside of context.

Remember, when someone tries to give you something, or you try to give *yourself* something, you have a *choice* – to give reception or give *rejection*.

In as much as many people need to learn to be better receivers, they also need to learn to be better "rejectors."

Someone says, "You're an idiot! You're unworthy of anything! You're stupid, ugly, you smell bad, and no one likes you!"

Do you ever find yourself giving reception to that if someone says it to you?

Do you ever find yourself giving reception to that if you say it to *yourself?*

In other words, do you buy into it and say it's true for you? If you're in any way offended or triggered by the harsh words and labels of others, it means you have received them on some level.

You can hear a crazy person on the street say, "You're stupid" and laugh it off. It's just the projections of a crazy person. Then you hear a friend say "You're stupid!" and it ruins your whole day, you cry yourself to sleep that night, and it takes three years of therapy to fully get over.

To receive those things means you have given up choice in what others, or you, wish to label yourself.

Do you ever do something stupid, and instead of saying, "What I *did* was stupid" decide to say to yourself, "*I'm* stupid?"

If so, you've bought into the bullshit that you are your actions. Instead of receiving lessons from your mistakes, you gave rejection to the lessons and instead gave reception to an identity from those mistakes. In other words, instead of going "What can I learn from this?" you asked "Who can I BE from this?"

What can I learn from this? I did something stupid... so I won't make that mistake again.

Who can I be from this? I did something stupid... so this must mean I'm stupid.

You can choose either question, but you may not choose the answer your brain gives you. If you choose to ask, "What's wrong with me?" then your brain will come up with answers for you.

What's wrong with me? *Well gee... let me count the ways. I don't look nearly as good as my friends, I can't stop binge watching Netflix while my life passes me by, and when that person just waved I waved back* *like a dumbass not realizing they were waving at the person behind me so now I'm just going to pretend to scratch my head but they totally know what I did and I can't even hide it because I'm an idiot and everyone hates me.*

You choose to ask the question, but you can't always choose the answer. Much like I can choose to eat doughnuts all day and not exercise, but I can't choose not to let my body turn to shit by this choice. Choose to ask better quality questions if you want to receive better quality answers.

I see this self-labeling based on actions even among those who are very intelligent and do a lot of personal development. They say to themselves, I must take responsibility, so I will blame myself.

However, this self-blame and identification with one's actions is what I call "false personal responsibility" or "pseudo-personal responsibility."

When someone makes a mistake and goes, "Oh gee, I'm an idiot!" they're *not* taking personal responsibility. If someone is an idiot, they're not, in their mind, responsible for the idiotic things they do. They can subconsciously go, "It's OK to keep doing idiotic things because I am an idiot, after all. No one can really blame a stupid person for doing stupid things. That would be like blaming a wild animal for doing as a wild animal does and attacking people."

It's essentially saying, "This is just the way I am! I can't help myself! I can't *choose* otherwise!" By blaming their identity, they've removed responsibility. They don't have to stop doing stupid things if they're "stupid" because now they're just living up to their identity.

If you ever tell yourself, "I'm hopeless. I'm unworthy. I'm stupid. I'm a failure. I'm unlovable. I'm undatable," then you've excused yourself of your choices. You've given your choices over to an identity that YOU chose to create!

The mind game is this: "What I do determines who I am. I can't choose who I am, and therefore I'm not responsible for what I do. I have no choice in my actions because my identity decides for me."

Ab. So. Lute. Bull. Shit.

It's common in our world to think what you have and what you do defines who you are. But being is the source of your doing which determines what you have. The order is Be, Do, Have – not Have, Do, Be. At least, from one perspective. *You should know by now that it's rarely just one way.*

What you do is a reflection of who you're choosing to be at any given moment in time. To confuse what you do with who you are is mistaking the reflection of a person in the mirror for the real person. A brain trick. An illusion. *Like being in a house of mirrors at a carnival and losing site of what's real and what's just a reflection.*

The brain doesn't know that what it's seeing is a reflection and not the real deal. It says, "But I can prove I'm an idiot, unworthy, and unlovable! Look at all the stupid things I do. Look at how no one cares about me. Look at how I fail myself and others. Look. Look. **Look**!! It's right *there*! I can see it's real!!" All the while, your silly little brain doesn't know it's looking at reflections and mistaking them for reality.

Yet if you were to reach out and try to touch the person you see in the mirror, you'd hit a barrier. You can't actually feel the person because they're not real, but rather just a reflection. If you were to break this mirror, you'd realize it was just an illusion. It was just bullshit.

> *Are you willing to break through your bullshit to see it's just an illusion? Or do you want to let your brain deceive you without questioning it?*

Why would You play this game of mirrors? Well, think about it... how else can You see Yourself from the outside? How else can

You see Yourself from the front, back, sides, top, and bottom? How else can You explore Yourself from the outside looking in without having something reflecting You back to Yourself?

> *What if All of this is just a game of You reflecting You back to Yourself to see what could not be seen from within You?*
>
> *What if Others outside of you are just reflections of what is within Yourself?*

What if you've forgotten that you're in a house of mirrors, and the whole time you're confusing reflections for reality? Wouldn't you be confused? Wouldn't you need to test what you see by touching the illusion to discover, "Oh yes! I forgot... I'm just playing the game of mirrors!"

If you're in a house of mirrors and realize you're in a house of mirrors, then it just simply becomes a game, an amusement, an experience. A part of you knows that the illusions are just illusions. Even with this knowing that you're looking at illusions, you may get confused, but isn't it OK that you get lost and confused temporarily, because, eventually, you'll find your way out of the game? Eventually you'll look back and go, "Well, wasn't that fun?"

A reflection isn't real, and neither is a projection. This means you can choose to reject the projections others and you put on yourself.

You can reject, "You're an idiot" when someone says it to you or when you say it to yourself.

Or, like watching a movie from a projector, you can suspend reality and go along with the projections. Let yourself get lost in it for the enjoyment of it, all the while you know deep inside it's just a movie. Just a projection on a screen. You can safely return to "reality" without being lost forever in what was just a game you wanted to experience for a moment.

This means you can receive the projection, "You're a great person!" should you choose to play along with that. You can choose to receive or reject whatever projections you want, but don't confuse them for reality. They're just a projection that you're playing along with like playing along with a movie you see. You may laugh, cry, and experience all the emotions watching this movie... but still you know what you see isn't really "real."

Rejection is just the other side of the coin of reception. You must reject many things in order to receive one thing. In other words, whenever you say "yes" to something, you're saying "no" to many other things in that moment.

Remember that it's all just for a moment. To say yes to an inhale is not to "reject" exhaling... except for that moment. To say "no" to helping a friend because you have something else important to do isn't to "reject" helping friends forever, just for that moment. To charge significant money for a service isn't to "reject" charity forever, just for that moment.

Yet you must remember this when you feel like "no" means rejecting something outright. Have you ever thought, "They told me 'no,' so they're rejecting *me*." "I asked them out on a date, I asked them for a favor, I asked them to buy my product, and they told me no so *this means* I'm being rejected."

Those in sales have learned a "no" may be nothing more than a "not now" or "I don't know enough yet." Taken too far, some sales people can be pushy, but then again, sometimes people need to be pushed to get through their own bullshit.

> *Genesis, to generate or create what you desire, is "to know/no." Knowing allows you to choose "yes" to what you'd like to create. "Noing" allows you to choose to give rejection by saying "no" to what interferes with your creation.*

If you believe that rejection is bad and take "no" as equaling long-standing rejection, then you'll now have an avoidance to saying "no." You'll "reject rejection" if you will. This makes it impossible to effectively make wise choices. It makes it impossible to reject an old game in favor of a new game.

Whether it shows up as difficulty telling people "no" to their requests, difficulty telling yourself "no" to temptations you face, difficulty rejecting the clothes that pile up in your closet even though you haven't worn that one shirt in like 17 years, or anything else, the avoidance of rejection leads to an accumulation of bullshit that's long overdue for being tossed out, or isn't worthy of taking in to begin with.

But Derek... I'm confused. I thought it's not about rejection, but integration. I thought it's not about making yourself or others wrong, but adding something else to it. You know I love logic. I can't see the logic of saying you must learn to reject, and yet earlier saying it's not about rejection but integration.

Thank you for sharing, mind. I can appreciate your confusion. It doesn't seem totally logical, does it? Yet remember we're only playing games of perception. I can look at one side of a door and say it's white, and another person looks at the other side of the door and says it's black. We're both right... because it's a door that's been painted two different colors. Integration means to not "reject rejection." This is logical, right?

If you've been telling yourself any excuse like, "I can't because I don't have enough money," this is the game you've chosen for a *moment*. You can choose to *reject* this "what is" game, your old story, and receive the "what could be" game, a new story.

Is there a way to play both games of "what is" and "what could be" without rejecting either? A way to not make it either/or but rather both? Perhaps you may discover a way to "play both" by the end of this book...

When someone comes to me with their bullshit, as a loving and caring true friend, I can reject their bullshit and give them truth. Give them something else to consider. I don't have to receive anyone else's bullshit, and I don't have to receive my own mind's bullshit either. Our minds may attempt to give us BS, it's our choice whether or not to receive it.

Those who only choose to receive and not reject can become overly sensitive to others. "Oh... this offends me! I'm sensitive to your negative words and hostile energy. It disrupts my aura! I don't have on my protective crystal to ward off negative vibrations. You should be more considerate of how you are affecting me!!"

Bullshit.

Who is it that's responsible for whether or not one is so frickin' receptive that they're taking on other people's bullshit and are offended by it? Is it the fault of the people giving offense? Or is it the fault of the person choosing to take offense?

This doesn't mean it's totally awesome and cool for people to be disrespectful, but *they* are the ones to accept responsibility for what they choose to do and the consequences it brings.

You can choose whether or not you're taking offense. Why would you choose to give your power to another to allow them to bring you down? Wouldn't you rather the keep power of choice, the ability to choose how you respond, for yourself? You're always welcome to respond with, "I'm *not* going to stand here and take this," and walk away without holding onto anything they projected, should you choose. You're always welcome to ask yourself when someone attempts to make you feel bad, "Do I want to let them have power over me, or do I want to choose to keep the power to feel good for myself?"

This is not meant to disrespect those who are highly sensitive individuals. I'm naturally prone to being on the sensitive side myself. It's a great gift – *at times*. I can tell myself, "I'm sensitive," and it's a great game to play – *at times.* Just like "I'm empathetic," "I'm open," and "I'm receptive" are all wonderful projections – *at times.*

All of these things are like breathing; useful... *until* you need to hold your breath. At that time of being underwater, it would be destructive to play the "breathing is good" game. But still, the "breathing is good" game is only to be rejected for some moments before it would be wise to play it again and come up for air.

CHAPTER 32

Breaking The Addiction Of Slavery

If we let labels define us, then what do we make of the label "addict?" Is this a cop-out, like saying, "I'm stupid and therefore can do stupid things?" Does labeling someone an addict make it a self-fulfilling prophecy? Or is it insensitive to not recognize that some people literally don't choose out of complete free will but rather from subconscious drives and neurological programming?

This is as much a book about where you *don't* have choice as it is about where you do have choice. An addict does and doesn't have a choice as I indicated earlier in this book. The question is, what do they have a choice in? What *don't* they have a choice in?

On one side of the coin, there are those who see the word "addict" as well as the word "disease" as disempowering. They say, "Once a person gives themselves this label of addict and say it's the disease's fault, this both lets the addict off the hook and takes away their sense of control." These people recognize that we have a choice in how we label ourselves, and this labeling carries a kind of power behind it. They would say, "Let's not label one an addict because then that gives power to the addiction and not the person."

I myself seem to have indicated that giving ourselves a label potentially removes responsibility, so I can appreciate this viewpoint.

I recognize its truth, partial as it may be, as nearly all viewpoints are partial.

On the other side of the coin, there are those who say science indicates our willpower is limited. Many times, choices that seem to be made out of free will are really just subconscious, emotional drives. The addict would never willingly choose to engage in their addiction. They're powerless to consciously overcome the overriding power of their biology.

I have a great appreciation for psychology and the power of the subconscious mind, so I can appreciate this viewpoint. I recognize its truth, partial as it may be, as nearly all viewpoints are partial.

It's true an addict may not *willingly* choose all their *behaviors*. Their early choices, perhaps made willingly, perhaps not, put shackles on them. At one point, they may have freely chosen what shackled them, what would become their addiction, perhaps simply out of ignorance. Or the shackles may have been put upon them without choice, like a baby born to a drug-addicted mother. No matter how much they fight against those shackles, sometimes the limits of human will and strength won't be enough to break them. They cannot break of the bonds of addiction.

The addict may not have choice in whether or not they "have" their sickness willingly. They may not have choice whether or not to "do" their addiction willingly. They may not even have choice in whether or not to "be" an addict. In this respect, we can all feel compassion for the addict who is enslaved to their addiction unwillingly.

Yet despite all of this, the addict still has a choice now.

The addict may choose to "have" a different environment in a rehabilitation center away from their drug of choice. They may choose to "do" by getting help and treatment. They may choose to "be" compassionate and forgiving towards themselves. In other words, they may choose to "be" OK with not "being" OK.

They may not choose their identity of "addict," but still they may choose whether or not to be limited to this identity. They may realize, just like what we "have" and "do" is a reflection and not reality, who we are "being" is a reflection, and not reality.

It may even be possible, through the right therapy, to do as the scientist Jeremiah did, and remove the poison from the water and restore one's state of purity.

This requires recognition that the parts both do and don't make for the whole. Does the addict have purity within their poison? Is an addict doomed to remain an addict, or is there possibility for something else, even if one can't see it now? Is it possible through the right approaches to remove the poison of addiction? Addiction may be a reality, but does that mean it's the only possibility?

This isn't just a choice for an addict, it's a choice for all of us, as we're all addicts to our insatiable human needs and drives. Will you be bound by your needs and appetites? Will you be bound by what you have? Will you be bound by what you do? Will you be bound by who you are?

Or are all those things just temporary? Will you realize that these things, the current "reality," can be replaced with a new possibility? Are you willing to see the purity within your own poison? Are you willing to see the purity in another's poison? Will you break the mirrors and see that they're just a reflection of what's real, but not reality? Will you break through your bullshit to see it's all just an illusion? Will you break through what you cling to because your mind tells you it's real, in order to prove to yourself that it's just a delusion, a mind trick, a game?

The addict, you, now have a choice – ***Will I be a slave to who I am, or will I be beyond who I am?***

Let this sink in...

We have an addiction to addiction. An addiction to slavery. An addiction to be controllers and yet being controlled by what we wish to control. It's a human condition that makes people give up their choices for the illusion of comfort, connection, significance, and excitement.

This addiction to slavery is a condition that tries to force others to do as one wishes. It's a human condition that tries to *force oneself* to do as one wishes. It's trying to be a master when all it really does is make the person a slave.

This master and slave idea isn't limited to dictators and their willing order followers. It's an everyday occurrence.

Look at how many people have relationships in which they don't like what someone else is doing, but they go along with it. Too scared to speak up for fear of rejection. Too scared to put up boundaries and say "No more!" Too unwilling to reject someone's bullshit because that would be uncomfortable or unsafe. Addicted to being a slave to this other person's choices to fulfill their insatiable desires for comfort, safety, connection, significance, and excitement.

Yet the other person in the tango is too scared to give up control. Too scared this person will leave them and make them insignificant, so they play mind games to manipulate them. They threaten, actively or passively, to remove connection from their slave. Perhaps even threaten with physical force to get the other person to follow along, "or else…"

Yet they're not a master, but a slave too, for they need their slave to feel power. They are a slave to their own appetites for comfort, connection, significance, and excitement. They need someone following their orders because without the order "follower/taker," the order "giver" is powerless, insignificant, unconnected, uncomfortable, and bored.

This is a game of force. Sometimes physical force of violence, other times psychological force of depriving one of their basic human *emotional needs*.

Master: "If you don't do what I say, I'm going to shame you so that you don't feel a sense of connection."

Slave: "If I don't do what they say, it could be chaos, and I'll lose my sense of certainty."

There is no true "master" in this game because each person is a slave to the other, or more accurately, a slave to their own appetites to fulfill the needs we all have.

This game playing out on a grand scale may be seen with war mongers and slave traders. There are those literally forced into slavery, and this is not a "game," the slaves wish to play willingly. Much like you may find yourself not willingly complying to the commands of others, but going along unwillingly because of a threat of force against you or loved ones. A threat of violence, or simply a threat of having your emotional needs starved.

This "master and slave" game takes place on an even more subtle level. It takes place within the relationship between you and your own mind.

The question is, is your mind the master or the slave?

Are you giving and taking orders with yourself unwillingly? Are you in a battle with your mind trying to make yourself change, to "get it right," and to try to force yourself to put down that damn doughnut when you know it's just going to go straight to your waist?

Perhaps you don't want to play the "master and slave" game with your mind. It's your choice after all, right?

Have you decided you simply want to make the mind your friend? Someone you lead, but whom you let follow along willingly? And should your mind wish to go another way, that's fine, but you will still go the way you know to go regardless of whether or not your mind is on board. Are you OK doing as you choose, and letting your mind do as it chooses?

Rather than trying to force yourself to be better, are you asking yourself what is in your best good? *Deciding* which game to play? *Choosing* to unleash your greatness?

This is a game of power. Power to choose. Power to choose to align yourself to something beyond your own limited mind.

So now you have a choice. ***Do you play the game of slavery, or do you play the game of choice?***

CHAPTER 33

Removing Your Own Shackles

If you wish to play the game of choice, you must know the words of force vs. the words of power.

I warned of the deadly words, "I know that." These words, even if true, can potentially get you caught up in pride.

However, there are three words that can be far deadlier if you wish to play the game of choice. Three words that I catch myself saying even after all these years of warning others of their danger.

You may shudder with fear as you hear these words…

Or you may go, "What's the big deal?"

The words are:

"I have to."

I'm trembling even as I write them.…

Can you feel the sense of choice being removed from you as you utter the words "I have to?" Can you feel how you lack power when you say them?

What they lack in power of choice, they make up for in force. They can be spoken to "force" yourself into doing something. Yet with this force, you remove your sense of power to choose.

"I have to" is possibly the most poisonous phrase of disempowerment. Similarly, the words "I can't" are also disempowering due to the removal of the feeling of choice.

Research indicates those who use the words "I can't" are less likely to resist junk food temptation compared to those who use the more empowering words "I don't."

When you use force rather than choice, it triggers something psychologists call reactance. This is your "anti-slavery" mechanism built within you that says, "You don't own me! It's *my* life, I do what I want! Whateva!"

We don't like it when people try to force things upon us because, surprise, surprise, it removes the ability to choose. As you should know by now, this is the same regardless of whether or not someone else tries to force you to do something, or whether you try to force yourself to do something.

Of course, those who don't choose to get control over their reactance may simply rebel against anything they're told to do. Then they're just as easily manipulated as the "sheep" they scorn because all one has to do is use reverse psychology to control them. Tell them not to do something, and they'll rebel against it and do it. Tell them to do something, and they'll rebel against that and not do it. Blind rebels aren't any less enslaved than blind followers.

"You should buy this other book instead of Derek Doepker's book... that dude doesn't know what he's talking about"

"Pssh... Don't tell me how to live my life! I do what I want! I'm totally not going to buy the book you say and will buy Derek's instead. No one can tell me what to do!!"

#Muahaha #SillyRebel #YouAreMyPuppet #IOwnYou

"I have to" can't be true because you don't "have to" do anything, remember?

Someone puts a gun to your head and attempts to force you to do something?

You don't "have to" go along. I'm not saying it's wise, I'm just saying there's a choice to take the bullet.

Therefore, "I have to" is bullshit.

Potentially...

Now you might be thinking, "Ok Derek... I know what you like to do. You're going to probably get me all riled up about how 'bad' these words are, and then come in and say, 'I have to' isn't necessary good or bad, right?"

Well done... you have learned well, young grasshopper.

I hope you're starting to not take things at face value. I hope you realize "I have to" isn't ever true, but also is true. Four-value logic, remember?

How is "I have to," at least potentially, a true statement?

We just need to add more "truth" to it.

I have to *IF*...

"I have to eat broccoli *IF* I would like to have broccoli be eaten by me."

Yeah, it sounds a little funny, but it's true right?

Let's make it more practical...

I have to hold my breath... *IF* I wish to avoid choking right now being underwater.

I have to get my friend a gift... *IF* I want to give them the joy of receiving an awesome gift from me.

I have to do what this person with a gun to my head says... *IF* I don't want to get shot in the face.

I have to make myself weaker temporarily... *IF* I wish to develop the strength that follows from lifting these weights.

I have to be in a state of love... *IF* I wish to overcome my fears and unleash my greatness.

Why look at things this way? Isn't this kind of a common sense thing that doesn't really need explaining?

On one hand, I could tell you to simply stop saying the words "I have to." This is often what I recommend people do in favor of replacing them with the words "I choose to" or "I will."

"I can't" becomes "I don't" or "I won't."

This is useful and a great game to play.

It does work.

But wouldn't it be even more empowering to allow yourself to not only say these words, but have them give you a greater sense of choice instead of a lesser sense of choice? What if the words, "I have to" could be used to increase your awareness to what's possible instead of cutting off possibilities?

Words are limiters, and they may bind you – if you choose to let them. However, remember even limiters can be tools for greater freedom. Even the resistance of dumbbells, which make you weaker when you lift them, can be used to make you stronger over time.

So what's another game, an "exercise," if you will, that will turn the force and resistance of "I have to" into something that actually makes you stronger?

Here's another empowering game you may choose to play...

Rather than rejecting "I have to" altogether, you may start integrating greater truth into it.

"I have to get this project done by the end of the week."

Oh, I said "I have to..." what does this mean? What are the conditions that makes this true? I have to get this project done by the end of the week IF...

"I want to keep my job."

Oh, OK. Is this really true?

"Yes. I'm told I will be fired if I don't have this project done."

OK. So really I'm choosing to keep my job. Do I really want my job? Is there something else I can choose?

Why do all of this exploration?

So you start to gain greater awareness of why you're choosing what you choose. You start to see other possibilities.

Maybe one hates their job and it wouldn't be so bad to lose it.

"I'm doing this project just to keep a job I hate. I think it's about time to tell my boss I quit and spend the time I would have spent working on this stupid project to start my own business and spend more time with my family."

Your "I have to" statements become a window into your motivations, what you're valuing, what you're making matter the most in your life at this moment. You might be enlightened by what you find.

To play this game, all you do is add any of the following words after the words "I have to..."

- If...
- Because...
- In order to...
- When...
- Since...

Or any other type of variation.

I have to feed my kids **because**...

"It's my job as a parent, and I'm not going to let them starve. I love them. I want them to live."

No shit, right? This is obvious. But the beauty isn't what's on the surface. If you stop here, you're missing the point...

"I feed my kids because I love them and I can't imagine my life without them. I'm so grateful for them. I can't take them for granted, because they could be taken from me at any time. But for now, I have a choice to feed them. Because someone fed me when I was helpless as a kid, this is the reason I'm here now. I have to because I choose to play the game of giving and receiving, and this is what a giver and receiver would do. They would pay it forward out of gratitude, not out of expectation of return."

Well now, ain't that some shit? You've just turned an "I have to" into a profound exploration of your motivations of being driven by unconditional love and being a "giver and receiver."

If you use "I have to" as a trigger to explore your motivations and conditions deeply, you not only can find out if your motivations are BS, but also if your motivations are genuine and something to be grateful for. Not a bad game to play, right?

Figure out the conditions that make the "I have to" true for you in this moment. With awareness of the conditions, you may then ask, "Is this always true? What is another truth? Is this the only way to meet this condition? Is there a better way?"

"I have to smoke this cigarette if I want to feel relief right now."

Is this the only way to meet this condition of feeling relief, or is there another possibility?

"Well… I guess I could take a minute to mediate, and that might bring me relief."

What if there is no other possibility you can think of? You may try, "If there is a possibility, what would it be?" "Can I allow myself to be open to new possibilities even if I can't see one that exists right now?"

This will help you discover if there are other better "apples" you may eat besides the ones you're eating. Apples that are available if you just choose to reach up and grab them from the tree.

Granted, this is often more easily done with a coach. If you'd like to explore your possibilities with me, you may contact me to see if my coaching is currently open and if I'm taking on new clients. Send an email to derek@derekdoepker.com Subject: "Coaching availability"

CHAPTER 34

You're Wrong

Many people who are addicted to their slavery are really saying the following...

"I have to in order to avoid taking personal responsibility, so I can keep blaming my circumstances, and because I wish to remain a slave to letting my mind and fears choose for me instead of choosing for myself."

Crazy, right? Who in their *right mind* would think that?

The answer is nearly *everyone* – myself included, at times. At the very least, you will regularly be tempted to play the slavery game.

Your "right mind" wants to be right all the time. This is why it will look for any way it can avoid taking responsibility for being wrong. Slavery, by rejecting personal responsibility, is really saying, "I don't want to make a mistake, and since mistakes are unavoidable when making choices, I choose not to choose. I choose to avoid being wrong by letting other people and things, including my mind and fears, choose for me. Then I can blame them."

The "choosing not to choose" game is useful for never being wrong. As soon as you accept responsibility for your choices and free yourself from enslavement, you accept personal responsibility for being wrong. Whether you ever actually are wrong or make a mistake might be debatable, but it sure feels like there's a risk of it being wrong whenever you are going to make any choice.

So what if you're wrong?

What's wrong with being wrong?

Your decisions don't define you, correct?

So even if one says, "You ARE wrong," it really just means "your choices are wrong." You are a "chooser," but you are not your choices.

But Derek... You can say what you do doesn't define you, but doesn't doing something wrong, by logical definition, make you a "wrongdoer?" It's not right, by definition, to be a wrongdoer. I wouldn't be OK with this! I'm so scared of being wrong! It's against everything I stand for!

Yes, mind, being wrong does mean you're a wrongdoer – from one point of view. However, I can play a game you can't... I can be OK with not being OK. I can make it alright to be a wrongdoer. After all, don't we all make mistakes? Aren't we all wrongdoers? I can choose to play the game of forgiveness and perhaps find wrongness isn't what is wrong. Maybe if I choose forgiveness... choose to see we're all fallible human beings with minds that play games and addictions that drive us, then perhaps in this unity as wrongdoers, I'll find the feeling of connection that I haven't been able to get from all these other games I've been playing. But I must choose to play this game without you, mind... it's not a game you know how to play. I'm not even sure if forgiveness is a "game" at all.

Is it so wrong to be "wrong?" To be a "wrongdoer?" To lose and be a "loser?"

What if I proudly say, "I'm a wrongdoer! I'm a loser! I'm a failure! I'm a mistake maker!"

Who gives a shit!?

Aren't all these things true for you too? Don't we share good company with everyone else on the planet if we're losers, wrongdoers, and failures? Just think, you can say, "That Derek guy that wrote this book is a loser too, and that dude's a total badass, so I guess it's not such a bad thing to be a loser!" #LookAtTheBrightSide

Are we bound by these things, or are we something more than these labels? Are you something more than who you "be?" Are you something more than even your identity?

Why does one reject "being wrong" or being a "wrongdoer" if it's a label that can apply to anyone?

If you hold onto pride, a game of the mind, that needs to make you "right," then someone or something else must be "wrong." A master and slave paradigm looked at a whole other way.

But remember, there is no master. The person who needs to be right is now more enslaved than ever. They are enslaved by the shackles of the fear of making a mistake. They must project "wrongness" on to everyone else, including their own mind, in order to maintain a feeling, an illusion, of "rightness."

Yet it's futile, because their game will eventually make them "wrong" at some point whether they want to be or not. They will certainly be wrong by another person playing the "right vs. wrong" game.

Right vs. wrong. Winning vs. losing. Success vs. failure.

How often are these things, in fact, bullshit? True in some ways, total illusions in other ways.

You have many choices. However, avoiding mistakes is not a choice you have the privilege of making. Your brain is an assumption-forming and meaning-making machine with inherent biases that will eventually cause you to err in your judgement. The sooner you can embrace telling yourself "I'm wrong, and I'm a wrongdoer" and not make yourself wrong for it, the sooner you'll be free from your bullshit.

One side of society says you must win to be a winner. Second place is first loser. They label based on outcome.

Another portion says, "Let's get rid of games where there is winning and losing because it hurts kids' self-esteem. Let's not label based on outcome, but rather let's say we're all winners no matter what."

One side is attached to labeling based on outcome, another side resists it. Could they both be full of shit?

Those who label on outcome may be driven to win at all costs and believe this to be a good thing. Through their hard work, they do win the games and become "winners." Then they recognize their own success, and this makes them work even harder. They work their way to the top and become champions. Seeing themselves as champions, they know they have unleashed their greatness, so they become *proud*.

Then they fall. They *always* fall. Their winning and being a "winner" kept them from striving to unleash even more of their greatness, and this was their downfall.

Those who make it not at all about winning and losing accept all for their inherent greatness. No one is defined by the outcome of the game. Some people are naturally better athletes, but others are naturally better scholars. They realize they don't have to do anything to be great, they just are great. They settle for mediocrity because this doesn't hinder them from recognizing the greatness within, so even in their mediocrity they become *proud*.

Then they fall. They *always* fall. Their acceptance of being "great," as is, kept them from striving to unleash even more of their greatness, and this was their downfall.

Each side is recognizing a truth. Each side is ignoring a truth.

Outcomes matter. Good intentions aren't enough. Play to win. Let competition and limitation be resistance that strengthens you. Others will try to destroy you if you don't reject their game. Let fear of losing make you smarter, better, greater.

Being matters. Intentions are the root of everything. It's not whether you win or lose, it's how you play the game. Failure doesn't define you, you define you. You don't become great, you recognize you already are great. Greatness is within you now should you wish to unleash it, and unleashing means you must give others the recognition of their greatness. It's about being great together, and not dominating anyone else.

Which side is true? Which side is false? Is neither side true? Are both sides true?

What if your identity is one who "strives to do right," yet recognizes that you will sometimes do wrong?

What if your identity is one who "strives to gain knowledge," yet recognizes that there are many ways you're still ignorant?

What if your identity is one who "strives to be grateful," yet recognizes that you'll still fall into expectation and resentment?

What if You are beyond not only what you have and what you do, but even beyond who you're being in any moment?

What if who you are isn't who You are? What if who You are is more than who you are?

I say this...

> **Be hungrier for improvement than approval. Be hungrier for lessons than successes.**

To be OK with being wrong, and yet still striving always for constant improvement, is the foundation of Growth Mindset, a concept popularized by Carol Dweck in her book *Mindset*.

In the next part of the book, we're going to really focus on how to both be a badass as well as constantly striving to be even more of a badass without letting the fact that "you're a badass" go to your head. We're going to balance both truths of "You're great as is" and yet "Greatness is what you do."

CHAPTER 35

How To Be Even More Of A Badass, Do Even More Badass Shit, And Have An Even More Badass Life

"It's my modesty that makes me such a badass. It's the fact that I always remain humble by not letting anything go to my head that is the reason I'm kind of a big deal." – Derek Doepker

Most of my friends can tell you, this is *exactly* the kind of thing I would say.

A reason I write books on how to overcome pride and be humble is because, let's face it, I'm just a little more humble than everyone else, and people need to learn a lesson in humility from me. #JustSayin

I'm joking, of course. The whole writing about pride thing is partly my own therapy because I can be full of myself and get caught up in pride like anyone else, but I'm not *that* full of myself.

Yet there is a paradoxical truth to the idea that it's one's humility, vulnerability, and restraint that actually gives them great power and makes them "kind of a big deal." It has been scientifically shown that admitting your mistakes and showing your flaws, when combined with demonstrating great value and accomplishments, can make one more relatable, likeable, and better able to develop greater rapport.

Just showing the world how much your shit is jacked up won't work. Just acting like your shit doesn't stink won't work either. Having a combination of the two is where it's at. It's about having some of each.

Sometimes you need to experience physical weakness for a little bit to have greater physical strength. Sometimes in relationships you need to be weak and vulnerable, so people go, "Oh, they're just like me!" and then you gain the power to connect with them and help them. You gain the "strength" of likability, connection, and influence.

Of course, if you cling to vulnerability, like going to one side of a slingshot and never releasing it, by only talking about how imperfect and flawed you are, the connection is lost. People go, "What does this person have to offer? Their life is more screwed up than mine! I better stay away so their bad luck doesn't rub off on me."

So think about this for a moment…

Many people are trying to demonstrate how perfect they are and avoid being wrong and exposing their wrongness to others, and yet it's this very act of exposing one's flaws that allows one to have a *deeper connection* with the very people they want connection from. It's like wanting to be stronger, but never lifting a weight for fear that lifting the weight will make one weaker. It's short-sighted. It's actually required to get weaker to get stronger.

Not only that, but ask yourself, why would you want everyone's approval? I love all people, but I sure as hell don't "like" all people. I most definitely don't want to be around all people out there.

A mask is worn for fear of people seeing the "real you." Yet even if you choose to wear a mask, some people won't love your mask. Some people won't relate to your mask. Your mask will disconnect you from ever having truly fulfilling and connected relationships, and the need for connection is the very freakin' reason you're wearing a mask in the first place! #YousCrayCray #ButImGuiltyToo

What if you took off the mask knowing some people will find the "real you" ugly, and others will find the "real you" beautiful? Wouldn't you want to hang out with the people who think you're hot stuff and avoid the people who think you's nasty? If you can't choose to please everyone, would you rather choose to please the people who actually love you, or the people who only love the mask you're wearing? That mask was getting all sweaty and nasty anyway. #LetThatShitAirOutForOnce

Those who have embraced their own imperfections will often be willing to embrace yours. Trying to make yourself appear perfect to these people is silly because they already know you're flawed just like they are.

There will be those who judge you for your flaws, and they are usually people who haven't accepted their own flaws. The funny thing is, those people often end up being total a-holes that are so wrapped up in their own BS that you wouldn't want them in your life anyway.

The more you expose your imperfections to show your genuine self, the more you'll attract people who genuinely love you. The more you hide your true self, the more you attract other fake people. Since you won't please everyone, you must ask, would I rather have what's genuine or what's fake?

By now I hope it goes without saying that everything about your relationship with others relates to the relationship you have with yourself and vice versa.

Willingness to admit you're not perfect and be OK with it is one part of growth mindset. "I'm not OK *now* and that's OK. Who I am now, what I've done, and what I have doesn't constrain me. I am beyond all of that. Mistakes have been made and will continue to be made."

Your logical mind *can* accept failure as part of a feedback process. This isn't a new way of thinking. It's how you started out. A baby is by default in growth mindset.

Does the baby go, "Welp, I fell for the third effin' time. I'm done with this shit! Walking just isn't my thing. Not sure how all the other babies do it… they must have better parents. Dammit if only I could afford to hire better parents. Those rich babies have all the luck."

Or…

Is a baby, rather than using its mind to make itself wrong, asking "What did I learn? How do I correct this? What else can I try?"

The baby craves *feedback*. The person dedicated to unleashing their greatness, who also has this mindset of growth, also craves feedback.

What does this look like?

YOU'RE WRONG!

"Great! What makes me wrong, and how can I do better?"

If the words "you're wrong" strike you with any type of negative emotion, this is where your lingering "fixed mindset" is holding on tight.

A fixed mindset is bullshit. A fixed mindset says this is the way things are, and I must keep things this way.

Telling a kid they're stupid leads them to adopt this identity. Then guess what? They do stupid things.

Praising a kid for being smart leads them to adopt this identity. Then guess what? They do smart things… and only smart things… which is stupid.

The "smart" kid will only do the things that make them feel smart – the things they excel at. If they try something and feel like an idiot, they go, "This can't be right. I'm smart, but I can't figure this out. I better not even try. It conflicts with my sense of identity."

Replace "smart" with any identity trait of your choice.

"You're so considerate."

Is "considerate" a good thing? What if the person now takes everyone's needs into consideration in place of or in addition to their own, then they're overwhelmed with trying to consider everyone's needs, taking on too much responsibility, and now they're in over their heads and can't consider anything because they reach the point of "Screw it all! To hell with everyone! Argh!!"

You see, "fixed mindset" is like fixed breathing (here we go again). Breathing is "good" until... well you know the rest.

Everything in this universe is changing, so the idea of anything being "fixed" is inherently false. It's a useful mind game so we think, "If there have always been four seasons, and it takes 365.25 days to rotate around the sun, I'm pretty sure nature isn't going to throw in an extra random ass partial season and 87.9264 days next year just for shits and giggles. Things will probably remain constant."

Yet from a higher perspective, everything that is, is only "For *now*." "For the time being." "Momentarily." You see this theme come up over and over again, and maybe that's because it applies to everything. It's about breaking the bullshit of permanence and recognizing the truth of constant change. When you embrace the idea that things are always changing, why would you cling onto anything, including an identity?

Those in a growth mindset love feedback and crave it so much that being told they're wrong is like being told, "Congratulations! You just hit the jackpot! You were getting bored of things seeming to be too much the same, too stagnant, too consistent in a universe that's always changing and constantly expanding at this time... but now you're going to discover the way you can expand even more! Now you're going to discover a way to let go of whatever you've been so you can be something even greater!"

> *Those in a growth mindset are in alignment with the principles of the Universe.*

#ItsNotWooWoo #ItsScience #OkItsKindOfWooWoo

Those in a growth mindset seek out new knowledge. They test their current ways of doing things to see if there's an even better way. They assume their current assumptions of what is and isn't possible are wrong. They judge their judgments.

Those who choose to be in growth mindset surround themselves with mentors, coaches, and peers to learn from. They especially surround themselves with people who are willing to say, "You're wrong!" to expose their blind spots. Or at the very least, people who are willing to say, "Here's an even better way."

How can one restore this state of being where failure isn't seen as failure, but only feedback? How does one actually overcome their fear of failure? I questioned this myself, and then I realized the times when I have been able to do this most effectively are when I applied something I call "CSM."

CHAPTER 36

CSM – My Secret Weapon For Overcoming Fear Of Failure

Those in a growth mindset are willing to learn from the mistakes of others so that they don't have to make all those mistakes themselves.

However, they're still willing to make their own mistakes in order to grow. The human need for contribution means you want to contribute something to others. So what if we tap into both needs?

I've found when I made my failures not just about my own growth, but about failing in order to help others avoid the mistakes I made, I was able to overcome many of my fears. I was now failing for both my own growth and the growth of those that I cared about, even if those people are complete strangers I've yet to meet.

This idea of being willing to fail to help others is how I came up with "CSM." If you look closely at my story for how I came up with the book *Why You're Stuck*, it was born out of a desire to use my experience of being stuck to teach others why we get stuck and how to get unstuck. Although I was in the midst of "stuckness" when I came up with the idea for the book, it was the act of documenting my experience to help others that actually pulled me out of that state.

I built my most successful business showing authors how I successfully went from a broke valet parker to a #1 bestselling author by creating a course that was a case study of a particular book's success. I showed others what to do and not to do.

When I realized my greatest breakthroughs had come when I went beyond myself and took what I was going through as a "game" or an "experiment" or... wait for it... a "case study," I came up with a concept called "**Case Study Mindset.**"

You're likely to be more willing to face fear, including fear of failure, if it's not just about you. I'm willing to run into a burning building to save a friend.

> *If fear exists within you, then just get outside of yourself to get outside of your fear.*

It is this simple.

Would you face your fears to save those you love? Would you endure discomfort to ease the discomfort of someone you truly love? CSM uses this power of loving others and being willing to sacrifice for them to transcend your own fear.

Let's look at what "true" love is, as this world often tosses the word around a lot. The need for "love" can be defined as a need for connection. I will give love to get love, meet my needs, and feel good.

This type of love, however, isn't the kind of love we're talking about. Anyone can "love" under the condition that it will make them feel good. This kind of conditional "give and take" love will not be enough to transcend fear. You must tap into the "give and receive" love of contribution, of true service to another without needing to get something back.

True love *as a human being* necessitates potential suffering. You cannot have genuine love for another in *this world* without either you or them likely suffering when the other is in pain or when they're gone – especially in their death.

True love is an act of great courage. Its beauty lies in the understanding that those who choose true love have agreed, "This love matters more than the suffering we must endure because of it."

Now you might be wondering, "I thought 'true love' wouldn't have suffering because it's totally selfless and holds no expectation? Isn't it only 'selfish' love that desires to be close to another person which creates suffering when you disconnect? If you 'really love someone,' you wouldn't hurt if they're gone because you'd set them free. True love can only ever be joy, bliss, and peace."

I hear this quite often by people defending the idea that, "True love has no suffering!" when I've proposed this idea of suffering coming with love. This is both true and false depending on what point of view you're coming from.

You see, it's true from a "higher perspective" that there is no suffering in true unconditional love and it's only wonderful feelings. The thing is, we're in a human condition. This means when a human being feels "true love," it comes packaged together with "human love."

Does suffering for the loss of a child mean it wasn't "true love" but "selfish" love?

Does losing the life of a close friend and feeling pain mean you just didn't "love them truly enough?"

Does seeing someone you love crying and in pain lead you to also feel pain? Does suffering with them mean you don't "truly love" them?

Does seeing any fellow human being tortured and being powerless to stop it cause you pain? Wouldn't any well-adjusted human being suffer with empathy seeing such a thing?

I know this may be obvious to many, particularly those more grounded in everyday physical reality. But some truly can't fathom the idea of "true love" and pain and suffering co-existing. They continuously say to themselves, "Any pain I feel means I'm not spiritual or enlightened or truly loving enough." This applies to any area of their life. They are so focused on the abstract concept of "true love" that they overlook the practical reality of how it shows up in daily life.

> *Don't confuse the perfect essence of something with the flawed expression and perceived experience of it.*

You have human needs that, when you love someone, even unconditionally, this love is still felt in the conditional nature of your humanity. You'll have a need for connection with them. Not meeting the need of being close to those you love will cause suffering, and yet it's the "true love" beyond all of this that allows you to endure the suffering.

If you *are* with them, and they are hurting, then you may hurt when they hurt. Does seeing people starving to death and suffering cause your heart to ache? If so, is this actually a sign that you have so much love you feel empathetic?

If you fail to recognize the truth of your humanity, of your weakness, you can make yourself "wrong" for mourning the loss of a loved one or suffering with another you love. You can fail to recognize that "true love" coincides with "human love."

Without recognizing how the two co-exist, one may say to themselves, "If I feel suffering because of not being with this person or because I know they're in pain, then I must not actually truly love them because true love would have no suffering."

Perhaps if you meditate on a mountain long enough, you'll transcend your human needs and not feel any suffering ever again. Everything said is always "potentially." But in the meantime, true love is probably going to hurt from time to time. And remember, "It's OK to not be OK."

Now some may say, "I'm willing to suffer for another." Yet don't deceive yourself into thinking this automatically means this is really loving them as much as you could. This just means you're willing to be a martyr, perhaps to feel connection and significance, and not *completely* out of unconditional love. To say "I truly love another simply because I'm willing to suffer for them" is, potentially, bull-shit. It doesn't mean you don't love them, or even love them a lot, but it's still not a complete "giving and receiving" type of love.

True love isn't just about suffering yourself out of love for an-other. True love is about allowing another to receive suffering. It's about being willing to let others endure suffering on your behalf.

What do I mean?

I noticed for many years I would have a hard time getting close to some people, especially in a romantic relationship aspect. The fear that I had wasn't mostly that I would suffer and have my heart broken. It was primarily that a bond would be created, and then the other person would end up suffering if I were to break the bond because it didn't work out.

My biggest fear wasn't having my own heart broken. I feared having someone else I care about and love having their heart bro-ken "because of me." I feared I would be the cause of their suffering. I thought it would be "good" to keep from getting too close in order to prevent their suffering. Yet all I was doing was, in a sense, trying to make a choice for them on whether or not they could love me and therefore potentially suffer due to this love.

I couldn't necessarily control whether I fell in love with someone or they fell in love with me. To "fall" in love just happens and seems to be coming from a place of helplessness, of vulnerability. So in order to exercise control, I would take a preventative approach by not getting too close to begin with. "Better safe than sorry."

Then I had to remind myself of this sobering reality...

I cannot choose for another if they wish to love me. If they wish to suffer in their love for me, I must be willing to allow them to make that choice to suffer. To deny anyone their "right to suffer" is really denying them their "right to love" since loving often involves suffering.

Now I know this sounds controversial if you don't get the deeper message. Technically, I didn't do anything "wrong" by not choosing to allow people to get close to me. What I did do, though, was cost both them and me the experience of feeling a deeper love. The more I rejected potential suffering, either mine or theirs, the more I rejected love. The attempt to "protect another from themselves" was essentially an attempt to prevent a love from flourishing.

You do have every right to choose who you do and don't want to love. You have every right to get close or not to get close to someone. Just realize that each of these choices has a price. The price of avoiding suffering at all costs is to avoid love at all costs

This shows up at the extreme when people close off, lash out, or do any other type of destructive behavior to push others away. "I'm going to *force* them not to love me." Of course, you can't actually force another person not to love you. They make that choice for themselves. This idea is about the attempt, the manipulation, and the desire to control others by withholding love, even in a mis-guided attempt to protect them, in order that they are "forced" into not loving you – and of course, they still may choose to love you anyway.

If one does love you, you can accept or reject their love as is your choice, but if you're rejecting their love, do you truly love them as much as you could? In a more everyday sense, if someone offers you help out of love, do you turn it down to "not be a burden" and thereby reject their offering of love? You may choose to do this as is your right, but is it really loving to tell another person, "You're not allowed to sacrifice for me, only I'm allowed to sacrifice for you?" thereby making it one-sided?

It's when your choices attempt to persuade another's choices that you must be careful. While it's fine to try to persuade a person to make a particular choice in *their* best interest, it would be very dan-gerous to start to say, "I need to persuade this person not to truly love me." It's in the attempt to proactively keep someone from making the choice to love you that you run into problems.

> *What if trying to keep another from suffering willingly for you is on one level trying to keep a person from loving you?*

If loving entails the potential for suffering, the moment you allow someone to love you, you must allow them to potentially suffer because of their love for you. You must be willing to say, "I love you so much that I will allow *you* to suffer in your love for me."

Ask yourself, "Do I love them enough to allow them to suffer for me? To allow them to sacrifice for me? To allow their heart to be broken for mine? To allow them to make their own choice to love me and possibly suffer for this choice?"

> *To give your life for another is love, but never forget that true love means you're also willing to allow another to give their life for you.*

It's give *and **receive**,* remember?

Think of how much you'd sacrifice to help others you love and fill them with joy. Now imagine your "future self" is another person you can help. Another person you can suffer for.

How would your life be different six months from now if you made those same sacrifices to help out your future self and put a smile on their face?

The deception is that sacrificing for others is good, but sacrificing for yourself is bad. Yet if you're not taking care of yourself as you are now and growing into your greater potential, how can you show up in the world as your greatest self to help others unleash *their* greatness?

Growth is essentially nothing more than showing love for your future self; the willingness to sacrifice from "present self" for the good of your future self. An unwillingness to sacrifice right now is like being an ass to your future self and screwing them over. It's like saying, "I'm gonna just be super comfortable now even though it's totally going to screw you over, future self. Deal with it." #DontBeAnAss #WhatDidYourFutureSelfEverDoToYou

Would you suffer willingly now out of love for your future self?

If you can find gratitude for how your "past self" hooked you up for your current reality, then from this state you can "pay it forward" and hook up your future self. This is the essence of growth. "What am I grateful for that I've done in the past? How can I pay it forward to me in the future?"

I point this out because CSM is about being willing to fail so that you can share your lessons with others so that they can grow. However you will receive the lessons too. This, in turn, helps *you grow*. It's an act of love for others and for "future you."

What does Case Study Mindset look like practically speaking?

• A blog documenting one's weight loss journey.

• A book documenting 50 different experiments in one's online business.

• An online journal about one's coping with addiction.

• A YouTube video blog about the ups and downs of being a new parent.

• Facebook updates about all the silly things one's cat does. Actually, not sure if this counts as a case study, but I love silly cat videos so I encourage people to make them and share them with me. Facebook.com/DerekDoepker

Case studies are great when they talk about what works and also *what doesn't work*. Even if you don't share too much about what doesn't work, if you're like me, you may find that you're at least far more *willing* to try things and fail because it's all about making a good case study. You'll be motivated to try new things so your case study isn't super boring and useless.

Will everyone want to see your case study? Hell no. Some people will think you're arrogant or stupid for doing this. Don't worry, they're probably not people you want to party with anyway.

I started writing this book as a case study to share the process of writing and releasing a book with other authors. By creating a case study, it got me off my ass from thinking about the book to actually writing it, trying many new outside-the-box promotional methods, and the rest is history. Or it will be when this book is the most epic bestselling book of all time. #FingersCrossed

Which reminds me, are you enjoying this book?

Sharing a review and spreading the word of how a particular book positively impacted your life would almost be like... a... "case study," which would be something I'm sure you realize by now could totally rock your socks off. #JustSayin #HintHint #WinkWink #NudgeNudge

Many times people typically don't want to fail, but most loving people do want to help others, including their future self, and would be willing to sacrifice to do so.

If you're willing to be the one to fail so others don't have to...

If you're willing to sacrifice now to totally rock the world of the future you...

If you choose to be the leader, a trailblazer who ventures forward boldly to uncharted territory to help those who are too scared to go...

This is greatness.

You will be rewarded for it.

Do you choose to be a leader out of love?

CHAPTER 37

"I Don't Know" And That's...

Those in a growth mindset are just as comfortable with questions, if not more so, than answers. They can turn confusion into curiosity. My frustration and confusion about why people are so full of shit, myself included, spurs me on a journey to uncover answers from psychology.

Did you notice this book is approximately ¼ questions? Does the constant question-asking get on your nerves because you just want a quick fix set of answers, or are you stimulated by the exploration and uncertainty the questions provide?

If it's the former, that's a fixed mindset that wants the answer now. But how can one be on a search for truth if they feel they already know it all? Isn't that... pride?

The idea that you don't know what you don't know can spur a childlike curiosity. I don't need to teach you how to do this. I'm really only reminding you that you have this within you. Do you choose to go back to the way you were? Do you choose to be a "big baby" that's curious about learning how to walk instead of a big baby that whines about not having everything all figured out right now?

The moment you have an answer, you can either settle with the answer or be stimulated to ask a new question. One great question for any answer is, "Is this always true?" Each new answer brings with it a whole new set of questions. The question is, are you more concerned with rightness or greatness? Pride leads to wanting to be right and be seen as great, while meekness is the attribute of those who are truly great.

The meek are not weak, but rather those with great power under restraint who don't let it go to their heads and need to show it off. They are *willing* to show and demonstrate their greatness to others to inspire and make an impact, but they are also *willing* to restrain it if it's for the greater good in that moment. They are grateful for their knowledge because at any moment it could be taken. They are grateful not just for what they've learned, but for what they may continue to learn; continue to learn not just for their own benefit, but to serve others. They are humble, modest, teachable, grateful, giving, courageous, caring, curious, and *willing*.

There are many different answers for "what" you may do, and rarely is one answer always the right answer. However, if instead of asking "What do I do?" you start with "How do I intend to be?" this can lead to far better decisions.

Do you intend to be proud or meek?

If you intend to be meek, might it not be wise to study others who demonstrate this quality, such as great leaders like Gandhi and Martin Luther King? Would it be wise to surround yourself with people who have great power and knowledge but who keep it under restraint and use it only for good as role models? Would it be wise to actually practice meekness rather than intellectualize it and just talk about it?

My answer is damn straight it would be. This book is just a reminder of how to find answers. It's up to you to seek them out and keep seeking them out. All the while, you should be continuously asking, "What's my lesson here? What else can I discover? What does this mean? Why? How? When is this true? When is it not true? How can I do this even better? What's another way? Why did this work for them? What's the same or similar with these things? What's different and a key distinction between these things?"

Lessons feed you more than successes. Be hungrier for lessons more than for successes, and you'll never stop growing. Improvement is the ultimate accomplishment achieved by those who make feedback matter more than the failure they must endure to get it.

The problem for many people is they think their problem is the problem. Whatever you say your problem is, isn't the real problem. If it were, you would have already solved it.

"I don't know what to do to achieve my goal." – That's not the problem. The problem is that you haven't gone to the library to read a book on this or gotten a coach or a mentor. Or the problem is that you really do know what to do but are scared that you don't have all the answers and fear making a mistake, and therefore you don't know how to redirect your thinking. Or the problem is that if you do this, you're worried people might think that you're stupid, and that would be embarrassing, and therefore you need to find a suitable way of meeting your need for connection and approval that doesn't hinder you achieving your goal.

"I know what to do but I can't get myself to do it because I'm unmotivated." – That's not the problem, the problem is that you're ignorant about human psychology and need to study how to work with your psychology rather than against it. Or the problem is that you don't realize you can start by making gradual adjustments instead of making drastic changes. Or the problem is that you are making gradual adjustments, and it would be easier if you DID dive into it head first. Or the problem is that you're intellectualizing what to do and haven't learned how to get into your heart to care enough about something outside of yourself that will enable you to overcome your fears.

There is no one-size-fits-all answer, as you can see here, and we all have our blind spots. This is why even I have coaches. I get caught up in "I don't know," and they dig deeper to help me see the "real" problem.

Let's look at what might be considered a big problem, and that is not even knowing what one wants. Not even being able to say, "This is my problem." Instead, it's more like, "Something is off, but I don't know what it is. I don't know what's wrong, or even what I want. I know my problem isn't the problem, because I don't even know what my problem is!"

"I don't know what my problem is. I have no goal. I don't know what I want or don't want, and that's a problem." – No, not having a goal or a clear vision isn't a problem. You feeling like you need to know what to do right now is the problem. What's wrong with the excitement and adventure of figuring out what you want? Essentially, you already answered that you want to *gain clarity*. Gaining clarity can be achieved by trying new things, reading books, hanging out with people who may inspire you, and so on. To gain clarity starts with being OK with confusion and letting it stimulate your curiosity to ask:

- If I did know what I want, what would it be?
- If I did know a place to start looking for answers, where would it be?
- What if I try this thing that's been in the back of my mind calling me for a while?
- What's something else I can do out of the ordinary that may give me even more clarity?
- Can I allow myself to be OK with not having answers but simply with sitting with the questions of life for a while?

> **What if being unclear is the exact catalyst you need to gain greater clarity through curiosity?**

Here's a newsflash. Even the most well put together and successful people don't always know what they want or what their next big thing is. Even the most successful people have times of uncertainty and darkness. It's *because* of their ability to go into darkness, be OK with it, and move through it that they're successful. Strong people aren't strong because they don't experience weakness, they're strong *precisely because* they're willing to endure weakness at times by challenging themselves with resistance.

> *Uncertainty is the resistance that must be endured for a breakthrough of newfound answers.*

Failure and wrongness are simply opportunities for new learning. Maybe you did everything right, and it was just the wrong timing, so now you've learned a lesson about timing. Maybe you did everything right, and it just didn't work out because of bad luck. It happens. Regardless, there's always a lesson.

If you don't know the lesson, then does that make you uncomfortable, want to place blame, and make someone "wrong?" Or, if you don't know the lesson, does this just make you even hungrier to dig deeper and go, "What could the lesson be? How can I make this into something for my growth and benefit proactively? Who might have an insight, show me something I'm not seeing, and help me see my blind spots?"

"I don't know," and that's *exactly* what's right! *This is growth mindset.*

Do you choose to make "I don't know" the right answer?

> *What if being great isn't always a matter of constantly doing great things, but rather being OK with not doing great things while you discover how to unleash even more of your greatness?*

CHAPTER 38

You're Awesome... But Don't Let It Go To Your Head

Growth mindset entails a willingness to see failures as feedback. It entails seeing old discoveries simply as catalysts for new discoveries. It is the process of expansion and evolution that is the way of nature. It requires a humility and willingness to let go of pride. Pride that yearns to always be right, settle with an answer, and rest complacently in one's current state of success.

Yet there's another part, which is recognizing your inherent greatness, your rightness, your successfulness, and ultimately your greatest potential. Recognizing your "True Self." Recognizing your inner badass, if you will.

You have to see that you have greatness within you if you wish to unleash more of it. This is called "unleash your greatness," after all and not "make yourself great eventually over time if you're lucky and all the stars and planets align and I hope you picked the right parents because not everyone's genetically gifted for it and oops you messed it up already with that thing you did that one night that you hope no one finds out about better luck next life."

"I'm great." Appreciation or pride?

You see the dilemma?

How can you praise yourself, acknowledge yourself when you are right, dare I say be *proud* of your accomplishments, and yet not have pride?

The answer is...

You can't.

You *will* experience pride. There is actually no choice in this matter. You don't have to *stay* in pride, but to think "I'm above ever being proud. I got this whole pride thing handled, and it's never going to be an issue for me cause I'm totally badass at being humble," would be, well... pride!

So ask yourself, if pride isn't necessarily a "bad" thing because nothing is good or bad out of context, then how might pride actually be a benefit? What if pride can help you grow? What if pride actually can, potentially, help you be more humble?

> *It's through overcoming the resistance of vices that one cultivates and strengthens virtues.*

In this sense, even vices aren't "good" or "bad." They're only an issue if you fall and remain victim to them. But to have pride creep up on you and pull you towards complacency is, in itself, simply an opportunity – an opportunity to make a choice. Do I give into the pride I'm feeling, or do I acknowledge it and keep moving towards growth and meekness?

This is what's meant when people give a compliment and say, "But don't let it go to your head." In other words, don't let it inflate your ego too much so that the ego takes over. In a sense, your ego isn't bad or something to be avoided. It's impossible to eliminate your ego, so don't even try. It simply needs to be balanced with something greater than your ego, your "True Self," if you will.

This is important because those who pride themselves on saying, "I'm smart!" "I'm awesome!" "I'm great!" run the risk of getting caught up in those things and sabotaging their own success with their positive affirmations. Their positivity backfires. Visualizing successful outcomes has even been shown to lead to over-confidence and less success.

(See bonus video at BreakThroughYourBS.com/Bonus)

And yet, at the same time, the recognition that you're great seems to be needed to have the confidence to pursue great things. We do want to positively affirm ourselves. We do want to see that a great outcome is a possibility. We do want to believe in our current greatness and that even more great things are in store for us.

Those who say, "I pretty much totally suck at life, and it's hopeless for things to get better," may be technically more "modest," but it's obviously not going to get them anywhere. They'll give up before they even get started.

What's the difference between someone who says, "I'm great!" and lets it go to their head and sabotage their success vs. someone who says "I'm great!" and uses that as a positive affirmation for spurring even more success?

The question is, where is this statement coming from? What else is it *balanced* with? What is the sub-context behind it? It's critical that you stop taking things at the surface level and dig deeper if you wish to be wise and effective.

If I say, "I'm right, AND I'm wrong." I'm balanced. I'm whole. I recognize that I'm right at times and wrong at times. I'm likely "right" about some things I believe right now, but I also recognize that I have blind spots and am pretty much guaranteed to be "wrong" about some things I believe. I know, and I don't know. I'm awesome, and I have a lot of work to do on myself.

It's "whole picture" thinking. It's Yin and Yang harmonizing each other. It's pretty much what this whole book is about.

Remember, if you wish to remain strong and are *unwilling* to be weak, you'll never get *stronger.* If you can't let go of being "great," you may never be even greater. One must let go of what they desire, if only for a moment, to get it. To enter into weakness in order to enter into even more strength.

Yet if you wish to remain weak, or believe you're too weak to even try, you'll also never get stronger. You must have the desire for strength to pursue it and endure the pain that comes with cultivating it. You must realize you have some strength that exists within you now before you even attempt to pick up a dumbbell to get even stronger.

You must see the movement, the dynamic that exists in all things to be effective. Appreciating the universe is about expansion and contraction. Energy in motion. Nothing is fixed, everything is moving. The attempt to remain in a particular state or with a particular identity is like a clock that is stuck at one point in time because the clock said, "Oh, this is the right time, so I'm just going to stay here forever."

This is critical to appreciate when you think about your mood. That is, your emotional and physical state, which I'll simply refer to as "state." Remember this...

States don't stick.

If you're in a bad mood, you can change it. You can: Move your body. Smile. Do a fist pump and say, "Hell yeah, baby!!" Dance. Put on good music. Use empowering language that shows where you have choice and *reframes* a situation. Ask yourself quality questions like, "What am I grateful for? How can I turn this situation into something that's beneficial?"

The fact that your state is so important and that it's constantly fluctuating is why I'm such a big advocate of health and fitness. Your physical health affects how you think and feel. Nothing in this book matters if you're so unhealthy and brain dead that you can't act upon it or think clearly about it. Many people would solve a lot of their problems if they just got more sleep and didn't treat their bodies like shit.

Your state affects your ability to discover answers. If you see questions in this book, and your brain starts to go, "Durrr, I don't know," then you're too brain-fried in the moment to get creative and empowering answers and be effective. Change your state, and then come back to the questions.

A poor state doesn't just affect the answers you get, it affects how you approach any situation and what you get out of it.

I was at a seminar once where I needed to pay $5 if I wanted to get in the room because I showed up late after a break. I started to feel upset about this, but then I asked myself, "If I go into the room too upset to even pay attention to the lessons I paid thousands of dollars to get because I "lost" $5, isn't that silly? Aren't I just compounding my loss by adding the cost of a poor state to a meager financial loss? If I'm paying $1 per minute to be here, and I let ten minutes go by grumbling to myself about the $5 loss, and not even paying attention to what's going on, then wouldn't I be *choosing to take from myself* $10 worth of this experience?"

I used this type of mental reframing to proactively choose to be in a better state because I know there's a serious cost to being in a poor state – the cost is losing out on the experience of appreciating what's showing up in life right now.

You can reframe any situation like this to improve your state. Shit happens, so do I want to add more shit to the shit by being in a poor state, which is basically me robbing from my own happiness? Or would I prefer to keep my state high since that's one thing I do have control over?

> **If life gives you shit, don't give a shit. Adding your own shit to the shit you've been given leads to a really shitty life.**

But Derek... I thought you said you can't "not" give a shit. I thought you said we are going to give at least a little bit of a shit, so this makes "don't give a shit" contradictory. Aren't we confusing the readers at this point?

Thank you for sharing mind. I trust the readers can see beyond the surface at this point. It's technically true from one perspective we're pretty much guaranteed to give a shit when life throws shit our way. It's natural and human. Sometimes things are made simple for brevity, but one must still consider what's implied with a statement. In this case, we will almost always still give a shit regardless of whether or not it makes sense to or not, so the key is to reframe the situation to give more of a shit about something else.

It's important to be considerate of your state when making decisions, as choices are primarily based on emotions. The good news is, you can choose to change your emotional state, and therefore, in a sense, proactively choose what kind of "emotional decisions" you make.

It's unwise to ask if I want to work out after hours of Netflix binging. I'll be at rest and want to stay at rest, possibly getting up only to grab some more ice cream. It makes more sense to get up, dance for a couple minutes, get the blood flowing and my body moving, and then ask, "So can I go do that workout now?" Think your answer is going to be different by putting a quick-fix dance session in between Netflixing and question-asking? You can bet your bottom dollar it does.

Do a fist pump and jumping jacks in the middle of a crowd, and look like an idiot if this is what it takes to save yourself from making a devastating, critical decision simply due to a poor state.

If you're looking for an order of priorities when deciding what to do, it's this:

1. What am I *being asked* to do by The Creator or a "Higher Power?" What do I already know is right to do now?

2. How can I boost my state so that I think and feel great?

3. How can I serve others?

4. How can I serve my future self?"

Managing your state is more of a priority than even serving others or your future self. Without the ability to manage your state with quality questions, the right type of language, and adjusting your physiology through movement, diet, exercise, sleep, and more, you'll never tap into your creative potential and drive to make all this other stuff happen. The mistake some make is they're trying to lift others up so much that they become so tired and helpless that no one benefits.

If you want more resources on the actual order of priorities and tactics for these things, I recommend checking out the book *Why You're Stuck* at ExcuseProof.com/stuck and the work of Brandon Broadwater at ExcuseProof.com/event.

You can choose your emotional state to a large degree. You might not help if you get in a poor state, but you can help if you remain in a poor state. If you're in a good mood, remember this won't stick either. It will fade. It's unwise to get too complacent expecting your great mood, creativity, and drive to last.

This is all important to understand for when you find yourself in a state of pride and complacency. There's a slingshot of pride on one side, and growth on the other. You can go into pride for a moment and let the feeling of success motivate you to have even more success.

The key is, after you move into pride, let that shit go. Don't let it go to your head. *Enjoy it for a moment and release into growth.* Go, "I've done something great and learned a great lesson. This is awesome! I can do this! I love this feeling of success in learning a lesson, and now I'm hungrier for even more success! Now it's time to start growing again!"

Celebrate your successes if you want more success! This is critical. You're motivated by wins. You need them to be inspired! Find every little thing you're doing right, and praise it. I really believe it's my ability to say, "Hell yeah Derek you da man!" that's been responsible for a lot of my success when I've had a win. It's also been responsible for a lot of my complacency when I didn't let it go and let myself rest in my success for too long.

Yes, you are motivated by challenges too. However, you need *both* success to make you think, "I can do it!" and challenge and "failure" to ask, "Now, how can I do even better?" It's integrated thinking, not choosing just one or the other.

This means, define your success not just as getting a desired outcome, but as your "effort" and "striving" to achieve success. Success isn't only when one loses weight or makes money, it's when they do the workout they didn't feel like doing, or attend a networking meeting when they could have stayed home. All of these things are successes. All of these things are wins. Are you choosing to give yourself recognition and appreciation for each of your wins? The wins of outcome, and the wins of striving, and the wins of intending to show up in your greatness? Are you reminding yourself to do this by giving others recognition and appreciation for each of their wins?

This praising effort is what Carol Dweck found was a key distinction with growth mindset. When parents praised their kids for attributes, like "you're smart," it led to more of a fixed mindset. When parents praised their kids for effort and striving, like "great work," this led to more of a growth mindset.

> *You might not ever be told by another that you're the shit for striving, but remember you can always choose to recognize yourself as being the shit for striving.*

In here, I playfully refer to "being" the shit for "doing" the effort of striving. This is, I believe, an important integration of being and doing.

If you're just focusing on the challenge part of growth by saying, "I'm such a loser, and I have to get my shit together," this is attempting to change through force of guilt, not power of choice. It's lifting a heavy dumbbell to get stronger, and then forgetting you actually need to put it down to let yourself rest, recover, and grow. Constant unending challenge isn't the way to growth.

Would saying "you're a loser and can't do anything right" work to motivate another person? Would telling someone all the ways they're failing motivate them?

Sometimes...

Those inspired by challenges may say, "If you tell me I can't do something, I'm going to *prove* you wrong!" Yet the only reason this works is because they recognize how they've already been successful. They have enough, dare I say, pride in themselves to take failure as an obstacle to conquer rather than be conquered by.

The masculine often responds better to challenge while the feminine responds better to praise. However, we all need both challenge and appreciation to stimulate growth to varying degrees. Just like we need both resistance and recovery to strengthen a muscle.

The real question is, does your current approach work on you? How would you want someone else to motivate you? Would someone telling you to "Stop doing that! Get your shit together, and do this instead!" inspire you?

What if someone didn't say you were wrong but simply recommended an *even better* way?

Case in point, I have a resting asshole face. I could probably work to change it, but for now it's what I'm working with. Well-meaning people sometimes come up to me out of the blue and say, "Smile!"

Uhh... sorry? I wasn't aware I was doing something wrong by sitting here minding my own business with a neutral look on my face.

This doesn't motivate me to change. If anything I'm more upset for these people "making me wrong" by implying that me not smiling is somehow bad, and I should be doing something else instead. Of course, this idea they're "making me wrong" isn't reality, it's just a mind game. But seriously, who feels the need to tell another person what to do with their face? #ItsMyBodyIDoWhatIWant

What I can imagine would work quite well to motivate me to smile is someone saying, "Derek, I love how calm, cool, and collected you are. I also love that you have an extreme sexy smile. When you let it out, my heart swoons. *wink*" I should note that it's a hot girl saying this to me in my imagination, so bear that in mind.

Would I be likely to *naturally* let out a smile in this moment, and would I be more likely to smile on an ongoing basis after hearing this? Damn straight. Notice this works because I'm not being made "wrong" for being the way I am and doing what I'm doing. It's more like, "You're great now, and here's another way you can be even greater. Here's something else to add more greatness to your existing greatness."

> *The longest relationship you're ever going to have is with yourself. How would you feel if another person talked to you the way you talk to yourself? Do you treat yourself the way you want others to treat you?*

Choose to celebrate both what you've done and what you're capable of doing. See how much of your capacity you've already fulfilled, how much of your greatness you've already unleashed. Yet continue to hold in your mind the image of how much more greatness you still have left within you. It's 10x, 100x, 1,000,000x greater than whatever you think it is. Never settle for where you're at when you realize you were meant for so much more while also recognizing that where you're at is exactly where you need to be to make the next step towards even more greatness.

See the current reality and the future possibility. Accept where you're at but never settle for it, for all things in nature must change. To wish to remain the same as you are now is to violate the very nature of your being as one that must evolve or die.

Realize this...

Pride is not a choice for greatness.

This has a dual meaning...

If you're moving towards growth, realize that there will be a natural tendency to end up in pride at some point. You will, inevitably, find yourself suddenly waking up one day and going, "Damn. I'm pretty great, aren't I? Look at all I've accomplished. Look at all the successes I've had because I challenged myself and have grown so much." You were moving toward growth, and as a result, the slingshot released, and you find yourself in pride. It's the human condition. You can't choose not to end up in pride at some point. Sometimes thoughts and feelings come up without our choosing. It's in how we respond to these things where choice lies.

So now you have a choice. The choice is not, "How can I never feel pride?" Your choice is this: *When* I experience pride... do I choose to *remain* in pride or *move back* towards growth?

Consider holding your breath again, but see it this time not from a place of choice. If you're going underwater, might you instinctually hold your breath without consciously choosing to do so? Do you "decide" to hold your breath or is it almost automatic?

Pride, and fear for that matter, and many other so called "bad" emotions may almost be seen as automatic reactions to the environment you're in. You can use these as tools to dive into waters and uncover treasures hidden underneath the surface. Yet you must never hold onto pride or fear, for if you don't let them go, eventually they would choke the life out of you.

Pride is not a choice for achieving greatness. Pride is inevitable, and yet you must also choose never to remain in pride, but rather to move toward meekness and growth to continuously unleash even more your greatness.

CHAPTER 39

Being Is Doing Is Having – Having Is Doing Is Being

You're in a house of mirrors, remember?

I mentioned that what shows up in life often stems from your way of being, which determines what you do, and ultimately what you have.

However, this is a two-way street. What you Have affects what you Do and who you Be – *if you choose.*

Let's look at how "having" affects your "being" and "doing."

You can have an outcome which affects what you decide to do. If a person does a workout program for six months, and not a single thing has changed in their body, wouldn't it be stupid to keep doing the same thing? Wouldn't it be wise to look at the results they have and at least consider, "Is this because I haven't given it enough time and effort to see results (which is sometimes the case), or is it because what I'm doing just isn't working? Could the things I'm doing that used to work no longer be the best things for me to do right now?"

You can have an environment that you put yourself in or that you've been put into by force. Research shows that one's environment, through the power of mirror neurons, does have a psychological and emotional impact on a person. If one has a poor environment, shitty friends they hang out with, and only have access to terrible foods, all of these things will affect what one does and who they are – if they choose.

Do you notice that you naturally start to take on the mannerisms of people you hang out with? One can choose contrary to their environmental influence, but willpower can only go so far. Rather than fight against a poor environment with limited willpower, wouldn't it be easier to use the willpower you have to make a choice to have an environment that almost effortlessly leads to being, doing, and having what you desire?

"Environment is stronger than willpower." – Yogananda

But Derek... I can't always change my environment. It's nice to say have a great environment, surround yourself with people who have what you want, and be around people who uplift you. However I can't totally avoid people in my life who are negative.

Yes mind, thank you for sharing. Something isn't necessarily "good" or "bad" until one responds to it a particular way. Challenging and "negative" people can help one grow and develop compassion, so I don't have to get rid of them in my life altogether. However, let's play the game of investing in and exposing myself to books, seminars, mentors, coaches, podcasts, blogs, meetup groups, and other sources of positive influence to add more good to my environment. Let's play the game of rejecting, at times, the negative influences both in people and things that challenge me beyond my current capacity until I grow enough to handle them.

What you do also affects who you be. If one starts exercising, then this would start to create an identity of being an "exerciser" or "health conscious." Then this identity creates a momentum to exercise even more. What you do is reinforcing or creating your identity – who you "be."

This is why taking even the smallest steps in the direction of what you want is critical. These tiny steps may appear insignificant because they don't create a big outcome in what you have right away. However, their significance is in their power to start to shift your identity.

Momentum generates motivation. Even tiny steps in the right direction shifts your state, so you want to do even more. Once you get started, then you want to keep going. Success breeds success.

This is the idea of a micro-commitment or micro-habit as I outline in my book *The Healthy Habit Revolution: Create Better Habits in 5 Minutes a Day available* at ExcuseProof.com/revolution #AnotherShamelessPlug #ItsMyBookIDoWhatIWant

All things works together. Everything affects everything else, and usually in a two-way street sort of way. What you do with your physical body affects your emotions. Your emotions affect your physical body. How you think affects how you feel, and how you feel affects how you think.

There is an order of priorities where some things matter more than others, but just because something matters more or is a starting point, doesn't mean other things in a chain don't cycle back.

A wise order of significance is: Start by doing what you already know to do. If you have a particular faith, this would be aligning to the Creator's (whatever term you use) wishes. You may also think of this as not asking, "What will I do?" but rather responding to the question of "Will you do this?" being asked of you by something beyond you.

> *"Have the courage to follow your heart and intuition. They somehow already know what you truly want to become. Everything else is secondary." – Steve Jobs*

Then do what you need to do for your own state. Then serve others. *Then* serve your future self by growing. It's wise to start with what you know to do before trying to get new information.

Too often people get themselves stuck trying to get new information, which is important for growth, at the expense of doing what they *already know.*

You'll have the most positive impact if you prioritize those closest to you. In other words, it's unwise to try to save strangers you've never met if it means letting your family and friends suffer. If I'm spreading the word about this book to "save the world," and my mom needs me to stop and help her, she gets first priority.

If I'm in a business, my team and employees would matter more than even the customers. As Richard Branson says, "Put your staff first, customers second, and shareholders third." While a business principle, it's really a life principle about focusing first on those closest to you whom you have the most impact on and let it spread from there.

Remember, the person you have the most impact on and choice with is *yourself.* Treat yourself well and let your unleashed greatness unleash the greatness in others. If I'm attempting to help my friends, I can sacrifice from myself in the short-term, but if I sacrifice from my long-term needs, then I'm doing them and myself a disservice. I must prioritize myself, then those closest to me, and only after this, then spread out from there, if I wish to be effective.

Realize too that unleashing your greatness may make others uncomfortable. It may feel like doing a disservice to some to be your fully awesome great self. They may be intimidated by it and may even attempt to shame you. They may project their insecurities on you and say "You're proud! You're arrogant! You're wrong for showing up as being so great! Take it down a notch, you show-off! Being great is *forbidden!*"

Realize, though, that there's a slingshot with your influence in them. While you may "make" them uncomfortable, although it's their choice to be uncomfortable from one perspective, still consider that this for them may only be temporary discomfort that actually leads them to more comfort and joy if they decide to get over their pride and be inspired by you.

You may plant a seed in them of what's possible by your example. They may see how they're not stepping into their own greatness when they see you in yours. You are being a *mirror* to them showing what they couldn't see from the inside looking out. They start to see their own unfulfilled potential that isn't being fulfilled due to their choices. They may fight it and reject it momentarily, but still it lingers in the back of their mind.

A seed starts to grow and that resentment turns to appreciation. They may eventually turn around and say, "You know what... I was actually the one being proud. You showed me how I wasn't stepping up and, once I got over my ego, I became inspired by your example. Now I'm going to be more like you and unleash more of my greatness."

Being a health and fitness coach, I see a common scenario. Someone is first shamed by their peers for suddenly eating a salad every day for lunch. They're picked on and mocked. But then months go by, and eventually some of their peers open up to them and say, "You know... I'm actually kind of impressed by your commitment. I want to start eating better myself. Do you have any tips for me?"

Don't confuse a current reality for a potential possibility in what you see in others. Your greatness may plant a seed. Sometimes to plant a seed you gotta dig up some dirt. You're going to dig up some dirt in some people when you are being great, but you'll plant a seed of what's possible for them in their mind. They'll see the gap between what they are and what they could be. This may be uncomfortable for them, but *it may also be exactly what they need to be set free.*

Do you love them enough to suffer yourself being ridiculed, and allow them to suffer the discomfort of seeing their untapped greatness, in order to set them free?

If they choose to get over their pride, then they'll nourish the seed that you chose to plant by your example. At which point, you played a critical role in unleashing their greatness. They're still responsible for nourishing the seed within them, but it was you who *chose* to plant the seed of what's possible by your example.

> *If you want to plant the seed of greatness in others, realize that you're going to dig up some of their dirt and get your hands dirty. Are you willing to endure their potential resentment for a moment to receive their recognition and appreciation for a lifetime?*

CHAPTER 40

It's All Coming Together

T he growth mindset is also sometimes referred to as "progress" mindset. Growth and progress are action-oriented words. They're a *process*. "Doing" words. They imply something that's in motion, like the Universe, constantly expanding and *evolving*. You are evolved, but only because you are evolving. Take the "evolved' part in isolation of the on-going process that's occurring, and you're tempted to think, "That's it, I've made it!"

It's not "I'm great," but rather "I'm *doing* greatness." "I'm *striving* for even more greatness." "I'm *experiencing* the greatness I have now." It's all of the above. It's an "ing" word that's about the process, not the current state.

This doesn't mean you can't say "I'm great." The question is, is that all there is to the story? This is one piece, but not the whole.

Can you see the wholeness from the pieces? Can you see the big picture without isolating only one detail?

Our good old friend Jeremiah seemed to do the opposite when he separated the poison from the purity. He respected that the parts *didn't* make for the whole. Can you separate the poison from the purity? Can you separate the parts from the whole? Can you make distinctions and see differences between things? This is a critical game to play.

One can only see a part and say, "True love is pure joy and bliss. There can be no suffering with only true love." It's true that there's only purity and bliss in true love. It's like pure water and sustains our life. Still, *from our experience on this Earth*, there is something suspended in this love called human needs from a human mind. This means that we typically experience suffering along with love – at least at some points in time, such as when we see those we love in pain. Is it the love itself causing the suffering, or what the love comes along with?

Suffering gets suspended in love, like a poison suspended in water, when we are human. The air you breathe and food you eat is tainted with small amounts of toxins, but this air and food still keeps you alive. Your body has means of filtering toxins out with your lungs and the liver. In much the same way the love we experience on this earth is almost always a bit "tainted" when it's mixed with our human condition, yet still essential and life giving. The love is "pure bliss" in isolation, but this isolation is hard to achieve without processing. Love shows up mixed with "humanness" which is, from one perspective, why something as perfect as love can hurt at times as well as heal. For instance, to see someone I love and feel bonded to them means that I hurt when I see them suffering.

Perhaps there's something even perfect about this imperfection in the way we experience a perfect love as imperfect beings. Can we separate the poison from the purity and transcend this suffering to find only the pure, true love without the pain and suffering? This is a question you may wish to consider.

Jeremiah didn't just see the parts though. He respected the "wholeness" of the poison and the water in their original slime state. He didn't touch the slime and go, "Well, since it's part water, and water is pure, this slime won't hurt me." He appreciated that the slime could hurt him if he wasn't careful, just like we know love hurts if we're not careful because it's been tainted with our human condition.

But in order to save his life and the life of the villagers, out of love, he boldly entered into the forbidden cave that all feared to see if there existed purity within a tainted slime. Jeremiah was *willing in his greatness* to see the wholeness of a pure, life-giving water, willing to see the pure love if you will, within a poisonous slime. Then through processing it out, there was ultimately perfection. A perfectly pure water was always there in the slime, but there simply needed someone to *choose* to see it and draw it out before perfection existed as a separate whole from the slime.

The *before* was imperfection. The *after* was perfection. The gap in the middle is the processing. Do you forget about the middle state, where the slime was being processed and having its poison removed? Or did you just focus on the before and after? Don't we often leave the processing part out of the story and only see the before and/or after? Yet it's the story of the processing that's the entire basis of all our favorite stories, The Hero's Journey.

Are you comparing your "before" to someone else's "after?" Are you forgetting when you see their greatness that they too struggled? Do you forget that those who are strong were once terribly weak, if even for a moment? For they had to be. One cannot be great without going through the trials of weakness, uncertainty, confusion, despair, darkness, depression, hardship, mind games, deceptions, wrongdoing, mistakes, vulnerability, selfish appetites, sadness, anger, misery, grief, guilt, overanalyzing, carelessness, addiction, discomfort, pain, pride, and anything else life can throw at you to challenge you. This is because there is no challenge too great to be overcome by the greatness that exists within each one of us – *so long as one is willing to get the help they need*, as true greatness is not ever to be taken in isolation from others.

Are these trials, which are so often avoided because they're considered "bad," what makes a person mediocre or insignificant if they endure them? Or are these trials the very means the great used to unleash their greatness? Is it perhaps only the willingness to endure these trials, and not the outcome, that is in itself the ultimate "being" of greatness?

You are a work in progress, going through a filter called life to separate your vices from your virtues to work towards a greater potential, a greater purity. You are being processed, you are processing, and you have this process you experience called growth. It's all one.

> *Forgiveness is a filter by which you may let go of the poison for the purity.*

You and your greatness are not independent of those outside of you. You cannot reach your true potential without the guidance and help from others and without helping others reach their potential. You and your greatness are not in isolation from the whole. You are one piece of everything, and without you, everything is not "Everything." Without others, you can never be everything.

What if in helping another unleash their greatness, you're unleashing yours? What if in your humility to receive help and allow another's strength to shine, you find it is this very act that shows you your own true strength?

Consider…

Would I allow myself to give my greatness to others? Would I allow myself to receive the greatness from another? What if there is no distinction or difference between the two? What if it's all the same?

> *What if the way to unleash your greatness is to ask, how can I unleash our greatness?*

Can you combine the parts to see a whole? Can you combine your being, doing, and having? Can you see both your pieces, your vices and virtues, and yet still see the perfection in the wholeness?

Can you use this division you see and this wholeness you see as motivation to create resolution among the parts of you that conflict?

With everything, there are only pieces. With "Everything," there are no pieces.

A day isn't just THE day, but also the day *and* the night. To look at a "whole person" is not to see them as a collection of some cells and molecules. It's not to confuse their hand with "them." It's not to confuse the thoughts with the thinker who has them. It's to see something in its entirety with no division of parts, for all parts are one. The ocean is not bajillions of droplets of water, but "the ocean."

No shit, right?

Well then, let me ask...

How responsible is the organ of your brain for your body's life?

100% responsible? 10% responsible?

At least we can agree it's 100% essential, true?

How responsible is your heart for your life?

How responsible are your lungs for your life?

If we start dividing things up and go, "Well, the brain is about 25% responsible, the heart 24%, the lungs 17%, blood vessels are pretty important, so let's say 19%, and so on," – would this make any kind of practical sense? Aren't I just pulling numbers out of my ass? Wouldn't you end up 100% dead without any of these things?

But do people do this division of responsibility in their daily lives?

I've heard it said, "Nutrition is 80% responsible for the results you get in your health." Great! Now try going without sleep, stressing yourself out like crazy, and drinking poison and see what happens to your health. That 80% you have on point don't mean shit yo.

Division of responsibility is a useful *game* to play to realize nutrition might have a bigger impact than something like exercise. I love 80/20 thinking, which is looking for the 20% of things you do that get 80% of results. It's a game of "what matters more," which is critical for making decisions that are all essentially a matter of prioritization. Never forget, though, it's not true or false; it's just a game of the mind.

If one divides responsibility and doesn't recognize how each part may be ***100% essential to the whole***, it can lead to a flaw in thinking, a blind spot, of telling oneself, "Well, this is only 5% responsible, so I can go without it." Or alternatively, "Since this is only responsible for 5% of my results, I'll half-ass it, and that's cool. I'm going to do what that Derek guy told me in a book and make it insignificant by saying it's just 5%. It's only a little thing."

It would be like saying, "My brain, heart, and lungs are the most important parts of my body, so this means I can go without nerves, blood, and muscles, or at least they don't have to do their job 100%." In other words, it's stupid and destructive.

If your body parts were little people, how would you want them working for you?

How would you feel about your lungs if they said this…

"I'm *just* lungs. The brain and heart seem to get all the recognition. I'm just one organ, I'm not really 100% responsible for this whole "keeping the body alive" thing. If those damn muscles didn't keep acting up, I wouldn't have to bust my ass so much. Maybe they just need to cut that shit out and give me a break once in a while. Why should I have to work so hard? I'll go ahead and take a break for today."

Or what if your lungs said this…

"I'm just lungs. I know I'm essential, so I won't quit. But I'm only like 17% responsible for the life of this body, so I'll only work about 17% as hard. If this body doesn't get enough oxygen, maybe the heart just needs to pump a little harder. The heart has been slacking off recently and using the excuse that it has a 'condition.' Bullshit. I think it's just a lazy bum."

How's it going to work out for you if your organs think like this?

Now what if your lungs thought like this...

"I'm the lungs, and dammit, I'm kind of a big deal. If I'm not here, the whole thing falls apart. I'm 100% essential, so I'll take 100% responsibility for doing my job. If other organs don't step up or cause me to work harder, well then, I'll just deal with it. The brain can sort that shit out, but I'm going to do whatever it takes that's within my power to keep this ship sailing. If I even just let myself slack off, that's going to negatively affect everything else, including the amount of oxygen I *receive for myself.*"

Wouldn't you want each part of your body taking 100% responsibility for the life of the whole body? It doesn't make practical sense to the logical mind to say the heart is 100% responsible and the brain is 100% responsible because that's 200%. Yet when looked at from the standpoint that each part is essential, if any part slacks off too much, it could potentially destroy everything. If one part does slack off, would any part be justified in doing less than 100% simply because another part is slacking off? Would it be wise for an organ to cop out of their job because "everyone else isn't doing their job 100%, so I might as well not even try?"

However, do people ever do this?

"I should call this person, but you know what, the phone goes both ways. They don't ever call me. Relationships are 50/50. If they don't call me, well then, dammit, why should I call them? Why should I be the one taking more responsibility? Screw that and screw them!"

Meanwhile, the other person is thinking about calling and is telling themselves this exact same bullshit story. It's a game we can play, but what does it bring about? Death of the relationship. Death of a team. Death of even ourselves sometimes.

What if someone said, "I'm 100% responsible for this relationship with this person, with this team, with this body of mine, and with anything else that shows up in my life that I relate to?"

Wouldn't they then say, "I want to talk to this person, so I'm going to be the one to take responsibility and make the move to call. I'm going to be proactive. I'm going to let them know how I feel, what I want, and make things happen. It's *their choice* how they respond to me, *but I'm going to be a leader in my life.* I'm going to do whatever it takes to make this whole thing work. There's no blame on them; it's just my responsibility."

How do you want the organs in your body to be?

Do you want your lungs to give up because your heart is slacking? Or would you rather have your lungs step it up to give your heart just a little more time to restore itself, for maybe the current reality of your heart being sick isn't the future possibility of it being healed. Wouldn't you want every piece in you to keep fighting for life for as long as possible to give the broken parts a chance to heal and potentially save you from destruction? If anything gave up before it needed to or stopped playing at 100%, might the whole body needlessly die when it could have been saved?

Are you doing what you want your own organs to do in the "body" of your relationships and the world? If what you see in your world is dying, are you going to look to another to step up, or would it only make sense for you to step up, take 100% responsibility, and live boldly in your greatness doing whatever it takes to keep the whole ship sailing? Will you face your fears, work extra hard, and do more than you "should need to" in order to give others a chance to heal, all in order to save the whole? Will you let others work harder for you and suffer on your behalf when you're weak and broken so you have a chance to heal, all in order to save the whole?

You are one part of many, and through this thinking of yourself as "only one part," it has the potential to make you feel insignificant.

You can use this "insignificance game" to scoff off some of your responsibility and feel justified. Yet all you're doing is slowly or quickly destroying the whole that you're a part of.

But you think...

"Anyone can do what I do. I'm not special. What I do doesn't matter."

There are many doctors out there, but if there's only one doctor on an airplane when someone needs a doctor to save their life, that doctor becomes the only doctor in the world that matters. Only they, in that moment, can save this life.

To the people you know, your family, friends, or someone you've yet to meet, you may be the one person, the only person, who in some moment can save their life – physically, emotionally, or spiritually.

Your gift of healing may be an open heart, kind words, empathy, compassion, speaking the truth with love, holding their hand, sharing a smile, giving a lesson learned from your hardships, or simply being present when no one else is. Can't these things too save a life?

You are just one person among many, and you may only offer one thing. Yet to another person, you and your gift, in one moment, may be everything.

There are those out there who would have not taken their life if they were just given a smile.

What if the smile you put on someone's face or the moment you cared about some stranger saved a life? Would you ever know?

You can assume you don't matter, you can assume you do. It's your choice. There's no way to know unless someone tells you. Unless someone comes back and said, "That time you were there for me meant everything."

If you need to remind yourself that you matter, ask yourself, "Am I reminding *others* they matter? Have I told the people in my life that I love that they're significant and they mean everything to me?

What if in my act of giving significance to others, I reflect back my own significance to myself?"

Your organs might not have total conscious choice in how they function, but *you* do. *You* have choice. Therefore, you may choose to take responsibility, even as one of many *essential* parts, for the whole. Not for the purpose of beating yourself or others up if the whole fails, but rather so you can say, "I did everything I could. Now let the dominos fall how they may, and I will rest knowing through my *willingness* to take 100% responsibility, I have acted with greatness."

Remember this...

> *Everything is made up of little things. Therefore, quite literally, the little things are everything.*

Every moment is just a "little thing" that makes up the entirety of your life. Every big thing you accomplish is just a series of little steps. A collection of little parts. With this comes ease in knowing that "greatness" is often just a series of insignificant steps. Showing up just one day at a time. Giving just one smile at a time. Being there for maybe just one person in a moment. Yet through these little things, something great is created out of all of it. Like tiny "insignificant" cells creating all that you are.

This means greatness doesn't need to be overwhelming. You can often take small, gradual steps to greatness, although you may need to be willing to make great leaps of faith from time to time. You can put yourself at ease remembering you can't do everything, but you can do anything just one thing at a time.

As much as this relieves pressure to have to make huge drastic changes in your life at all times, it increases the pressure as well. The "little things" now become significant. You can't show up half-assing little things without consequence because that means you're, in a sense, half-assing everything. You still gotta play full out at each moment for greatness. You'll fail at this time and time again, but then the question is, how quickly do you get back up? How much do you play full on in getting up off your ass after you fail and fall? This getting back up quickly too, is greatness.

You can say the little things are each an essential part of the whole, but even this too is but a mind game. We can safely take "pieces of water" from the ocean without affecting the whole ocean, because we realize we're just taking out a part, and it doesn't destroy the whole.

This ability to not confuse the whole for the parts is what allows one to see that the poisonous slime isn't just poison, but rather part poison and part purity. Each moment is but a part, and doesn't define the whole. To not breathe isn't to never breathe. It's just but for a moment, a part of eternity, that something is true before something else becomes true. And yet you may still find there is one whole truth that is unceasing and unchanging.

Can you see it both ways?

> *When you focus on how we're all different, you no longer appreciate how we're all the same. When you focus on how we're all the same, you no longer appreciate how we're all unique.*

These are the games of the mind. You can see the whole as nothing but pieces, or you can see nothing of the pieces because you only see the wholeness. You can make anything insignificant, if you want. You can make anything significant, if you want.

You can say "Only great leaders who moved millions into action and changed nations" are great, and no one else. Or you can also say, "The mom who works tirelessly to give her kids a great life" is as great and significant as anyone else, for it was her role as a mother that played an essential part in her kids growing up to be greater leaders who moved millions.

Your mind can choose either. Either way can be bullshit. Either way can show a beautiful truth.

Isn't this amazing? Isn't it amazing the games you can play?

Still these games can be deadly when misapplied. One may do what I did at one point and say, "Who am I but one insignificant person? Who am I but one drop in the ocean, which can safely be removed, and the whole ocean won't be affected. No one would miss it. No one would see it's gone. The world will keep turning."

Or I can say, "Who am I if not an essential part of this whole of my family? What am I if not absolutely critical to the people who need to hear the message I have to share, and they'll only get it if they hear it in my voice? Even if I'm only one piece of the puzzle, doesn't that mean the puzzle could never be complete without me?"

This helps me escape feeling insignificant, but then could I swing towards pride if I start to see myself as too significant? Might I tell myself I'm "significant enough" so I don't need to keep unleashing my greatness?

Don't I need to look at others and make them both significant and insignificant? If I give them *too much* significance, might I say, "This all rests on their shoulders. It's the President's responsibility. It's my friend's responsibility. It's my team's responsibility."

If, however, I make them insignificant, might I say, "They don't matter. I don't need them. It's all about me and what I do."

Would either of these one-sided approaches work?

Are you special? Are we all special? If we're all special, does that mean nobody is special?

Are you the same as your neighbor? Do you share the same questioning mind? The same human needs? The same desire to love and be loved?

Or are you different because you eat different apples? Because you make different things matter? Because one is man, and one is woman. One is from here, and another is from there. One believes this, and another believes that.

Are we separate or united? Can you see both? Can you appreciate both?

What if "whole" and "part" are just games of the mind?

What if "same" and "different" are just games of the mind?

What if a "setback from success" is the same as a "setup for success?"

What if one's poisonous state is different than one's pure potential?

What if pride, growth, being, doing, having, succeeding, failing, mistakes, accomplishments, and all the words we use to label things are just games of the mind that can never fully express the higher truth they're attempting to convey?

What if "you" are just a game beyond the mind being played by You?

What if everything is nothing without You?

What if you are nothing without everything else?

Are you willing to play the game of appreciating and integrating all the games?

If it's a choice in what you choose to be... how do you choose to be?

Do you choose to be as Jeremiah, and let your love give you the courage to *break through* the gate holding you back from entering the cave you fear most? Will you venture into the place that can cause you the most suffering, in order to see if there exists something that can save your life within what could potentially destroy you?

Do you choose to see with eyes like Jeremiah, which show you despite your imperfect tainted state, that You are not the poison, but rather the pure water? Are you willing to draw out this purity? Do you choose to see that others are not their temporary imperfect state, not the poison, but rather the pure water? Are you willing to see the purity they cannot even see in themselves? Are you willing to draw out the purity from within them? Are you willing to play the game of mirrors and reflect back their own greatness to them?

Remember, you are in a house of mirrors.

What you see is what you are reflecting.

What do you choose to reflect – poison or purity?

CHAPTER 41

Remembrance Meditation

I give thanks for darkness
For it reminds me to use my light inside

I give thanks for weakness
For it reminds me to allow another's strength to shine

I give thanks for imperfection
For it reminds me of work I can do

I give thanks for confusion
For it reminds me to relentlessly seek truth

I give thanks for persecution
For it reminds me what I stand for

I give thanks for struggle
For it reminds me I have strength

I give thanks for all losses
For they remind me that everything's borrowed graciously from
creation

I give thanks for fear
For it reminds me of the power of imagination

I give thanks for pain
For it reminds me to feel compassion for suffering

I give thanks for death
For it reminds me of each breaths' sweetness

I give thanks for a broken heart
For it reminds me of the limitless strength of love

I give thanks for dependence
For it reminds me all is one

I give thanks for all things
For in all things, there is balance

And in balance is perfection
And in perfection there is God

CHAPTER 42

A Journey Through WTF

Your Destination

As our journey in this book starts to wrap up, I must prepare you for the journey you're about to face.

This is a journey of unleashing even more of your greatness.

But let's take it down a notch and say it's just about accomplishing some goal you have in your life within the next few months to few years. A "next step" milestone that you have in mind. Not the "be all and end all" goal for your life.

It could be any goal like to lose 20 pounds, to start a successful business, to write a book, to go get 1,000 of your friends to buy *this* book because "it's totes amazeballs," or anything else.

Can you see the goal in your mind's eye? Is it crystal clear in your imagination?

If it's not crystal clear, then perhaps figure out something more short-term. Instead of a destination of fulfilling your life's mission which you haven't even figured out what that is yet, perhaps you just see yourself reading books or trying new experiences to gain clarity.

This vision is your "destination." It's something that gets you up off your ass. It's something that gets you out of your status quo.

You don't have to stay at this destination forever, but at least vacation there to break up your routine.

Notice how you can actually "see" it, but it's only seen in your imagination. A potential possibility – not reality.

Your Departure Point

Your departure point is, as you guessed in, where you're at now.

You may think the "here and now" is relatively steady, unless your life is currently in chaos. Same job. Same friends. Same shit, different day. It's the status quo.

For many, this is a comfortable mediocrity. Although things might even be uncomfortably shitty, one may be certain about what kind of shit they're dealing with. They know how to handle this shit, and that provides a certain comfort even in the midst of pain. "Better the hell I know than the hell I don't know."

Yet just like a city, buildings come up and come down. Restaurants open and close. You may stay in the same spot, but the spot still changes around you. The illusion of consistency, over enough years passing, may be seen for the delusion it is if you pay attention. Or it may become obvious when some loud-ass neighbors move in and start blasting their music every night.
#PunkAssKidsNeedToLearnSomeManners

What does your departure point look like?

Just look around... what do you see?

Where are you at?

Who are you being?

Who do you hang around with most of the time?

What does your daily life look like?

Is it consistent or chaotic?

When do you feel great about life?

When do you feel mediocre and "meh?"

When do you feel like shit?

How do you interact with people?

How do they interact with you?

Why did you choose this life?

Did you even feel you had a choice, or is this a life that was "forced" upon you?

How does your departure point make you feel?

Obviously something's a little "off" or not what it "could be." You probably wouldn't be reading this book if you didn't realize things could be at least a little better.

Things may even be "dangerously" comfortable. You may get a lingering sense, that even though everything is "OK" now, things will change.

Or perhaps you're in a terrible place, and you can't wait to get out of here.

Maybe it's none of this, but you just want to check out a different place for a while. Take a vacation.

Consider, though...

If you could be anywhere in the world, is this where you'd be? If you could be anyone, is this who you would be? How would you be living? Would you be hanging out with the same people?

Did your past self hook you up with awesome things because of some of their decisions? Did your past self screw you over with some of their decisions?

What decisions don't you like made by your past self? Suspend the "I have no regrets" game, and explore, "If there was something I would have done differently, what would it be?"

Now what lessons can you learn from those choices so your present self doesn't make the same mistakes?

What good decisions did your past self make that you're grateful for? Would you be willing to make similar good decisions to pay it forward to your future self out of gratitude?

Right now, you probably have a pretty good idea of what your current reality looks and feels like.

You're holding two clear visions now. One vision is with your mind's eye, a future possibility that you can see clearly in your imagination. It's the top of a mountain. You can't see it with your physical eyes, and yet you know it's there because all mountains have a top. This is your destination.

The other vision is with your physical eyes and senses. You look around and see a present reality. It's somewhere just outside the bottom of the destination mountain. You now realize you're going to have to go on a journey to climb this mountain if you wish to reach your destination.

The WTF Zone

Now there's a gap between these two places of your departure point and your destination point, between your origin settlement and the peak of this mountaintop you wish to climb where your destination resides.

This gap is dark because you can't see it with your physical eyes. You also can't quite make it out in your imagination, although your imagination tries to paint a picture with a lot of "What if" questions.

This place between your departure point and your destination point, the gap between the two, is what I call the "WTF zone." It's because you have no idea what the eff is there. And this scares you.

Good things? Bad things? Scary monsters that will eat you?

You really have no idea. This uncertainty is why many people never venture into the "WTF zone." That is, unless they have a high need for variety and don't mind unpredictability.

If you're not one of those people who loves the unexpected, then my role is to enlighten you about what you can expect in the WTF zone so you'll be more certain, albeit never absolutely certain, about WTF you're getting into by journeying through "WTF."

Preparing For The Journey

There will be a few things you'll want to have prepared before you go out on the journey. Don't worry if you don't have all of these things before venturing out to WTF, you can find all of them in the middle of WTF as well.

If you don't know how to find these things, I'm going to grant you a special magic power that will serve you well now, and during your time in WTF.

It's called: "Just Frickin' Ask Someone Where To Find These Things."

Now granted, this magic power doesn't always work, but I've found if you keep trying it over and over, like blowing in an old NES cartridge repeatedly, this sorcery will eventually pay off.

Sometimes you need to use a variation of the spell called: "Just Frickin Ask Someone If They Know Someone Who Might Know Where To Find These Things, And Remember Google Is Your Friend."

While not perfect magic, the power of these spells is never to be underappreciated.

Map

Many would overcome their fear of venturing into the WTF zone if they just got a map.

Do you realize that others have ventured out there into WTF and made maps? Maybe they didn't start at the same point you did and they took a slightly different path, but a lot of the territory has already been mapped out.

If one is to travel through WTF, they would be wise to pick up a map to see what the landscape entails. They'll find maps at the library, online, and other places in various forms of books, case studies, training programs, and more from fellow travelers who've made safe passage to the destination of choice and created a map along their way.

Now granted, maps are limited. They only show the path the individual mapmaker took, and it might be different from the exact path a traveler wishes to take or is even capable of taking. Nevertheless, a map goes a long way to giving a traveler, you, a greater feeling of certainty before and during the journey.

Compass

If you're going on the journey, you'll need a compass to figure out where you're at. While the direction you need to go will likely continuously change, a compass always points to true north.

A compass comes in the form of true principles. Principles are big picture "rules of the game," so to speak. They don't provide an exact answer, but they always provide an answer of wisdom. They point you in the right direction.

"Get myself into a peak state before making a critical decision" – will be a wise choice, and not steer you wrong.

"Take 100% responsibility" – will keep you oriented.

Companion

A companion is someone who will travel with you so you're not alone. They can point out pitfalls in your blind spots – if they're a true companion.

Be careful of companions that only point out good things and not pitfalls. Or who just want to shoot the shit and aren't actually interested in your wellbeing. They're not a true companion.

A *true* companion will always be willing to say, "Yo, watch your step, dumbass, you're about to fall into a hole!" They won't worry about hurting your feelings as much as they worry about you not jacking your shit up by doing something dumb and being blinded by BS.

Flashlight

A flashlight helps you see in the dark. It only lights up where you point it at though.

It's the power of an "enlightening" question that gets your mind to see things that were once dark. You'd be wise to keep a flashlight and point it around in different directions.

Here are some places you can point your flashlight:

- What's my lesson here?
- If I did know what to do, what would it be?
- Who might know the solution?
- What's a good question to ask myself right now in this situation?

Be sure to keep the flashlight charged up, or it won't work. You can recharge a flashlight by ramping up your body's energy state. Get up, move your body, get the blood flowing, put a big smile on your face, do 10 jumping jacks, dance. Anything that gets the energy flowing in your body to create a positive state will add more juice to your flashlight. This is #Science

A Guide

A guide can potentially make your journey through WTF a breeze. They know the way, or at least they know a way. Their way might be blocked with a boulder that fell since they last traveled there, but generally speaking, if you find a *good* guide, they'll know the ins and outs of WTF, including the best and quickest ways up to your peak destination.

Be careful of a bad guide. Some guides offer their services, but they don't know what the hell they're talking about. Make sure they show you some evidence that they know how to get to where you're wanting to go.

A coach could be a guide, but more often a coach is like a companion with a flashlight of their own. They can help point out blind spots and light up things you're not seeing, but they don't always know the best path to your specific destination. Instead, they help you find the path for yourself – which can be an empowering way to take the journey.

A great guide would be a mentor who's been to your destination, possibly even multiple times from multiple different pathways. At the very least, they have one solid path to get to your destination.

Now granted, maybe they climbed up a rock face to get there, and you don't have the same strength and skillset to do this. It might be wise then to find a mentor who was similar in strength and skill when they started as you are now. Nevertheless, almost any good mentor will get you further along than you might get on your own.

Setting Your Intention

Before you start your journey, you must set your intention.

How do you wish to play the game? How do you wish to be on the journey?

There will be many paths to your destination. If you don't decide the way you're going to take the journey, you might meander around conflicted with so many different paths to choose from.

You must also get the courage to actually get up and leave your current departure point.

Consider...

Why do you wish to make the journey to this destination?

What will life be like in another year, or five years if things keep going the way they've been going currently?

How will your life look in another 10 years the way things have been going?

Remember, each decision, every choice, big or small, including the reason for leaving, may affect the outcome of the journey. Also remember, at any point in time, you may change your intentions.

What motivates you now doesn't have to be what motivates you later. Your way of being now doesn't have to be your way of being later. You always have a choice, including the choice to make a new choice.

Now you need to know what's inside the WTF zone so it doesn't catch you by surprise.

What's Inside WTF

Stepping Stones, Winding Roads, and Big Leaps

The path you follow could be solid or a bit rocky. Many times you'll have areas where it's stepping stones just hopping to one point, catching your balance, and then hopping to the next point. This is how most of the journey is.

Many times you'll be on a path that winds around a bend, and you can't see what's on the other side of it. Don't worry. Just keep looking at what's right in front of you now, and you'll get to where the path leads. Like driving a car at night, you can make a journey of hundreds of miles into an unknown darkness just by seeing the path that's lit up right in front of you.

However, sometimes you come to big leaps. You might be tempted to think, "Welp, this is the end of the road. I have to jump, and I'm not sure I can make this jump." You'll never get to your destination, though, if you don't take a leap of faith from time to time.

The good news is, you can be somewhat ready for them when they show up. When you're on your path, challenge yourself to jump along. Build up your strength. Do some exercise even when you don't "need to." This way, when you come across a big leap, you've strengthened your muscles and your courage.

Give yourself challenges willingly throughout life, and you'll be willing to conquer challenges thrust upon you by life.

The ultimate way to build the courage for leaps of faith is to remember, "When have I made a leap of faith before and it worked out?"

You'll find that if you go back in your past, there are many times you can recall doing what seemed impossible – and yet here you stand. You can look back and consider that 10 years ago you weren't nearly as capable as you are now, yet still somehow you made it here. You overcame what seemed like impossible jumps before, so you can do it again. Let this acknowledgement give you the courage to take your next leap of faith. Perhaps something is supporting you during this leap you don't even realize is there...

Roadblocks and Obstacles

From time to time you'll come across roadblocks and obstacles. Perhaps your map or guide prepared you for them, perhaps not. It doesn't matter, just know right now that they're going to come up.

The first way you can get through a roadblock or obstacle is to break through it. Perhaps get a few companions to help. Remember, you may just need to ask. It might not break right away, but it doesn't hurt to try – unless it's like solid concrete and you punch it and break your hand. #DontBeADumbass #UseCommonSense

The forceful approach may build up some strength. You could actually get pretty damn good at just busting through obstacles. *The key to effortlessness is relentless effort*. If you relentlessly practice breaking through any obstacle that comes your way, through great effort, eventually obstacles become almost effortless to overcome.

But you may wish to ask yourself, "Is it always wise to spend hours, days, or even years busting through an obstacle if I can just take five minutes to walk around it?"

You'll have to decide for yourself how you wish to choose to approach each obstacle, for each obstacle will be different.

The second way to handle something blocking your path is to simply find an alternative path or way around it. Realize that there are many paths to your destination. There are many different paths to the peak of the mountain. It's OK to quit on the path you are taking without quitting on the destination. In other words, don't think one single path is too legit to quit. #SeeWhatIDidThere #MCHammerReferenceInSelfHelp #ImWinningSoHardRightNow

> **Quit on the details, but not on the destination. Be willing to change your path without changing your priority.**

Loop Arounds

Sometimes your path won't make sense. Your destination is due north, but yet if you go straight north, it's a trap. If you head north at the crossroad, the path winds around and takes you south, away from where you're going and back off the mountain.

Sometimes where you need to go is in the *complete opposite* direction of the peak. You follow the "slingshot" trail that heads south for a moment, but then winds back around to take you back north towards the mountain top.

You'll realize, "I can't just head straight to where I want to go. I need to understand where the trails lead over time."

Base Camp

You may be tempted, after making progress for a while, to keep heading straight up to the top of the mountain. Yet if you go too quickly, you'll lose steam and burn out.

What you may need to do is head up for a bit, get acclimated to the higher altitude, and then come back down to base camp to rest up a bit.

This will teach you patience. It will teach you not to push beyond your physical capabilities. At times, it will teach you not to push beyond your emotional capabilities. Your desire to get to the top quickly is understandable, but foolish if not kept it check. Going too far too quickly may end up destroying you.

If you find it hard to breathe, you may ask, "Do I need to head back down *temporarily*, and make a base camp until I'm restored again to continue this journey?"

Settlements

As you continue on your journey, you will come across settlements. These are comfortable little spots that you may wish to take a break in. However, be warned, you may find this turns from a quick rest stop into a permanent settlement.

You see the journey is long and hard, and these settlements are cozy and comfortable. What's especially an issue at these settlements are settlers. Fellow travelers who've given up on their journey.

They'll start to say things to you like, "Oh, that place you want to go to, you can't make it. We've tried. It's just a bunch of BS. Anyone who sells you on the idea of getting to the peak is just a scammer. You don't want to go back out there. It's nice here. It's comfortable here. We like you here. Here, have a beer and stay with us."

This may be a very tempting offer to settle with the other settlers. The settlement is nice, albeit nothing to write home about. However, it's definitely more comfortable than the sometimes lonely journey traveling towards your destination. Maybe you were a little arrogant to think you could get to the peak. Isn't that pride? Isn't pride "bad?"

Now you have a choice. Do you wish to stay with the settlers, or continue the journey?

Should you decide to continue the journey, be warned... the settlers won't like that you are leaving them. You are pretty awesome after all, and gosh darnit people like you. Can you blame them for wanting you to stay?

Yet their friendliness turns to bitterness if you leave them. They'll shout at you as you walk away, "You're an idiot! You fool! You're going to get yourself killed out there!"

What you might find, though, is as you make your way out of the settlement, a few other settlers decide to venture out behind you. Inspired by your courage, they say to themselves, "You know what, I had given up and settled, but seeing this person continuing their journey has inspired me to continue my journey. Maybe there is a way to the peak after all."

Perhaps even a few of the settlers ask to join you. Remember though, choose your companions wisely. You're depending on them to point out the pitfalls. They can be the very reason you make it or the very reason you fall.

Robbers

Now at this point, you might be patting yourself on the back for your bravery, not letting the settlers get to you. Just when you start thinking, "Those settlers don't know what they're talking about," you get whacked on the back.

It's a robber, and he steals a bunch of your shit.

You can be prepared for this ahead of time.

Do you keep some extra food stored away in spots along your journey you can backtrack to and snag?

Do you know how to protect yourself and your assets?

Despite your best preparations, though, sometimes robberies happen. You may not always choose whether a robber gets you, but you can choose how you prepare for it and how you respond to it.

If you get robbed, do you hang your head in shame and return to a nearby settlement, too fearful to return to your journey?

Or do you still venture boldly forward saying, "This robber can take my belongings from me, but they can never take my choice from me to continue going forward. I'm choosing not to let them have power over how I run my life, but rather I'm keeping this power for myself. I choose to go forward greatly no matter what setbacks I have, for what looks like a setback may actually be a setup for a breakthrough *if I get the lesson* from this experience."

Voices

As you venture on the journey, you may hear voices come from deep within the woods beyond where you can see. These voices are sometimes helpful, sometimes harmful. Some may try to get you to go off your path, while others will steer you in the right direction.

You're never quite sure what to make of these voices. You may wish to learn to distinguish the voices. You notice that the loud voices seem to be the most dangerous. There's a still, soft, subtle, quiet voice you hear, that always seems to be steering you right.

Are the voices actually in your head? Are they outside of you? Are they voices of fear? Voices of wisdom? Voices of past conditioning? Echoes bouncing through the forest from a movie playing in a nearby settlement? Real people hiding in the woods messing with you, or perhaps actually trying to help?

Be careful of the voices you listen to. They may be what saves you or destroys you.

The Demon

There is one thing that you must be extremely careful of – the demon.

The demon has one purpose – to destroy you. The demon is named "Death."

One may trip and fall off a ledge in WTF. The demon will be there at the bottom to catch their fall. Into the hands of death this person will fall – a sad but sobering reality.

No amount of sunshine-and-rainbows thinking makes the demon not exist. It's there, it's real, and you know others who've fallen victim to the demon in WTF. This lingering thought that there's a real demon that may actually kill you is why WTF is so scary.

"Fear" sometimes gets mistakenly labeled as "false evidence appearing real." There is nothing "false" about the reality of death. Fear exists because it's protecting you from a potential reality – death and destruction.

This is your dilemma...

Should this fear consume you, you'll never reach your destination. You'd never venture out into WTF for fear the demon will get you.

Should you ignore this fear's warning when the demon is lurking nearby, you may find yourself carelessly and foolheartedly falling into the clutches of the demon.

Fear may be the very thing that stops you from reaching your destination, and yet it may be the very thing that keeps you alive on your journey to your destination.

Should this fear not be balanced with something else, it will paralyze you. A paralyzed person is an easy target for the demon. The very thing that's trying to save you from destruction may be the thing that brings it about.

What will get you to act in spite of this fear?

What is the other choice besides fear?

Why are you making this journey to begin with? Out of fear, or something else? Or a mix of feelings? Is there ever just one motivation?

Reaching Your Destination

If you actually step out and take the journey instead of sitting in a comfortable settlement talking about how "I could totally make the journey but uhh, you know, I just don't really feel like it 'cause I mean I have nothing to prove or anything…"

If you persevere in spite of roadblocks, robbers, and proud settlers…

If you make both the small steps and the great leaps of faith…

You will reach your destination. It will be glorious. You will be *proud*.

Now you have a choice.

You may choose to bask in your glory and make a settlement of your new destination. To settle at the peak of this mountain. To enjoy the wonderful new experience of being in a destination that's even more amazing than where you departed from.

Or you may look around… and see off in the distance another mountain to climb.

From this high altitude, you get a glimpse of what might be an even more amazing destination. Maybe you just get quickly bored of your newfound destination or realize it wasn't all it was cracked up to be in your imagination.

Do you settle, or do you climb a new peak?

Do you choose something else altogether?

The answer depends on the intention you set.

Back Into WTF

While many will find *comfort* with their newfound destination and prefer to stay at the top of the mountain, others may venture back into WTF to climb the next mountain. They say to themselves, "If I've done it once, I can do it again!" They love the feeling of pride and *significance* of reaching the top of mountains.

They'll repeat the same overall process, but this time, they may find the path this journey takes them on is more challenging. This time settling becomes more tempting as they can now just simply brag to the fellow settlers about their accomplishments and relive their glory days without needing a new mountain to climb.

But if they're motivated by the *growth* they'll experience, then the challenge, rather than being off-putting, will provide a tempting allure to become *even greater*. They'll have something to prove to themselves about what their potential truly is, and it doesn't matter if others recognize it or not.

Others may wish to venture out to WTF not to climb the next mountain, but simply to explore what's out there. Perhaps exploring lands beyond what can even be seen at the peak of the mountain. Perhaps swimming in lakes, bungee jumping off cliffs, and getting #TurntUp at some totally dope jungle parties. Perhaps coming across hidden temples and finding the whole world of WTF fascinating with its never-ending exciting *variety* of new discoveries.

Still others will venture back into WTF to hang out with other travelers. Perhaps it's lonely at the top and they want some friends to join them so that they feel *connected* and can share the experience of being at the peak of the mountain.

Or perhaps they help others get to the peak themselves because they remember what it was like to be in a settlement and have feelings of hopeless resignation. They know the people there secretly yearn to reach the top of this mountain, but no one showed them the way. They wish to *contribute* something to their fellow travelers by proclaiming, "I've been to the top of the mountain! I've come back down to show you the way so all people from this day forward may reach its peak!"

Finally, there are those who do not wish to play just one single game. Since we can change our intentions and what we make matter the most at any point in time, some may do a little of each of these things. They adventure for a while with no particular destination, just enjoying the exciting things they come across. Then they may decide to take on a new mountain to climb to grow themselves and sense that feeling of accomplishment. After a while they may settle comfortably but then eventually grow restless. They decide they want to make a contribution and start creating maps of what they've discovered in WTF and become a part-time WTF tour guide in their later years.

There are many ways to play the game. There are many intentions that can be set. The journey of WTF is a journey of choice.

How do you choose to journey? How do you wish to be in your adventures in WTF?

It Always Ends The Same...

There are those who choose not to venture back out into WTF. They make their destination a settlement. They get comfortable at the top of their mountain. Just getting to this peak was enough, and now they're safe. They're out of WTF.

They sit back, crack open a beer, and turn on *Fast and Furious 7*.

No more getting lost. No more having to figure out the unknown. No more fear of robbers taking their stuff.

And best of all, there's no demo...

Oh shitballs...

What's that?

The demon enters the house of the settler.

"What are you doing here?!" – shrieks the settler! "This isn't the WTF zone! You're supposed to be out there catching wandering travelers, not in here in my safe little settlement at the peak of the mountain!"

The demon lets out a menacing laugh. "You fool! Everywhere is the WTF zone. This is my land. ALL of it. Where you started, where you went, where you're at now is all my land. There was never any escaping me. I always find those I hunt for – *always*."

The fate of the comfortable settler is the same fate of the thrill-seeking adventurer or social butterfly. They (and you) always face the demon. It *always* catches you.

It's all WTF. There is no "zone" of danger and "zone" of safety. There is no more assurance of certainty of what's going to happen in a settlement vs a winding road or peak of a mountain. The demon finds you on the rocky bridges, swimming in the lakes, or in the comfort of your own home watching *Fast and Furious 7*. The demon catches some when they're young and some when their old. The demon catches those who are just one step away from the peak and catches those who've never even stepped foot out of their comfortable settlement of origin.

Each traveler and non-traveler alike eventually faces the demon.

Some may even catch a glimpse on their journey of the demon and live to tell about it. Yet it's only for a moment that they're spared. The demon will find them again.

When one sees the demon, they start to ask themselves questions. One traveler who caught a glimpse of the demon but escaped its grasp, Brendon Burchard asked himself, "Did I live? Did I love? Did I matter?"

All who face the demon ask their own version of these questions. *The demon comes closer...*

If I always meet the demon no matter what, what's the meaning of all of this? *The demon comes closer...*

Was it about the strength I developed and possessions I accumulated? What does this matter if I'm now about to lose it all anyway? *The demon comes closer...*

What good was it to settle here if I'm going to die here? Was there something else I wish I could have done or seen before now?

The demon comes closer...

Did I leave the stove on? Oh shit, that doesn't matter now...

The demon comes closer...

Who did I become on my adventure? Am I proud of how I will be remembered? Will those who mourn my loss say, "They were great!" or "Yeah umm, I guess they we're kind of sort of OK?"

The demon comes closer...

Was it about the impact I left on others that will live on even after I'm gone? Will my choices be an inspiration to those who remain? What am I leaving behind?

The demon comes closer...

Why did I make the choices I made? What was motivating me? What does this matter now?

The demon comes closer...

Do the people I care about know how much I appreciate them? Did I tell them they matter? Did I make peace, or is there still a grudge I hold that's now too late to resolve?

The demon comes closer...

Can I fight this demon? Can I still escape it? Maybe if I...

The demon grips your neck...

This pain is too much! I want to die now! I'm ready, why isn't it killing me yet? Please God, just make the pain stop...

The demon lifts you up, your body goes weak, and it stares into your eyes as it chokes the last bit of life out of you...

Yet even now you have a choice...

Do you see the choice?

Your body is too weak to even move.

Are you prepared for this choice?

It's the choice all your acts of courage or cowardice prepared you for. All your leaps of faith or stumbles of trepidation moved you to one side of a spectrum or another.

Do you know where your power lies?

Did you make your choices willingly or have them "made for you" unwillingly?

Do you know how you wish to be?

Why did you ever leave any settlement? Why did you ever stay when you did?

Do you know what you'll choose?

All the choices were shaping you.

All your intentions were coloring your actions.

All of them moving you, preparing you, to make your one final choice.

The final choice you have now.

The only choice that remains before the demon ends your life.

Do you look upon the demon with fear or love?

CHAPTER 43

A Look Back At Your Adventure

D o you see the significance of your final choice?
Here's a little exploration to consider.
Is fear good or bad?

It depends...

Does it keep you safe?

Potentially.

Does it endanger you?

Potentially.

Can it motivate you to greatness?

Potentially.

Can it paralyze you in mediocrity?

Potentially.

All potentials based on choices.

You learned in this book a way you can use fear to motivate you to greatness. This is a useful game to play.

Now there are those who say that if you're totally present, living in the moment, and completely trusting, you won't have fear. Fear they may say, is "bad." "One must not choose from a place of fear."

This is true from *one perspective.* By now, you should know that I also like to take a practical perspective as well.

What are the odds you're never going to have fear and remain completely present at all times? Mediate on a mountain top long enough, and you might transcend your human conditioning. In the meantime, you probably have fear, so you might as well use it to serve you. It is there to keep you safe from death, after all.

Fear may be the very force that gets someone up *off* their ass and moving into greatness. Fear may be the very thing that keeps them *on* their ass in mediocrity. It's their choice of how to direct the fear that makes the difference.

Fear keeps people alive so they can keep making choices, keep growing, keep doing great things. Fear of loss keeps the surgeon sharp so they don't lose a patient to carelessness.

However, fear *alone* will not be enough to live greatly. Too much fear and one becomes paralyzed. One runs at every sound of the bushes shaking and wonders, "Is that the demon! OMG! I better go run and hide and stay in a nice cozy settlement! Maybe we better just drop a bunch of bombs in the woods to kill the demon in case it's in there. I don't even care if it was just a cute little baby bunny going to its little happy bunny family."

Fear, like all emotions, can serve you or enslave you. The question is, who is deciding what to do with fear? Does fear alone have power to destroy you or the rest of the world, or does one choose to give fear power? If you make fear your enemy, it may consume and destroy you with the power you choose to give it.

What if you appreciate fear and make it your friend? If you truly love someone, would you let them go when it's time to part ways without clinging to them?

Fear, while a potentially useful motivator and friend, isn't enough. There must be balance with something that leads and guides fear so it doesn't cause destruction.

What else is driving you?

What would get you to purposely venture into a land where a demon resides knowing it could spell death?

The first thing is the *awareness* that you can never hide from the demon. So it's pointless to try.

The second thing is, you guessed it, love.

Love for yourself. Love for others. Love for a cause greater than you. Love for excitement. Love for connection. Love for your future. Love for almost anything.

When you face a leap of faith, what happens inside of you?

Fear is telling you there's a demon down there. Fear is saying, "Don't jump! You may fall and the demon will get you!"

Yet, do you still jump? Is this an act of courage? What else besides fear is motivating you? If you have both fear of jumping and fear of not jumping, what is beyond the fear directing it?

What is an act of courage during a leap of faith if not an act of love?

What is an act of patience at base camp if not an act of love?

What is an act of perseverance after being robbed if not an act of love?

What is an act of willingness and trust if not an act of love?

All of these times that you act in spite of your fear, it's love that's moving you.

All of the times that you lead fear to motivate you to greatness instead of paralyze you, it was the love that had power over the fear. The love of your future self, love of others, love of your present self, and ultimately perhaps the love of something beyond you.

So what happens when you face the demon and it grabs you?

Do you feel fear?

If so, why?

Your fear keeps you safe on the journey. It keeps you from meeting the demon needlessly.

But when the demon has you in its clutches, why would you still ever feel fear if your fate is now sealed? There's no purpose in the fear protecting you from death when death is now inevitable. Fear in this moment doesn't give you an opportunity to live another day or to make another choice.

Fear is utterly useless once you're in the hands of the demon.

Yet it may still grip you if it's become a habit and a way of life.

Do you have a choice in all your emotions, or do they just happen?

Are your emotions like habits that are reinforced by your behaviors?

If fear is what's been driving you *primarily* – whether it's a fear of discomfort that keeps you in a settlement, or fear of "missing out on fun" so you go on an adventure, or any other type of fear...

If you made fear your way of life...

If you made your choices *more* out of fear instead of out of love...

Will you be able to let that fear go when it no longer serves you?

What will you do with your fear when you face the demon of death?

The demon of death of your life? The demon of death of a relationship? The demon of death of a business? The demon of death of your finances? The demon of death of your dreams? The demon of death of your ego?

Any demon of death that shows up in your life that your fear tries to protect you from – what will you choose when the demon has you in its hands and you realize there's no more escaping it?

Will you still choose fear when it no longer serves you?

Or... will you lovingly let your friend fear go when it no longer serves you?

Can you choose "not to choose" fear, or must you choose something else?

What do you choose instead?

Can you choose both fear and love?

Does it matter if you choose love?

Does it matter if you choose fear?

Is this death the end of all?

Or is this death just for a *moment?*
Are you in a house of mirrors?
Is what you see a reflection?
Does what you see change depending on your perspective?
Do you choose to look with love?
Does this change what you see?

CHAPTER 44

A Return To The Lake Of Greatness

You look upon The Lake of Greatness and feel fear even though it's all that can save you.

We fear our greatness for it seems overwhelming.

So overpowering that we feel it may consume us if we submerge ourselves in it.

If you remain in fear of greatness, you die... slowly.

If you're willing to dive in in spite of the fear, you may live.

If you embrace the fear and take the plunge...

You may hold your breath and hold onto only the air in your lungs...

Holding your breath, like fear, can keep you alive.

Fear can be a friend.

But only for a moment.

Then you must let the fear go if you wish to live.

Then you must always come up and let the air in if you wish to live.

Then you may forever nourish yourself in the waters of Greatness.

CHAPTER 45

Now – Here Is Where You Have A Choice

A great mind driven by fear may destroy the world.

A great mind driven by love may save the world.

Yet, "intelligent" decisions may be made by both minds.

Your great mind, if driven by fear, may destroy your world.

Your great mind, if driven by love, may save your world.

When do you love? *When* do you fear?

Do you love reality, but fear unknown possibilities?

Do you fear reality, and mentally escape to an imagined possibility you love?

The realist vs. the idealist – two games of the mind.

The realist in actuality doesn't truly see "what is." They only see what was.

As soon as the mind thinks about "what is," the moment has already passed. The realist only sees how things were, and then expects them to be. Clinging to their love of the past, if even only clinging to what was just a moment ago.

The idealist, when stuck in their idealism, escapes the moment to live in fantasy. How things "should be" or "could be." They prefer to retreat to their fantasy world where it's comfortable to escape the uncomfortable "reality" they sense before them.

Some like to go back and forth between both these games.

Neither one is real.

What is real is now. This moment. The present.

"There is nothing except the eternal now." – Alan Watts

If your mind is thinking about it, it's not *now*, but what just was or never was.

If your mind is thinking about it, it's not *now*, but what may be or may never be.

Those reliving their "glory years" are playing a game of the mind – for the only moment of glory is now.

Those who feel that they "missed their opportunity" are playing a game of the mind – for the opportunity always was and always ever will be here now. Perhaps the best opportunity is yet to come in a "new now."

Those playing "it should be" are playing a game of the mind – for nothing should be except what is here now.

Those who feel it "should have been" are playing a game of the mind – for they're missing their chance to pick "what can be" right in this moment, only to leave their future self repeating the same game of "should have been" in a never-ending mind game.

Now is the moment where "what is" and "what could be" merge. "What comes next" is based on your choice.

Reality and possibility "make love" through your choice in this moment to give birth to the next moment. Or should you choose, they may also "make fear" to give birth to the next moment as well.

What "next now" are you choosing?

Yes, this moment is but a moment, a piece. One drop in an ocean. Seemingly insignificantly different from the moments that immediately precede it and follow it.

And yet this moment is essential to the whole. One critical piece, like your brain or heart, to the whole body. Without this moment giving birth to the following moment through your choice, the whole thing dies.

This moment is the ultimate limiter of possibilities. Your mind can bombard you with thoughts and worries and "what ifs." It can make you think that there are a million choices to make at once.

Yet this moment frees you through its limitation. It removes all the stress and overwhelm, and shows you simply now have but just one choice to make.

While this moment is the ultimate limiter of possibilities, it is at the same time, the ultimate expander of possibilities. For all the possibilities exist in this moment for how you wish to be, do, and have.

How do you wish to experience this moment? You may see a picture one way in this moment, and you may see the same picture a completely different way in the next moment. You can play this game for eons of time, always seeing something different, and yet always looking at the same picture. Endless possibilities existing before you, and yet still limited to only what's here now.

What if you stripped everything down to this moment? With no greater context than what shows up here now, what context would you create?

Here's my choices…

Who? I

What? Am

When? Now

Where? Here

Why? To Love

How? Completely

"I am now here to love completely."

When you cut out all the fluff, the answers become clear.

Your mind cannot truly make sense out of the contradictions of life. You are always the same, yet you are always changing. Yet this moment shows you the truth behind this.

Your mind attempts to explain a limitless reality in limited terms. It attempts to explain through millions of words, pictures, and countless perspectives that which can be made so simple if you allow it to be.

Will you find the only place free of BS?

Do you choose now?

Will you be now?

Will you do now?

Will you have now?

I've said you must always make a choice. To choose "not to choose" is still a choice. Yet even still, this can be false from one perspective.

What if by "having to" make a choice, you are in a sense enslaved to choosing? Burdened by a need to constantly explore your options, weigh pros and cons, and make decisions that always entail getting it wrong from time to time?

But if there's only ever one option, you'll never be burdened with "having to" make another choice again. Wouldn't this limitation actually bring with it a freedom?

What if your great power lies not within your ability to choose, but in your ability to remove choice altogether and only have love?

You may find if you choose "no choice" but love, to only have the option of love now and always, this great limitation may in fact bring about your ultimate liberation.

CHAPTER 45

Always Changing, Always The Same

What is always changing and always the same?
Time, for one, likes to play this game

"What's the time?" One may wonder
Two answers come you may consider

Each moment is passing, never repeating
Yet "now" is the time, forever unchanging

"Who are you?" Another interesting question
No right or wrong, it's all perspective

I am me, as it shall always be
I could never be another, quite obviously

But surely I won't be who I was before
Each moment growing wiser, of this I'm sure

"Why are you here now?" You're asked
Answering this right is your most important task

To dance, to work, to eat, to play
The reasons keep changing from day to day

The mind gives many answers to you
But is there one answer that's always true?

Yes, it's the answer my heart speaks of
My reason for being is simply to love

CHAPTER 47

The End... Or A New Departure Point?

I hope to have left you with more questions than answers, in a paradoxical state of being clearer and yet more uncertain than when you started. Embrace this. It can be "good," depending on how you respond to it. This is not a book of action steps and checklists. I have plenty of other resources I've created with those things. It's a book on learning to grow beyond your BS because you'll probably always have it in this life, and this means learning to sit with uncertainty – temporarily.

You can look at the surface level of what's been presented here and get great lessons or go deeper and get different lessons. One isn't necessarily better or more "right" or "wrong" than another. This can be a book for achieving simple goals like "putting down the damn doughnuts and eating a carrot for once," more complex goals like starting a successful business, or even extremely lofty and somewhat vague goals like "living greatly."

This book is alive and dynamic with new discoveries as you read the parts multiple times and play a different game each time.

There were times that I sometimes made choices "either/or." You may wonder, "Is this an inaccurate manipulation of the possibilities?" The answer may be sometimes, but not always. Either/or is a legitimate and sometimes very practical way to think.

Can a person choose to only be either in a particular room or not in that room? Granted, the smartass solution is to stand in the doorway as "both." Yet consider, how many problems are created when people try to be half in and half out? What if someone needs you to be fully present with them, and you're only halfway there with them?" Can it truly be said one is "in the room" with them, so to speak? Or is "half out," from one perspective, really "all out?"

"Do I want to surf Facebook or write my book?" was a question I asked myself quite often. Are there more than two choices? Sure, but decision making is sometimes an art of selective focus and elimination of possibilities. That paradox of greater freedom through limitation.

You're BSing yourself if you're letting *your mind* limit you to two choices and *not allowing* other possibilities to exist, instead of *you* purposely limiting yourself to two choices as it serves you, while still maintaining the ability to remove this limitation should that serve you. It's like an actor who plays the role of "limitation," but who may stop playing the role at any time should they choose to, because they know they're only playing a role. Playing a game, if you will. Or watching a movie and getting into it, but still you know it's just a movie.

Don't get lost in your own magic. But then consider, are you both the magician *and* the magic? Are you both the magic and the magician? Are you both *in* a house of mirrors and *the* house of mirrors?

In more everyday terms, you may consider, "Am I asking what to create, or is the creation asking me to create it? If I'm taking 100% responsibility, what am I responding to? Can I be both to the asker and the answerer at the same time?"

There's no intellectual answer your mind provides that will satisfy these questions logically. Perhaps to even ask questions like these at this point in your journey would seem meaningless and overly philosophical, yet later, they're the exact questions you need to unlock something. That's what makes them beautiful.

This book is about teaching you how to dance. To realize that sometimes, there's no one right step. In making missteps though, you learn how to be a better dancer. At times, it's a freestyle dance just for shits and giggles alone in your room.

Still other times, it's a tango. You're dancing with a partner. Dancing with future and past. Dancing with you and another. Dancing with You and your mind.

In a tango, there is a leader. Not to be confused with master and slave, the leader and follower dynamic is different. It respects choice. The follower goes along because they are *willing*. The follower has trust that the leader has their best interest in mind. The follower may even benefit more in the short-term compared to the leader, as the leader may sacrifice their own short-term needs for the follower. Like a leader who eats last to ensure that all of their team gets fed first.

Yet remember, the leader doesn't sacrifice from themselves in the long-term, for they have to take care of themselves, or else the followers suffer. We must still feed ourselves to feed the hungry.

The effective leader sacrifices from themselves in the short-term, but never the long-term. Remember, you can hold your breath for a moment for the sake of your follower, but remember to come up for air. Never forget who the leader is and who the follower is.

A truly good leader, a leader who leads with humility and not pride, finds that through their "limitation" of *temporary* self-sacrifice, they'll end up with greater freedom. The follower, through their "limitation" of obedience, also ends up with greater freedom.

In the "master and slave" game, there is only greater enslavement for all. In the leader and follower game, when played correctly, when played from "give and receive" rather than "give and take," when driven primarily from love and not fear, there is only greater freedom for all.

Consider, is your mind the leader or the follower? Is your fear the leader or the follower? Are your stories, excuses, and justifications a leader or a follower? Or are these a master or a slave? Must you choose to change the game entirely to unlock new choices? To live with your mind or be lived by your mind, which do you choose?

I can think about the past and future instead of what's right in front of me, and at times, this is helpful. This doesn't automatically mean I'm not "living in the now." The question is, is it my mind that's taking me unwillingly into the past and the future? Is it reliving an experience or imagining something and playing it out over and over without my consent? Am I a "slave" to the mind and being dragged away from the present moment unwillingly?

Or am I proactively choosing to look back at the past and get a lesson now? Am I choosing to imagine a future and see what might be possible for me now to create this future? Am I being present with my reflection back or projection forward as conscious choice?

This book is about proactivity and being 100% responsible for your choices. However, this does not mean you're always free to choose willingly how you feel and sometimes even how you act.

From one point of view, we can affect our emotions, but sometimes things happen that trigger something inside of us. Emotions can come up without us saying, "Gee, I'm going to choose to feel really pissed off and hate my life right now! That sounds like a great idea!"

What do you do when you're triggered? This is your choice.

What do you do if you're triggered and you "lose control?" How you respond once you regain your composure? This is your choice. My suggestion is – *make it right.*

Even the addict who acts unwillingly still has choice somewhere.

Now remember this when you see others in their different states – for you may be tempted to say that their anger, resentment, attachment, fear, depression, or other things are "just their choices. They need to suck it up and choose to cheer up and be grateful."

This, too, is only one viewpoint, and when not balanced with love, may lead to judgment and failure to appreciate how all of us may fall for our mind games, and that all emotions may serve us depending on our *response* to them. This includes our response to our own emotions and the emotions of others.

Consider, are you not yourself occasionally unwillingly falling into poor states? Have you ever in the past? How would you want another to treat you for your weaknesses? Can you treat another in their weakness this way?

Don't confuse one's poison for "them." What if they are purity and the poison was simply added? They may have forgotten about their own purity because they only see themselves as poisonous slime. They may need to see their purity reflected back to them by you showing it to them. They're not necessarily bad, but rather simply forgetful, as we all are. They've forgotten that they're in a house of mirrors. Have you forgotten too?

Do you choose to draw out the purity within another? You may wish to ask, "*How do I* draw out the purity within another? Might it be the same means by which I draw it out of myself? Am I treating myself the way I want others to treat me? If I learn how to positively influence myself, am I learning how to positively influence another? Does this work both ways? Might it be wise to ask, "How do I positively influence both myself and others?"

Remember, now you have a choice in how you respond always.

You can choose how to look at a barren field.

You don't see anything growing, and you may say, "This sucks. There's nothing growing and so we're going to starve." Pessimism.

You don't see anything growing, and you may say, "I don't see anything growing on the surface, but maybe there's something growing underneath the surface I can't see yet!" Optimism.

Both viewpoints are potentially destructive.

If the pessimist says, "We're going to starve, so I'll passively sit back and await my fate."

Or...

If the optimist uses their wishful thinking to say, "I'll just passively sit back and let nature, others, or God take care of it."

Then both of them may starve.

The wise person says, "I only know that now I have a choice. I will choose to plant seeds and water them just to be sure."

The wise person doesn't make an assumption about the field bringing forth fruit either way, but they still must assume as we all do, that at least planting a seed and watering it would likely lead to something growing. They assume that the laws of nature didn't just decide to change overnight. They also assume, "There is potential here that's worth my effort to fulfill."

Thinking you're never going to assume anything, when assuming and judging is what your brain is designed to do, is ridiculous. Rather, it would be wiser to simply assume your assumptions are not necessarily reality. To judge your judgments.

You may choose to play the game of assuming that you're capable of growing more within you and more outside of you than what you see is here before you. The game of "there is always *far more* potential here worthy of my effort to fulfill." And when you can't assume one way or another, ask yourself, "Is it worth the leap of faith, as Jeremiah took, to find out? Wouldn't it be worth finding out, since my life, and the lives of all those I love, may depend on it?"

One may consider before even planting the field, "Is it I who asks whether to plant this field, or is it the field who's asking me if I'll plant it? Is the first question "Will I?" or "Will you?" Is it that I'm I asking or being asked? Am I questioning or responding? Am I requesting or being requested or both? May I choose how to play the game?"

Perhaps if you surrender asking your question for a moment, you'll quiet yourself long enough to hear the question asked of you.

There are many points of view, and each one brings a truth to the table. Each one is an essential significant part of the whole, and yet each one can be insignificant. Not all truths are equal. The truth that I'm wearing a white shirt as I type this is something I believe should matter less than the truth that children are being sold into sex slavery right now. Which truth do I choose to remember? Which truth do I choose to bring awareness of? Which truth do I choose to make matter more? Or perhaps, which truth is asking me to make it matter more?

What truths or points of view do you choose to make matter most right now?

Be careful not to let a point of view become a permanent way of life.

I have one point of view I'll offer for your consideration. It, too, is but a mind game, yet still an interesting one to play.

I have a dream that we will be neither united nor divided.

Because the ultimate paradox is that your perfection is different from my perfection, and your BS is the same as my BS. It's our perfection that divides us, and our BS that unites us.

I will see that your perfection is different from my perfection. While I am in some sense perfect, something is still missing without you. I will look at you and say, "Your gift is perfect and so is mine, and yet neither of us would be complete without each other. I appreciate your perfection, your gift, because it makes you different from me. I choose to make you special to me, and in this moment, I become special to you."

I will see that your BS makes you just like me. Rather than letting our BS, our bullshit, our belief systems, our blind spots divide us, we can look at one another and say, "You and I are one in being total bullshitters. Your mind plays the same games that my mind plays, even if we're playing different games at the same time."

If we only see how we're all different, we no longer appreciate how we're all the same. If we only see how we're all the same, we no longer appreciate how we're all unique.

Let's come together as one, and yet never forget that we are many. May the fact that your gift is unique make you significant, and the fact that BS is common to all, make this BS insignificant.

Why Did I Write This Book?

Simon Sinek says start with why. I'm ending with "why" because it's *my* book, I do what I want, and he can't tell me how to live my life. Also because some lessons here make more sense now that you have the entire context of this book. Plus, isn't the end just the start of something new?

Why did I write this book?

Many reasons, many partial truths. Many changing and evolving intentions over the course of time.

This book started out as a book called *Don't Do This...* with the intent to cover some self-help myths. I wanted to write a new book to make some more money and grow my business, but also because I'm passionate about personal development. I'm committed to empowerment, enlightenment, and compassion in all things I do. Although I'm a health and fitness author as well, that's really mostly a means of teaching principles of empowerment to those who'd rather learn how to get a six-pack than be one of "those people" who reads self-help books.

This book had pretty humble beginnings. Nothing special, but still a somewhat "pure intent" to serve others. A somewhat "tainted" intent as some may call it to make money – which of course is actually a potentially pure intent because money is useful for doing all kinds of good.

Yet something happened as I went on this journey. It happened when I started writing with the intention to help us collectively better understand ourselves so we may be more compassionate towards ourselves as well as others.

It evolved to be a book about choice. A book about finding freedom from the enslavement of our own minds so that we can find freedom from the shackles of fear that bind us in the world at large. A fear that divides us because of our differences, our BS. A fear that keeps people playing small so as not to offend others when it is this very playing small that is robbing the world of the gift it needs the most – the gift of showing that we don't have to keep living, or suffocating if you will, in fear that may destroy us. We can let go of holding our breaths in fear which may serve us but only for a moment, and choose to come up and breathe in even more of the air of Greatness which we need to live. We can now choose to love fully.

That's all choosing greatness is – choosing love. Choosing love not for a moment, but always. Always striving – actively. Making love your being, your doing, your having. Giving and receiving love freely. Always receiving love, never taking it. Always giving love, never rejecting it. Suffering along with the love if that what it entails as a human, but realizing that love in its pure state is nothing to fear, for it can only give life and never take from it. This means that choosing greatness can only give life to you and those you inspire. One's greatness can never take greatness from another.

We no longer need to fear our greatness. We no longer need to make it forbidden and lock it away in a cave behind gates of BS. The world appears to be dying, and we need to break through the gates to find the one thing that can save us. We must break through these gates with or without the permission of others, because all will thank us for this act of courage eventually.

We need to draw out the greatness, the purity, the love, when we discover it in ourselves. We need to draw out the love, the purity, the greatness, when we discover it in another. We need to remember, *it's always there, in all people*, waiting to be discovered and unleashed. We are not our poison, we are purity with poison to be filtered out by forgiveness.

Although I could have chosen to see myself as but one insignificant part in the whole body, I decided I was going to be significant and play at 100% to do whatever it takes to keep the body alive by offering my gift – writing a message that is beyond me. I needed to give this body, this world, a little longer to heal because I believe that it will heal.

I believe the darkness and division happening in the world right now doesn't need to be a setback, but a setup for a collective breakthrough – should we choose. We decide if this "world pain" is the end, or just one side of a slingshot about to release into world peace. I cannot choose for others, but I will choose to do everything I can as my one insignificant but essential self in this whole big thing. I will keep striving to play full out until the body heals or dies. I cannot choose what other parts do, what other people do, but I can always choose healing. I can always choose love.

With ever-evolving intentions, ideas started pouring into me. People showed up giving the exact words I needed to hear to inspire a new part of the work. Even reading words of hatred and division inspired new insights and served a useful purpose. I would start writing, and ideas way too freakin' smart for my brain would start flowing into and out of me. Separate pieces of this book started coming together to form a collective and unified whole that I could have never imagined or consciously created from the outset.

This book became a living embodiment of the very lessons it was teaching, for at some point it was no longer me writing it – it began to write itself. It began to show me its lessons. It began to show me how to unleash my own greatness. In my attempt to serve others and help them unleash their greatness, I found I was the one perhaps to be served the most.

I started to consider, "Am I the one who asked whether to write this book, or did this book, or something beyond this book, ask me if I would write it? Who asked the question first? Was the first choice I had to ask, or respond, or both, or neither?"

I'd say there are parts of this book that are "divinely inspired," but I don't know one way or another. What I do know is that this book is a result of a lot of wise outside sources, some I've met and some I've never seen, who have shared their lessons with me over the years, and I've been able to synthesize these lessons into something new – and add a lot more hashtags. #IDontEvenKnowWhyIEverStartedUsingHashtagsButIFeelLikeItsBecomeAThingForMeSoNowIKindOfHaveToOopsIMeanChooseToKeepOnUsingThemOMGArentISoZany

Why am I sharing this? Your journey may start with only modest intentions and aspirations, but it has to start somewhere. It may start with mostly fear driving you, but later something else matters more. If you stick along for the ride, you'll be guided along, one green light at a time, step by step into something far greater than you could have originally imagined.

I got this lesson clearly when I went wake surfing for the first time. The key to me finally getting up wasn't to put my feet flat on the board while in the water waiting for the boat to start. Instead, I had to lay down and surrender on my back, place only the smallest part of my heels on the board, and trust that I would be pulled up into the position I needed to be in if I just held on and trusted in the process.

I realized, I can't try to start like how I want to finish. I must trust that if I'm willing to choose to first surrender to something beyond myself, I will end up exactly where I need to be if I just keep choosing to hold onto something beyond myself. I must be willing. I must trust. I must have faith.

Are you willing to trust the process? Are you willing to see that it only takes one small step, one seed of good intention, one small act of courage, one almost insignificant desire to do good, to do love, and if you hold on, you may just find something or Someone beyond you pulls you up the rest of the way?

This is what I've found.

I intend for all these lessons in this book to serve you for your highest good.

I've shared them with you because I don't need to physically see you in order to see the greatness, the purity, the love within you that I wish to draw out.

So now you have a choice...

Do you choose to let this greatness, your love, You be unleashed?

I honor your truth and your choice.

You are but just one thing to me, and that thing is everything.

I love You. Now. Always.

Derek Doepker

Did You Love Break Through Your BS?

Thank you for investing in yourself and in this book.

You can stay in touch with me by making sure you get on the Break Through Your BS newsletter when you get your Break Through Your BS "Resource Guide" and video series at BreakThroughYourBS.com/Bonus

If you enjoyed this book, please share the word with others. It helps them, helps me, and you can even turn it into a mini-case study which helps you. Remember, when you have a pure intent to serve others, sometimes you may be the end up receiving even more.

You can leave a review for the book on Amazon with this easy link: BreakThroughYourBS.com/Review

If you thought this book totally sucked, I want to hear that too! Well, not really, but I'm open to growth. So if you have constructive feedback on how to make the book even better, please feel free to email that to me. Getting feedback for improvement is how I grow.

If you're interested in personal coaching, you may contact me about this as well. I occasionally offer highly discounted sessions for those in need. Fair warning, I will be a bit pricier than your run of the mill "life coach" due to the level of training I've received. I will challenge you. I will be your best friend but also a true companion who shows you the pitfalls you might be about to fall into. If you can't handle that, please find someone else.

You can send any messages to info@excuseproof.com

More Resources by Derek Doepker

ExcuseProof.com

The Healthy Habit Revolution – ExcuseProof.com/Revolution

Why You're Stuck – ExcuseProof.com/Stuck

50 Fitness Tips You Wish You Knew – ExcuseProof.com/50tips

How To Stick To A Diet – ExcuseProof.com/diet

Weight Loss Motivation Hacks – ExcuseProof.com/MotivationHacks

Badass Success Course To Take Things To The Next Level

Success Made Simple – Udemy.com/success-made-simple

A Few Recommended Resources (Affiliate Links)

Pivot book – ExcuseProof.com/Pivot

New Peak's Millionaire Mind Intensive – DerekDoepker.com/mmi

Brandon Broadwater's Seminars – ExcuseProof.com/event

REMINDER

Given will you be
Reception when you're ready
What you know right now
Right now means this is what's to know

Do you remember?
You're in a house of mirrors...

reflections perceived through a game played by You in

All This

This is All You playing a game of perceiving reflections

Made in the USA
Lexington, KY
29 August 2016